YO-BDB-086

mini·math for appraisers

by IRVIN E. JOHNSON

To my good friend
Valerie Chavarria
cordially
Irv Johnson
1/20/81

INTERNATIONAL ASSOCIATION OF ASSESSING OFFICERS
1313 EAST 60TH STREET, CHICAGO, ILLINOIS 60637

Second Printing.
© 1974 by the International Association of Assessing
Officers, 1313 East 60th Street, Chicago, Illinois 60637.

The material in this volume is presented for its thought
provoking and general educational values. The opinions
expressed herein, as well as those expressed in
previously published reports and publications, do not
necessarily represent a statement of policy of the
International Association of Assessing Officers.

Printed in the United States of America
ISBN Number: 0-88329-000-6
Library of Congress Catalog Card Number: 72-92138

CONTENTS

Introduction

"Mini-Math for Appraisers" is a book *about* numbers, a book *of* numbers—*special* numbers: compound interest factors and precomputed mortgage-equity over-all rates, and how to use them in analysis and valuation. Further, it has been designed especially for people who "hate" math.

Standard compound interest tables are some of the most useful, but least understood, of all appraisal tools. Most books on this subject, which probes and measures the time value of money, have been written by mathematicians for mathematicians. "Mini-Math" has been prepared by an appraiser for appraisers and other non-mathematicians. Since it was designed to express rather than impress, it is more practical than profound.

This book is the product of many years' experience in the fields of real estate, appraisal, research, investment analysis, teaching, writing, and lecturing. Portions of "Mini-Math" have appeared in the *Assessors Journal;* parts have been used by the Ventura County (California) assessor's office, the International Association of Assessing Officers, the Society of Real Estate Appraisers, and by college instructors, in real estate and appraisal classes.

Where there is "mini," there also must be "maxi." We suggest that the appraiser acquire more complete sets of the six standard compound interest and annuity tables, listed in monthly, quarterly, semi-annual and annual periods. An inexpensive set is published by the Center for Real Estate and Urban Economics, Institute of Urban and Regional Development, University of California, Berkeley, California. Their "Tables For Investment Analysis" by Paul F. Wendt and Alan R. Cerf sells for less than $5. The most comprehensive volume in this field is the "Financial Compound Interest and Annuity Tables," Financial Publishing Company, Boston; price is about $25 for the big "blue book."

Computations Without Algebra

Mini-math relates directly to the market and income approaches to value. Its principal function in comparative sales analysis is the computation of the cash equivalent of non-cash items—mainly, purchase money mortgages and trust deeds. Only by such a calculation can sales price be adjusted for terms. More than twenty procedures used in the analysis and discount of trust deeds and mortgages are outlined and illustrated.

Primary methods and techniques of the income approach are explained by example, with special attention given to the mortgage-equity technique. All computations of over-all rate, value, appreciation, loan amortization and yield on equity are made by using only the standard compound interest tables or their derivatives—totally precomputed over-all rates such as those beginning on pages 129-183. The OAR (Over-All Rate) Tables, appearing here in book form for the first time, penetrate the unsound barrier of complex calculations.

Just as there often is more than one trail to the top of the mountain, there may be more than one mathematical procedure leading to the computation of a value indicator. The mortgage-equity technique outlined in this book allows the appraiser to dispense with algebra, complicated equations, and special symbols. "Mortgage-equity" is frequently equated with "Ellwood." The appraisal profession owes a debt of gratitude to L.W. Ellwood, MAI, for his pioneering in this field and for his scholarly work built around the "Ellwood Tables."

Structure of Text

There is no single adjustment of a microscope or telescope to accommodate every eye. Mini-math may help some students and practising appraisers bring into focus what might otherwise have been blurred and obscure. Sequence of presentation in "Mini-Math" treats theory first, in Parts I and II; Part III discusses practice. The "Compound Interest and Annuity Tables," the "Over-All Rate Tables," and the "Supplemental Tables" follow. Here are a few suggestions for programming study:

- Go through Parts I and II in order presented.
- Study Part III by topics, according to your interests. Relate the discussions in Section 1 to the procedures and illustrations in Section 2. (Both sections in Part III are arranged alphabetically under the same general headings.)
- Whenever factors and mortgage-equity over-all rates are used in the text, verify by locating them in the tables.
- Make the actual calculations shown in the examples, and check for accuracy.
- Use an electronic calculator or slide rule, if available, for ease and speed in computation.
- If calculation is a "by hand" operation, rounding factors to three significant decimal places simplifies your arithmetic.
- Make some "trial runs," solving your own appraisal problems by following the appropriate procedures listed and illustrated in the summary of mini-math methods beginning on page 73.

"Mini-Math for Appraisers" has been prepared for appraisal practice, not just for study, and certainly not for "once over lightly" speed reading. An exploratory survey of the "Ready Reference Roster" in Part III, Section 2, will indicate the many types of computations the industrious student of mini-math can make with confidence and efficiency. Sections containing the "Summary of Mini-Math Methods," the "Compound Interest and Annuity Tables," the "OAR Tables," and the "Supplemental Tables" have been designed for quick reference and constitute the actual working parts of the book. Pages in these two parts of the text will, through continued reference and use by the appraiser, experience the greatest degree of physical depreciation; however, we foresee no probability of accelerated functional obsolescence.

Check and Double Check

While every attempt has been made to insure accuracy in the text and tables, we cannot guarantee complete freedom from fault. Variance in "rounding" factors in numerous steps of computation might account for slight differences between our calculations and yours. However, appraisal practice allows a reasonable range of tolerance; for the final step in computing any indicator of value is "rounding" to possibly the nearest $500 or $1,000 or more. If you discover a significant mistake, kindly do two things: (a) let us know; (b) consider that such an error has added the "human touch" to this book.

Where Credit Is Due

For his incisive review of the "Mini-Math" manuscript and for his constructive comments, special appreciation goes to Walter C. Hunter, ASA, MGA. Mr. Hunter is Assistant Assessor of Ventura County, California, and is a senior member of the American Society of Appraisers. He serves as national president of the Society of Governmental Appraisers and holds the first Master Governmental Appraiser (MGA) designation granted by the Society.

Recognition must also be given to Richard B. Tanner for programming the E.D.P. run of the Over-All Rate Tables used here. Mr. Tanner is research analyst in the office of Edwin B. Shriner, CAE, Assessor of Ventura County, California. An expression of appreciation is due this office for maintaining an atmosphere conducive to creative thinking and to the development of progressive procedures.

Compound Interest Is Simple—Almost

7 x 9 = 63. Right? Right!

.45 ÷ .15 = 3.0 Right? Right again.

Present worth equals future worth times a factor. True? True!

What we are attempting to demonstrate is simply this: You will have no actual difficulty in understanding the compound interest tables, over-all rates and mini-math methods, if you can:

1. Add, subtract, multiply and divide.
2. Place a decimal point where it belongs.
3. Follow simple directions.

The objective of this book is to uncomplicate the complicated. Mini-math is easier than you think. It's also easier *if* you think.

Irvin E. Johnson
Ventura, California
April 1972

PART 1
The Super Six Magic Multipliers

THE POSITIVE POWER OF COMPOUNDING

Standard compound interest and annuity tables are essential tools in the appraiser's kit. Their significance should be as familiar as the draftsman's pencil, the fifty foot tape—or the Golden Rule. Tables of both future and present worth show the tremendous power of compounding, which is a cardinal factor in the dynamics of investment, a factor of prime importance to both investors and appraisers.

This great cumulative force can be demonstrated in quite a surprising manner by reference to a widely publicized real estate transaction—the purchase of Manhattan Island from the Indians in 1626 for trinkets with a cash equivalent of $24. While that deal seems to have been all in favor of Peter Minuit and the Dutch colonists, look at the other side of the coin and consider the possibilities of investing and compounding the sale price.

Suppose the chief and his tribe decide to take the $24 in cash instead of trinkets, and invest it, perhaps establishing the First American Building and Loan Association. They further set a policy of compounding all earnings from the $24 for future generations, spending none of the interest from this special investment. What would it amount to by 1976, America's upcoming bi centennial year? If the $24 had earned 6% interest, compounded quarterly, it would have grown in the subsequent 350 years to more than $27 billion. Yes, $27 billion; there is no typographical error. Granted, 350 years is a long time, but if you are 35 years old, you have lived 10% of that period yourself. The astronomical sum to which the $24 could have grown at 6% compound interest exceeds the total current assessed value of the entire borough of Manhattan, including land and improvements.

To get a little more mileage out of the idea, presume that the $24 had earned 7½% returns compounded quarterly for 350 years. At that interest rate, by 1976 this investment would be worth $4 trillion! A trillion is almost impossible to comprehend or visualize, but here are a few units of comparison:

- In the mid 1960's the life insurance industry in America generated the first trillion dollar business.
- Total indebtedness in the United States, both public and private, is

5

estimated at $1.7 trillion.
- A single year's gross national product in America reached $1 trillion for the first time in 1971.

Contrast the $4 trillion with 7½% simple interest; $24 at 7½% simple interest would earn $1.80 a year, or a total of $630 in 350 years. Less than 4 cents a week, or a multi-trillion dollar fortune.) *Compounding* makes the difference.

Thus far, we have been more theoretical than practical in the effort to underline the importance and power of compounding. If colossal figures astound you, let's drop down to smaller numbers and note the potential power of doubling through compounding: Start with one penny, double it 27 times, and you'll be a millionaire, worth exactly $1,342,177.28!

Compound Interest Is Not So Complex

Because the appraiser is working with this tremendous power in dealing with the time value of money, he should comprehend something of its nature. He must know how to measure it, how to compute present and future worth, how to solve for rate or time. This—and more—he can do through understanding the six standard compound interest and annuity tables and using them efficiently.

If this discussion seems elementary, it is intended to be. This book was *not* written for the mathematician who thrives on complex equations. However, a review of fundamentals can be profitable to anyone, even the expert.

Compound interest, as we recall from grade school arithmetic, is interest calculated on an accumulation of principal and prior earned interest—not on original principal only. Compound interest is not paid when earned, but is added to the outstanding principal balance. Compound interest is thus computed on a periodically increasing base.

In contrast, simple interest is interest on original principal only. The base does not grow, for interest does not accumulate. It is paid and collected periodically as it is earned. For example: If $1,000 were invested at 5% simple interest for 5 years, it would earn .05 x $1,000, or $50 per year. Interest in the amount of $50 would be paid annually, for a total of 5 x $50, or $250. Principal amount at the end of the term would still be $1,000.

If $1,000 were invested at 5%, compounded annually for 5 years, accumulation would progress as follows:

Year	Interest Earned			Cumulative Principal Balance
0				$1,000.00
1	.05 x $1,000.00	=	$50.00	1,050.00
2	.05 x 1,050.00	=	52.50	1,102.50
3	.05 x 1,102.50	=	55.125	1,157.625
4	.05 x 1,157.625	=	57.88125	1,215.50625
5	.05 x 1,215.50625	=	60.77531	1,276.28156
			$276.28	

Note that simple interest remains constant period by period, while the amount of compound interest accelerates each succeeding period as the base grows. Simple interest would be graphed as a straight horizontal line. The progression of compound interest is curvilinear, since it generates a continuously increasing income stream. The following bar graphs point up visually the difference between simple and compound interest.

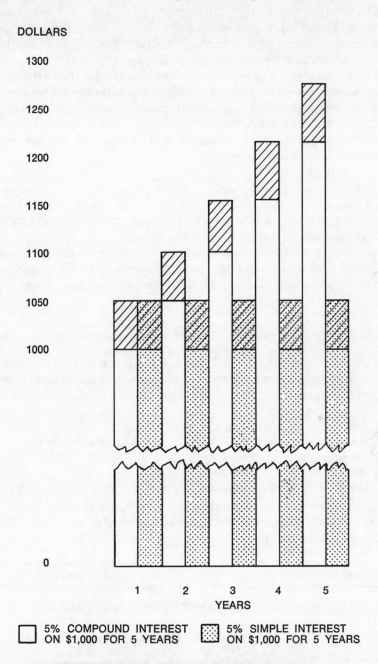

NOTE: Patterned areas at the tops of the bars represent interest earned annually. The unpatterned, lower portions of bars represent annual principal base.

Curvilinear progression of compound interest can be illustrated more vividly by a line graph that spans a longer period of time; say, 40 years. A

single initial investment of $1,000 at 5% compounded annually would grow
to $7,000 in 40 years. Of this amount, $6,000 is compound interest earned.
Simple interest would have remained at $50 a year for 40 years, earning a
total of $2,000. (See graph on facing page.)

Deposits of $1,000 each year at 5% compounded annually would grow to
$120,000 in 40 years. This series of periodic investments would earn
$80,000 in compound interest. (See graph on page 10.)

At 10% interest on $1,000, compounded annually for 40 years, the
curvilinear ascent skyrockets substantially. Computation shows growth of
the $1,000 to over $45,000 in that period of time. And $1,000 invested each
year at 10% for 40 years would amount to a hefty $442,000.

A greater divergence between simple and compound interest becomes
more apparent through an increase in:

- The amount invested;
- The rate of interest (or yield);
- The length of time involved.

Understandably, greater gains are realized on regular, periodic investments of
additional funds than on a single, initial investment.

A comprehension of elementary compound interest provides a knowledgeable basis for understanding the derivation, interrelationships, and
functions of the six standard compound interest and annuity tables.

THE "SUPER SIX"

Names of the tables vary in different texts, but the factors themselves are
uniform. We have listed our preferred terminology and the abbreviations that
will be used throughout the book. Also, other commonly used nomenclature
is noted:

Future Worth of 1 (FW 1)—Amount of 1
Future Worth of 1 Per Period (FW 1/P)—Amount of 1 Per Period
Sinking Fund (SF)
Present Worth of 1 (PW 1)—Reversion
Present Worth of 1 Per Period (PW 1/P)—Inwood Coefficient; Annuity
Periodic Repayment (PR)—Partial Payment; Loan Amortization

The following chart summarizes the basic function of each table and the
interrelationship between the tables.

Type of Table	What It Shows	Relation to Other Tables
FUTURE WORTH OF 1 (Amount Of 1)	Growth at compound interest of a single initial deposit or investment	$s = (1 + i)^n$ (Basic formula)
FUTURE WORTH OF 1 PER PERIOD (Amount Of 1 Per Period)	Growth at compound interest of a level series of periodic deposits	Sum of preceding FUTURE WORTH OF 1 factors plus 1

(Chart continues on page 11)

GROWTH OF $1,000 AT 5% INTEREST, COMPOUNDED ANNUALLY

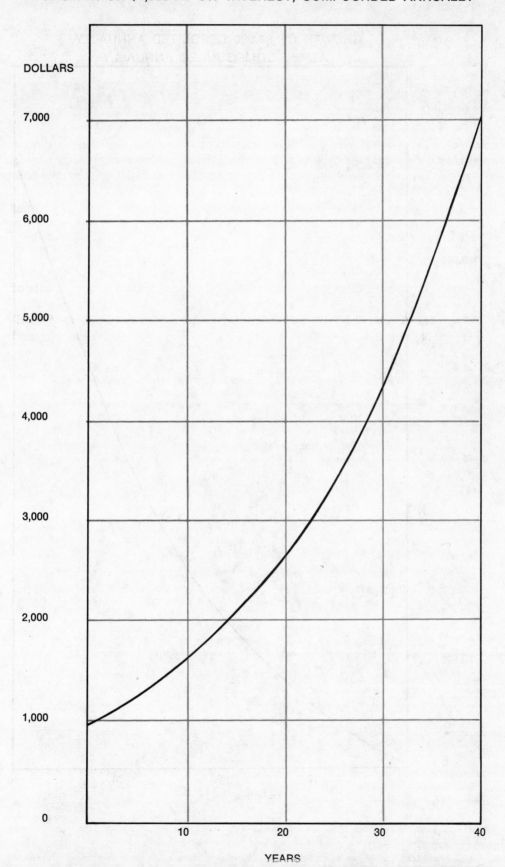

DOLLARS

7,000

6,000

5,000

4,000

3,000

2,000

1,000

0

10   20   30   40

YEARS

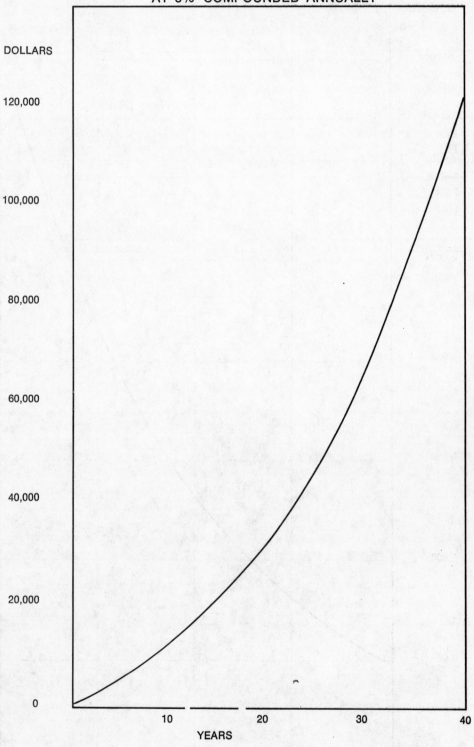

GROWTH OF $1,000 DEPOSITED ANNUALLY,
AT 5% COMPOUNDED ANNUALLY

Type of Table	What It Shows	Relation to Other Tables
SINKING FUND	Amount of periodic deposit required which will grow at compound interest to a specified future amount	Reciprocal of FUTURE WORTH OF 1 PER PERIOD (Or PERIODIC REPAYMENT minus i)
PRESENT WORTH OF 1	Present worth of a single future income payment	Reciprocal of FUTURE WORTH OF 1
PRESENT WORTH OF 1 PER PERIOD	Present worth of a series of future income payments	Sum of PRESENT WORTH OF 1 factors
PERIODIC REPAYMENT (Partial Payment)	Amount of periodic payment required to amortize a loan	Reciprocal of PRESENT WORTH OF 1 PER PERIOD (Or SINKING FUND plus i)

The same relationships are depicted in the following diagram:

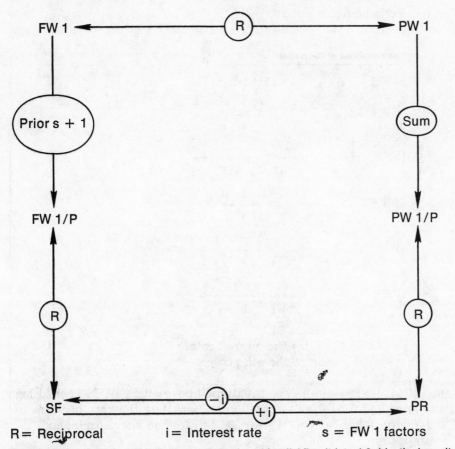

R = Reciprocal   i = Interest rate   s = FW 1 factors

NOTE: The reciprocal of any number may be found by dividing it into 1.0. Identical results are acheived by multiplying by a factor or by dividing by the reciprocal of the factor.

The following standard symbols representing the compound interest factors and the equations for their derivation are *not* used in "Mini-Math." They are included here only as a matter of reference for the benefit of the appraiser who encounters them in other published texts and tables.

The Factor	The Symbol for the Factor
Future Worth of 1	s
Future Worth of 1 Per Period	$s_{\overline{n}\rceil}$
Sinking Fund	$\dfrac{1}{s_{\overline{n}\rceil}}$
Present Worth of 1	v^n
Present Worth of 1 Per Period	$a_{\overline{n}\rceil}$
Periodic Repayment	$\dfrac{1}{a_{\overline{n}\rceil}}$

The Equations of Derivation

(FW 1) $\qquad s = (1 + i)^n$

(FW 1/P) $\qquad s_{\overline{n}\rceil} = \dfrac{(1 + i)^n - 1}{i}$

(SF) $\qquad \dfrac{1}{s_{\overline{n}\rceil}} = \dfrac{i}{(1 + i)^n - 1}$

(PW 1) $\qquad v^n = \dfrac{1}{(1 + i)^n}$

(PW 1/P) $\qquad a_{\overline{n}\rceil} = \dfrac{1 - v^n}{i}$

(PR) $\qquad \dfrac{1}{a_{\overline{n}\rceil}} = \dfrac{i}{1 - v^n}$

"1" represents $1.
"i" stands for the interest rate.
"n" means to the nth power.

A simplified version of the six equations above might be less confusing and more meaningful to the "average" appraiser. Here they are in terms of the FW 1 factor, PW 1 factor, "1" for $1, "i" for the interest rate, and "n" for the nth power:

$$FW\ 1 \quad = \quad (1 + i)^n$$

$$\text{FW 1/P} = \frac{\text{FW 1} - 1}{i}$$

$$\text{SF} = \frac{i}{\text{FW 1} - 1}$$

$$\text{PW 1} = \frac{1}{\text{FW 1}}$$

$$\text{PW 1/P} = \frac{1 - \text{PW 1}}{i}$$

$$\text{PR} = \frac{i}{1 - \text{PW 1}}$$

The sections that follow sketch briefly the derivations, interrelationships, and uses of the tables.

Future Worth of 1

Derivation of factor and relationship to other tables:

Formula for computing FW 1 factor is:

$s = (1.0 + i)^n$

The symbol "s" represents the FW 1 factor; "1.0" is one dollar, "i" stands for the interest rate; "n" indicates to the nth power.

For example: To find the FW 1 factor at 5% for 5 years:

$s = (1.0 + .05)^5$

$= 1.05 \times 1.05 \times 1.05 \times 1.05 \times 1.05$

$= 1.27628$

Note that the example showing the computation of 5% compound interest for 5 years on $1,000 corresponds: Divide $1,276.28 by 1,000, and you have the factor 1.27628 (rounded to 5 places). Fortunately, it is unnecessary to use the equation. The computations of compound interest have already been made for you and are built into the FW 1 factors given in standard tables.

FW 1 is the basic table of compound interest. From it all other tables are derived.

Principal use:

FW 1 factors, as multipliers, are used primarily in computing the growth of a single deposit or investment at compound interest, when interest or yield rate and time are given. Present worth (the original amount of deposit or investment) is multiplied by the FW 1 factor at the rate and for the time specified to calculate future worth.

For example: Find the estimated value of a parcel of land purchased for $15,000 and held for 12 years, located in an area where land values are increasing at an average rate of 9% per year, compounded.

Solution: Don't use the formula: $s = (1.0 + .09)^{12}$. Instead, look up the FW 1 factor at 9% for 12 years. You'll find it is 2.81266.

By multiplication: $15,000 x 2.81266 = $42,200 (rounded)

Future Worth Of 1 Per Period

Derivation and relationship to other tables:

FW 1/P factor is the sum of the preceding FW 1 factors, plus 1.0.

For example: The FW 1/P factor at 5% for 5 periods is the sum of the

FW 1 factors for periods 1 through 4, or 4.5256, plus 1.0, which is 5.5256.

It can also be derived by this equation:

$$\text{FW } 1/P = (\text{FW } 1 - 1.0) \div i$$
$$= (1.27628 - 1.0) \div .05$$
$$= .27628 \div .05$$
$$= 5.5256$$

The easy and only practical way is to use the prepared tables. But perhaps such a workout as this in calculating factors may engender, on behalf of the compound interest tables, a greater degree of understanding, respect and appreciation. The FW 1/P factors are the *reciprocals of the sinking fund factors.*

Principal use:

FW 1/P factors, as multipliers, calculate the growth of level series of periodic deposits or investments at compound interest. The dollar amount of one deposit is multiplied by the FW 1/P factor at the rate and for the time specified to compute the dollar amount to which the deposits will grow.

For example: A man deposits $50 monthly in an account paying 5½% compounded monthly. To what sum would his savings account grow in 25 years?

Solution: FW 1/P factor at 5½% for 300 monthly periods is 642.03743. Multiplying: $50 x 642.03743 = $32,101.87

Sinking Fund

Derivation and relationship to other tables:

We will illustrate three ways of deriving this versatile factor by computing the SF at 5% for 5 annual periods:

1. Since the SF is the reciprocal of the FW 1/P, the factor can be found by this formula:

   $$\text{SF} = 1.0 \div \text{FW } 1/P$$

   Substituting:

   $$\text{SF} = 1.0 \div 5.5256$$
   $$= .18097$$

2. The SF factor may also be derived directly from the corresponding FW 1 factor by a simple equation. Note that this formula contains the same members as the equation for the derivation of the FW 1/P, its reciprocal, except that division is reversed:

   $$\text{SF} = i \div (\text{FW } 1 - 1.0)$$

   Substituting

   $$\text{SF} = .05 \div (1.27628 - 1.0)$$
   $$= .05 \div .27628$$
   $$= .18097$$

3. The SF factor is the Periodic Repayment factor less the interest rate. (From the tables, the PR factor at 5% for 5 annual periods is found to be .23097.)

   $$\text{SF} = \text{PR} - i$$

   Substituting:

   $$\text{SF} = .23097 - .05$$
   $$= .18097$$

Principal use:

SF factors, as multipliers, compute the amount of periodic deposit required that will grow to a predetermined future amount, with interest rate and time period given.

For example: An investor plans to reroof an apartment complex in 10 years at an estimated cost of $10,000. What amount must be deposited quarterly for 10 years in a sinking fund savings account paying 5% compounded quarterly?

Solution: SF factor at 5% for 40 quarters is .01942.

Multiplying: $10,000 x .01942 = $194.20

Present Worth Of 1

Derivation and relationship to other tables:

The PW 1 factor is the reciprocal of the FW 1 factor. To find PW 1 at 5% for 5 periods, use this equation:

PW 1 = 1.0 ÷ FW 1

Substituting:

PW 1 = 1.0 ÷ 1.27628

= .78353

Principal use:

The PW 1 factor, as a multiplier, computes and deducts compound interest from known or assumed future worth, at a stipulated interest rate and for a given period of time, to determine present worth.

For example: It is estimated that land in the direction of the city's growth will be ripe for urban development in 7 years, at which time it will have a projected worth of $8,500 an acre. At a yield rate of 9%, what is its indicated present worth?

Solution: PW 1 factor at 9% for 7 years is .54703.

Multiplying: $8,500 x .54703 = $4,650 (rounded)

Present Worth Of 1 Per Period

Derivation and relationship to other tables:

The PW 1/P factor is the sum or cumulative total of the corresponding and preceding PW 1 factors. To illustrate, the PW 1/P factors at 5% for periods 1 through 5 may be found by simple addition:

Period	PW 1	PW 1/P
1	.95238	.95238
2	.90703	1.85941
3	.86384	2.72325
4	.82270	3.54595
5	.78353	4.32948
	4.32948	

A computation of the factor at 5% for period 5 by means of an equation illustrates a simpler way:

PW 1/P = (1.0 − PW 1) ÷ i

Substituting:

PW 1/P = (1.0 − .78353) ÷ .05

= .21647 ÷ .05

= 4.3294

Principal use:

The PW 1/P factor is used to compute the present worth of any level terminal series of future income payments, such as a lease or annuity of any type. The dollar amount of one periodic income payment is multiplied by the PW 1/P factor at the specified rate and for the given time period. The product is the present worth of the future income stream. (Adjustments can be made easily to accommodate graduated annuities or income streams with a deferred start.)

For example: A ground lease runs for 15 years at an annual rental of $12,000 net. Compute present worth at a yield of 7½%.

Solution: PW 1/P factor at 7½% for 15 years is 8.82712.

Multiplying: $12,000 x 8.82712 = $105,925

Periodic Repayment

Derivation and relationship to other tables:

The PR factor, like the Sinking Fund factor, is extremely versatile, and can be derived in three ways. Each method will be illustrated by computing the factor at 5% for 5 periods:

1. It is the reciprocal of the PW 1/P factor:

   PR = $1.0 \div$ PW 1/P

   Substituting:

   PR = $1.0 \div 4.32948$

       = .23097

2. It can be derived from the PW 1 factor:

   PR = $i \div (1.0 -$ PW 1)

   Substituting:

   PR = $.05 \div (1.0 - .78353)$

       = $.05 \div .21647$

       = .23097

3. It is the SF factor plus the interest rate:

   PR = SF + i

   Substituting:

   PR = .18097 + .05

       = .23097

Principal use:

The PR factor as a multiplier is used to calculate the amount of periodic payment required (principal and interest included) to amortize a loan or return a capital sum at a specified interest rate within a given period.

For example: What monthly payment would amortize a loan of $30,000 at 8% interest in 25 years?

Solution: PR factor at 8% for 300 monthly periods is .00772

Multiplying: $30,000 x .00772 = $231.60

READING THE TABLES

The "compleat appraiser" should read tables with full comprehension. The following is a representative set of the six standard tables arrayed in a logical sequence. Factors at 5% are given for periods 1 through 20:

COMPOUND INTEREST AND ANNUITY TABLES
5%

Period	FW 1	FW 1/P	SF	PW 1	PW 1/P	PR	Period
1	1.05000	1.00000	1.00000	.95238	.95238	1.05000	1
2	1.10250	2.05000	.48780	.90703	1.85941	.53780	2
3	1.15763	3.15250	.31721	.86384	2.72325	.36721	3
4	1.21551	4.31013	.23201	.82270	3.54595	.28201	4
5	1.27628	5.52563	.18097	.78353	4.32948	.23097	5
6	1.34010	6.80191	.14702	.74622	5.07569	.19702	6
7	1.40710	8.14201	.12282	.71068	5.78637	.17282	7
8	1.47746	9.54911	.10472	.67684	6.46321	.15472	8
9	1.55133	11.02656	.09069	.64461	7.10782	.14069	9
10	1.62889	12.57789	.07950	.61391	7.72173	.12950	10
11	1.71034	14.20679	.07039	.58468	8.30641	.12039	11
12	1.79586	15.91713	.06283	.55684	8.86325	.11283	12
13	1.88565	17.71298	.05646	.53032	9.39357	.10646	13
14	1.97993	19.59863	.05102	.50507	9.89864	.10102	14
15	2.07893	21.57856	.04634	.48102	10.37966	.09634	15
16	2.18287	23.65749	.04227	.45811	10.83777	.09227	16
17	2.29202	25.84037	.03870	.43630	11.27407	.08870	17
18	2.40662	28.13238	.03555	.41552	11.68959	.08555	18
19	2.52695	30.53900	.03275	.39573	12.08532	.08275	19
20	2.65330	33.06595	.03024	.37689	12.46221	.08024	20

The following exercise should help the student or appraiser acquire an understanding of the basic meanings and uses of the six tables. Take the line for Period 15 in the preceding 5% table and read across. For purposes of simplicity, relate the factors to $1,000 or $1,000 per period, using the factors as multipliers only.

FW 1   The factor of 2.07893 indicates that any deposit or value of $1,000 would grow in 15 years, at 5% compounded annually, to $2,078.93.

FW 1/P   Factor of 21.57856 shows that $1,000 deposited or invested at the end of each year for 15 years would generate an accumulation of $21,578.56, at 5%.

SF   The factor .04634, applied to a future worth of $1,000, shows that a deposit of $46.34 would be required at the end of each year to grow to $1,000 in 15 years at 5% compounded annually.

PW 1   As a multiplier, the factor .48102 gives $481.02 as the present worth of a single future income payment or reversion of $1,000 in 15 years at 5% interest or yield.

PW 1/P   Factor computes the present worth of an annuity of $1,000 a year for 15 years to be $10,379.66, at a rate of 5%.

PR   An annual payment of $96.34 would amortize a 5% loan of $1,000 in 15 years, the "loan constant" being 9.634%. (Note that the difference between the SF and PR factors is the interest rate: .05.)

In many situations the appraiser will encounter problems within problems. Occasion may require the use of all six tables in certain complex computations.

Annual Rates and Varying Compounding Periods

There are three variables in tables of compound interest and related derivatives: the interest rate, the compounding interval, and the term in periods. In the more complete tables, rates given cover a range from 1/12% to 100%, with compounding monthly, quarterly, semi-annually, or annually. The number of periods extends to 360 or more per table. The first step in the use of a factor is obviously the selection of the proper table. A consideration here is not only the interest rate, but also the compounding interval and the total number of periods. For example, in selecting a factor at 6%, there are these alternatives for a term of 25 years:

- 300 monthly periods.
- 100 quarterly periods.
- 50 semi-annual periods.
- 25 annual periods.

Factors would be selected from four separate tables, because of the different compounding intervals involved, even though the annual rate is 6% in each case. Monthly rate is ½%; quarterly, 1½%; semi-annual, 3%; and annual 6%. As a matter of procedure, we believe that all rates should be stated as annual rates, with the compounding interval being stipulated.

Basic Concepts

Fundamentals should be spelled out, not assumed. A reasonable degree of comprehension can be obtained by viewing the tables through a framework of the following points:

1. A factor is a percent, expressed as a decimal.
2. The tables are more commonly used in problem solving by:
   a. Multiplying by a factor.
   b. Dividing by a factor.
   c. Computing a factor and locating it in the tables to find rate or time.

   Present worth and future worth are computed by multiplying or dividing by a factor. Rate and time are found by dividing present worth by future worth, or vice versa, and locating the computed factor in the tables. Solving for time is a vertical search, since rate is known; computation of rate is a horizontal search, for time is given.
3. Special cases may call for adjusting a factor: adding or subtracting 1.0; adding or subtracting the interest rate; multiplying a factor by a percent; subtracting one factor from another; multiplying two factors, etc.
4. The computation of compound interest is built into each factor.
5. Multiplying or dividing by a factor does only one of two things:
   a. It adds compound interest to present worth, or
   b. It subtracts compound interest from future worth.
6. The six standard tables all involve the same basic ingredients:
   a. A present sum or stream (present worth).
   b. A future sum or stream (future worth).
   c. Compound interest at a specified rate.
   d. A given number of time periods (compounding intervals).

The usual problem, or segment of a problem, seeks a single unknown quantity, which can be found by use of the factors when the other three elements are given.

7. Future worth to be found equals present worth plus compound interest. It is original principal with future interest added.

8. Present worth to be computed equals future worth minus compound interest. It is original principal only.

9. "Discounting" an income sum or stream (receivable in the future) to its present worth, is the process of computing and subtracting compound interest so that original principal only remains.

10. Identical results are achieved by:
    a. Multiplying by a factor, or
    b. Dividing by its reciprocal and vice versa.

11. Basic equations of value are:
    Value = Income ÷ Rate
    or
    Value = Income x Factor

12. By expansion, the formula for computing present worth is:
    Value = Periodic Payment x PW 1/P + Reversion x PW 1
    (Reversion includes any single future terminal income payment or value.)

Ways and Means

While a factor is not a mystery number, it is a very special number—seemingly a magic number, accomplishing the difficult, or otherwise impossible, in an easy, almost effortless manner.

Because compounding is such a potent force, the analyst or appraiser should realize the importance of determining the proper factor. Choosing the wrong factor could compound his error. Selecting and using the right factor in a knowledgeable manner will never replace discreet judgment, but it can provide a most helpful instrument in the analysis of investments and the valuation of property.

PART 2
Mini-Math Takes Three

Tourists in Switzerland, visiting the Glacier Garden, are fascinated by the Lion of Lucerne. This famous statue of a dying lion protecting the Bourbon lily with its paw, was carved out of sandstone in 1821. Designed by the Danish sculptor Bertel Thorwaldsen, the heroic figure was dedicated to the memory of the Swiss Guards who perished while defending the Tuileries in Paris in 1792. The bas-relief, 28 feet long, is magnificent. An artist once commented, "The lion was there all the time. All the sculptor had to do was chisel away the excess stone."

The value of a parcel of real estate is expressed as a number. Measurements of the growth and time value of money are made by numbers. These values and measurements often can be computed most accurately and readily by the use of compound interest factors found in the prepared tables. These factors were not invented; they were discovered. The inter-relationships between the numbers have always existed; the excess numbers were chipped away, leaving as a residual the beautifully functional factors.

The appraiser who now meets or uses the compound interest tables for the first time can, by removing unawareness, indifference, or neglect, discover for himself the magic multipliers!

Shortcuts and Limitations

In Part I three sets of reciprocal tables are noted:
> FW 1 and PW 1.
> FW 1/P and SF.
> PW 1/P and PR.

Analysis also showed that the difference between the SF and PR is the interest rate. Because of these relationships, it is possible to use two or three tables to do the work of six. Mini-math takes three:
> PW 1.
> PW 1/P.
> PR.

Observation of mini-math's three tables reveals the *size limitations* on each type of factor:
- PW 1 is always less than 1.0. As the time period lengthens, the factor may be less than the interest rate.

21

- PW 1/P is always greater than 1.0 (except for Period 1), less than 1.0 per period, and less than the reciprocal of the interest rate.
- PR is always less than 1.0 (except for Period 1) and greater than the interest rate.

Also note the way in which progression to a greater number of periods and to a higher interest rate affects the size of the factor:

- As the number of time periods increases (rate remaining constant):
  a) PW 1 decreases.
  b) PW 1/P increases.
  c) PR decreases.
- As the interest rate increases (time period remaining constant):
  a) PW 1 decreases.
  b) PW 1/P decreases.
  c) PR increases.

The reciprocals — FW 1, FW 1/P, and SF — increase or decrease in reverse order.

Tie the observations of size and progression of the tables to the concept that the factors either add compound interest to present worth or subtract compound interest from future worth, and you will see that "it figures."

Double Duty Tables

The following outlines will show the regular function and the alternate function of each table in the mini-math trio.

Use this table	to find ...
PW 1 (PRESENT WORTH OF 1)	Present worth of a single future income payment
PW 1/P (PRESENT WORTH OF 1 PER PERIOD)	Present worth of a series of future income payments
PR (PERIODIC REPAYMENT, or Partial Payment)	Periodic payment required to amortize a principal sum

PW 1   PW 1/P   PR

└─────────── Sum ───────────↑   └─────── Reciprocal ───────↑

If you need ...	To find ...	Do this ...
FUTURE WORTH OF 1 (Amount of 1)	Growth of a single deposit or investment at compound interest	Divide by the PRESENT WORTH OF 1 factor
FUTURE WORTH OF 1 PER PERIOD (Amount Of 1 Per Period)	Growth of a level series of periodic deposits at compound interest	Subtract the interest rate (i) from the PERIODIC RE-PAYMENT factor and divide

If you need . . .	To find . . .	Do this . . .
SINKING FUND	Amount of periodic deposit required when future worth is given	Subtract the interest rate (i) from the PERIODIC RE-PAYMENT factor and multiply

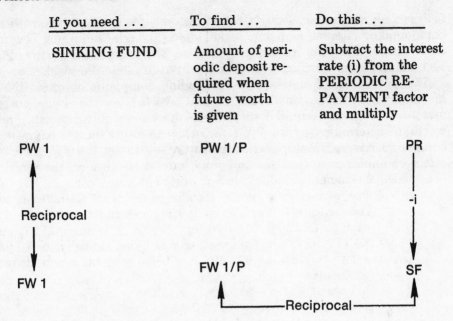

Factors and Reciprocals

By way of clarification: Webster defines "reciprocal" as used in mathematics as "the quotient of unity divided by any quantity" — unity being the number "1.0." The following principles are basic to an understanding of the relationship between a number and its reciprocal:

1. The reciprocal of any number is computed by dividing it into 1.0.
   For example, the reciprocal of 4 is $1 \div 4 = .25$
2. The product of 2 reciprocals is always 1.0.
   For example, $4 \times .25 = 1.0$
3. Identical answers may be found by multiplying by a number or by dividing by its reciprocal, and vice versa.
   For example $30 \times 4 \quad = 120$, and
        $30 \div .25 = 120$
        Also
        $60 \times .25 = 15$, and
        $60 \div 4 \quad = 15$

Each type of factor used in mini-math will be reviewed and explored separately.

PRESENT WORTH OF 1

Present worth tables are predicated on the principle that a payment due at some future time is worth less today and must therefore be discounted. One dollar payable one year from today, including 6% interest, is not worth $1 today. Precisely it is worth $0.9433962264; practically, it is worth 94 cents.

Present Worth of 1 factors frequently are referred to as the reversionary factors. They are used in the property reversion (residual) technique and in any valuation of a single terminal payment or worth. By use of the PW 1 factors one can value a single future income payment today, with rate, compounding interval, and time period given. A single "lump sum" payment at a future date will return the original single capital investment plus accumulated compound interest, which is in reality deferred yield.

The known is "future worth," including compound interest; the unknown, to be determined, is "present worth" — the initial original investment or value required to produce the known future worth. Present worth, as determined by the PW 1 factor, is the future income payment less compound interest. Multiplication of future worth by the PW 1 factor in effect computes and deducts compound interest in advance, the remainder being original principal or value (present worth) only.

For example: A single income payment of $10,000 is to be received in 15 years. In computing present worth at a yield rate of 6%, multiply $10,000 by the PW 1 factor .41727, giving $4,172.70. The 6% interest, compounded annually for 15 years, amounting to $5,827.30, has been computed and deducted from future worth.

Present worth = $10,000 x .41727
              = $4,172.70

You can look at it this way:

Present worth = Future worth — Compound interest
              = $10,000 — $5,827.30
              = $4,172.70

It is unnecessary to calculate the amount of interest, for the computation of compound interest is built into the factor.

The PW 1 factors are the reciprocals of the corresponding FW 1 factors. Dividing present worth by the PW 1 factor will give a result identical to multiplying by the FW 1 factor (its reciprocal) in computing the amount to which a single deposit or investment will grow at compound interest.

For example: To determine the amount to which $5,000 will increase in 10 years, in an account paying 5% compounded annually, divide $5,000 by the PW 1 factor, .61391, giving $8,144.52. Compound interest at 5% for 10 years, amounting to $3,144.52, has been computed and added to the original deposit (present worth).

Future worth = $5,000 ÷ .61391
             = $8,144.52

Future worth = Present worth + Compound interest
             = $5,000 + $3,144.52
             = $8,144.52

The PW 1 factor does double duty, for the same computation could have been made by multiplying present worth of $5,000 by the FW 1 factor, 1.62889. $5,000 x 1.62889 = $8,144.45. Slight difference is due to rounding factors to five decimal places.

Present worth tables are accurate measures of the time value of money at any given interest rate. (See diagram at the top of the facing page.)

The factors shown in the diagram for years 1 through 7 at 10% compounded annually, give the declining present worth of a single future income payment as the time period lengthens. For example, a payment of

PRESENT WORTH OF 1
10%

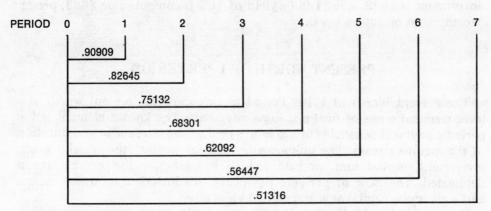

PERIOD 0   1   2   3   4   5   6   7

.90909
.82645
.75132
.68301
.62092
.56447
.51316

$1,000, due in one year, has a present worth of $909.09 at a yield rate of 10%:

$1,000 x .90909 = $909.09
Return *of* capital in 1 year: $909.09
Return *on* capital in 1 year: 90.91
                                   $1,000.00

Similarly, a single payment of $1,000, due in four years, has a present worth of $683 at a yield rate of 10%:

$1,000 x .68301 = $683
Return *of* capital in 4 years: $683
Return *on* capital in 4 years: 317
                                  $1,000

To convince any "Doubting Thomas," here's proof that the factors really work and are labor saving devices:

Year	10% Interest Compounded Annually	Present Worth Building Up To Future Worth
0		$683.00
1	$68.30	751.30
2	75.13	826.43
3	82.64	909.07
4	90.91	999.98
	.02 (adjustment)	
	$317.00	$1,000.00 (rounded)

At the ending of the first year, 10% interest on an investment of $683 amounts to $68.30. Since no payment is to be made until the end of four years, the $68.30 earned is added to $683. The base has built up to $751.30, on which 10% interest for the second year is computed. This pattern of compounding continues year by year. In four years at 10% interest compounded annually a present worth of $683 builds up to $1,000.

The preceding computations show that if an investor pays $683 (present worth) for a future payment or value of $1,000 (future worth) due in four years, he would receive a true 10% yield plus a recovery of capital. Since his investment is $683, not $1,000, yield of 10% is computed on $683, present worth — not on future worth.

PRESENT WORTH OF 1 PER PERIOD

The Present Worth of 1 Per Period factors show the present worth of a level terminal series of future income payments. The known element is the periodic payment schedule (future worth) — i.e., the size, shape and duration of the income stream. The unknown is "present worth:" the initial deposit, investment, capital sum, or value which will generate the income stream delineated. The flow of periodic payments will include a return *of* capital and a return *on* capital at any specified yield rate.

Present Worth of 1 Per Period tables are also known as the annuity tables. The PW 1/P factor is the Inwood coefficient.

The process of multiplying the amount of periodic payment by the PW 1/P factor computes present worth of the annuity by a determination and deduction of compound interest from the future income stream at whatever yield rate is indicated. Present worth is future worth minus compound interest. The factor will make this computation:

> *For example:* An annual income payment of $5,000 is to be received each year for 10 years. To compute its present worth at a yield rate of 9%, multiply $5,000 by 6.41766 (PW 1/P factor) giving $32,088. This process has computed and subtracted $17,912 earned interest (yield) from the total stream of $50,000.

Just as

> Future worth = $5,000 x 10
> = $50,000

So also

> Present worth = $5,000 x 6.41766
> = $32,088

And

> Present worth = Future worth — Compound interest
> = $50,000 — $17,912
> = $32,088

A level terminal income stream with no delayed start presents no particular problem in computation. For example, $5,000 per period for 4 consecutive periods, 10% yield rate, would be discounted to present worth in this manner:

$$\$5,000 \text{ x } 3.16987 = \$15,849.35$$

Four periodic payments of $5,000 would return $15,849.35 capital invested plus $4,150.65 yield at 10% for a total of $20,000. The two tables at the top of the facing page are evidence of this.

This, however, is the long way around. Since the PW 1/P factor for any period is the sum of the corresponding and preceding PW 1 factors, the easy, direct way in this representative problem is through single multiplication. The product of 3.16987 (PW 1/P) and $5,000 gives a present worth at 10%

Year	Payment	10% Yield	Principal Returned	Principal Balance
0	—	—	—	$15,849.35
1	$5,000	$1,584.94	$3,415.06	12,434.29
2	5,000	1,243.43	3,756.57	8,677.72
3	5,000	867.77	4,132.23	4,545.49
4	5,000	454.51*	4,545.49*	0
	$20,000	$4,150.65	$15,849.35	

$4,150.65 + $15,849.35 = $20,000

*Adjustment of $0.04 is made because of rounding.

The same answer could be found in the following manner:

Year	Present Worth of 1		Periodic Payment		Present Worth
1	.90909	x	$5,000	=	$4,545.45
2	.82645	x	5,000	=	4,132.25
3	.75132	x	5,000	=	3,756.60
4	.68301	x	5,000	=	3,415.05
	3.16987		$20,000		$15,849.35

for 4 periods, which is identical to the sum of all four present worth amounts, computed individually by use of the PW 1 factors for periods 1, 2, 3, and 4.

The following diagram shows the composition of the PW 1/P factors at 10% for periods 1 through 7, and the relationship of PW 1 factors to PW 1/P. The figures on the top horizontal line are the PW 1 factors for each period. On the following seven lines appear the PW 1/P factors, which are derived by adding the Pw 1 factors through each time period involved.

PRESENT WORTH OF 1 PER PERIOD
10%

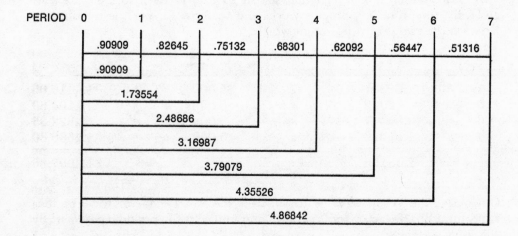

By way of further explanation, note:
    Period 2:   .90909 + .82645 = 1.73554
    Period 3:   .90909 + .82645 + .75132 = 2.48636
    Period 7:   .90909 + .82645 + .75132 + .68301 + .62092 + .56447 +
             .51316 = 4.86842

In the use of the PW 1/P factors, consideration should be given to two special situations:

1. A level terminal stream with a deferred start.
2. A "step-up" or "step-down" annuity, consisting of two or more consecutive streams on graduated levels, with or without a deferred start.

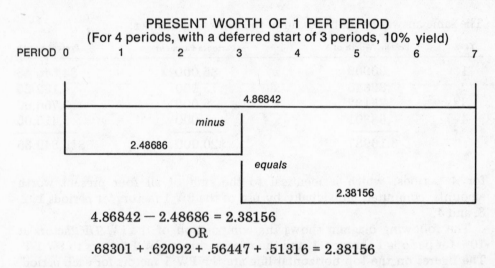

PRESENT WORTH OF 1 PER PERIOD
(For 4 periods, with a deferred start of 3 periods, 10% yield)

4.86842 − 2.48686 = 2.38156
OR
.68301 + .62092 + .56447 + .51316 = 2.38156

To illustrate, the present worth of $5,000 per period for 4 periods, with a deferred start of 3 periods, at a 10% yield rate is:

        Present worth = (4.86842 − 2.48686) x $5,000
                        = 2.38156 x $5,000
                        = $11,907.80

Another method, although impractical to use, is given to illustrate how and why the proceding process works and to show further the relationship between the two tables of present worth:

Period	PW 1 factor		Periodic Payment		Present Worth
4	.68301	x	$5,000	=	$3,415.05
5	.62092	x	5,000	=	3,104.60
6	.56447	x	5,000	=	2,822.35
7	.51316	x	5,000	=	2,565.80
	2.38156				$11,907.80

Obviously, the "easy way" is to subtract the PW 1/P factor for 3 periods from the PW 1/P factor for 7 periods, and multiply the periodic payment by the adjusted factor.

An alternate method of adjusting a factor for a deferred start is to select the PW 1/P factor as though there were no deferred start and multiply it by the PW 1 factor for the period of deferment.

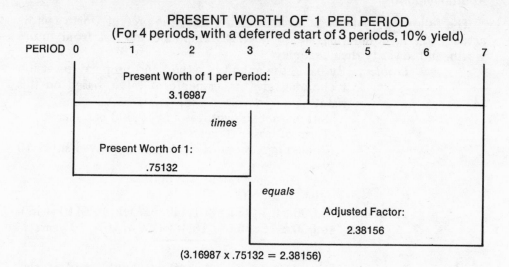

PRESENT WORTH OF 1 PER PERIOD
(For 4 periods, with a deferred start of 3 periods, 10% yield)

Present Worth of 1 per Period:
3.16987

times

Present Worth of 1:
.75132

equals

Adjusted Factor:
2.38156

(3.16987 x .75132 = 2.38156)

The last procedure illustrated would be of particular advantage in a situation in which its use would eliminate the necessity of extending the tables. The PW 1 factor discounts correctly for the deferred (future) start of a level terminal series of income payments, just as it discounts for a single future income payment. Each level segment of a graduated annuity should be treated as individual entity, with a final summation to be made.

For example: A lease calls for annual payments of $5,000 for the first 10 years, $6,500 for the next 10 years, and $8,000 for the following 5 years. Value the lease at a yield rate of 9%.

Method: Compute the initial 10 year stream in the usual way. Consider the $6,500 annual flow as a 10 period series with a 10 period deferred start. The last portion will be treated as a 5 year terminal stream with a 20 year deferred start. Factors can be adjusted by either of the two methods illustrated. The three separate amounts of present worth computed are to be added, as they constitute a single capital sum.

Solution:

PW 1/P factors at 9%:
Year 10   6.41766
Year 20   9.12855
Year 25   9.82258

Adjusted PW 1/P factors to be used as multipliers:
Years   1—10   6.41766 (no adjustment)
Years 11—20   9.12855 − 6.41766 = 2.71089
Years 21—25   9.82258 − 9.12855 =   .69403

Computation of present worth of the annuity:
$5,000 x 6.41766 = $32,088
   6,500 x 2.71089 =   17,621

$$8,000 \times .69403 = \underline{5,552}$$

$$\$55,261$$

Additional Proof

The following example is given to show what the present worth factors actually do in computing and deducting compound interest from future worth, and to verify their accuracy.

Problem: By using the annuity method and property reversion technique, give an estimate of value, based on this data:

Net-net-net straight lease[1] : $10,000 per year
Term of lease: 10 years
Remaining economic life of improvements: 10 years
Assumed land value: $40,000
Yield rate: 10%

Solution: $10,000 x 6.14457 = $61,446 (PW 1/P, 10%, 10 years)
40,000 x   .38554 = 15,422 (PW 1, 10%, 10 years)

$$\$76,868$$

Proof: If the factors do what they should, and if the computations are correct, $10,000 per year for 10 years should pay 10% yield and return the capital sum of $61,446, the principal amount outstanding decreasing to $0 by the end of 10 years.

Also, land worth $40,000 will revert to the lessor in 10 years. Present worth of the reversion, computed to be $15,422, should build up to $40,000 in 10 years, at 10% compounded annually.

Year	Payment	10% Yield	Principal Returned	Principal Balance
0				$61,446
1	$10,000	$6,145	$3,855	57,591
2	10,000	5,759	4,241	53,350
3	10,000	5,335	4,665	48,685
4	10,000	4,869	5,131	43,554
5	10,000	4,355	5,645	37,909
6	10,000	3,791	6,209	31,700
7	10,000	3,170	6,830	24,870
8	10,000	2,487	7,513	17,357
9	10,000	1,736	8,264	9,093
10	10,000	907*	9,093*	0
	$100,000	$38,554	$61,446	

Return *of* capital $61,446
Return *on* capital   38,554

*Adjust $2 for rounding. $100,000

---

[1] A net-net-net lease is one in which the lessee pays *all* expenses, including maintenance, insurance and property taxes.

Year	10% Yield (Deferred)	Principal Balance
0		$15,422
1	$1,542	16,964
2	1,696	18,660
3	1,866	20,526
4	2,053	22,579
5	2,258	24,837
6	2,484	27,321
7	2,732	30,053
8	3,005	33,058
9	3,306	36,364
10	3,636	40,000

A Matter of Reciprocity

The PW 1/P factor is the reciprocal of the Periodic Repayment factor. One table may substitute for the other by switching from multiplication to division, and vice versa.

> *For example:* Annual payment to amortize a loan of $35,000 at 8½% in 15 years is
> $35,000 ÷ 8.30424 = $4,214.71 (PW 1/P factor)
> or
> $35,000 x .12042 = $4,214.70 (PR factor)

On occasion, a dog-eared copy of present worth factors could prove to be the appraiser's best friend.

PERIODIC REPAYMENT (PARTIAL PAYMENT)

Factors in this table show the periodic payment required to amortize a loan or return a capital sum with interest in a specified time period at a given rate. The income stream is a level terminal one, and equal periodic payments include principal and interest. Each succeeding period a larger amount applies to principal and a smaller amount to interest, as interest is computed each period on the unpaid balance.

The amount of periodic payment is found by multiplying the original principal amount by the PR factor. Amortization schedules used by lending institutions are developed from this table. The PR factor computes and adds interest to the present worth (principal amount) of an amortized loan.

> *For example:* Annual payments to amortize a loan of $40,000 at 9% in 10 years are .15582 x $40,000 or $6,232.80. (Use PR factor at 9% for 10 periods.) Total payments to repay the loan are 10 x $6,232.80, or $62,328, of which $40,000 is principal and $22,328 earned interest, computed each period on a declining principal balance.

The PR factor is the reciprocal of the corresponding PW 1/P factor. It is also the Sinking Fund factor plus i (interest rate). The PR table is a versatile one, and, with slight adjustments, can perform the functions of three others:

1. Divide by the PR and you can make the same computations as

multiplying by the PW 1/P factor.

> *For example:* The present worth of an annual income stream of
> $8,000 for 5 years at a yield rate of 12% is:
>
> $8,000 ÷ .27741 = $28,838

2. Subtract the interest rate from the PR factor, multiply future worth by
   it, and you are actually using the Sinking Fund factor to determine the
   periodic deposit required.

   > *For example:* A depositor has a goal of accumulating $15,000
   > in 15 years by making annual deposits in a 5% savings account.
   > What amount of annual deposit is required?
   >
   > *Solution:*
   >
   > .09634 — .05 = .04634
   >
   > $15,000 x .04634 = $695.10

3. Subtract the interest rate from the PR factor, divide by it, and your
   computation is identical to multiplying by the Future Worth of 1 Per
   Period.

   > *For example:* An annual deposit of $1,500 is made in a savings
   > account paying 6%. To what amount would the account grow in
   > 8 years?
   >
   > *Solution:*
   >
   > .16104 — .06 = .10104
   >
   > $1,500 ÷ .10104 = $14,845.60

Interpolation by Simple Proportion

Factors for percentages not given in the tables used in mini-math may be
computed by interpolation. The method illustrated is quite accurate when
used with the PR factors, but somewhat less precise with the other tables.
Let's illustrate the procedure:

> *Problem:* Compute the PR factor at 9¾% for 10 annual periods.
>
> *Solution:* Tables in "Mini-Math" include 9% and 10%. The PR
> factor for 9¾% will lie at some point between. Find it
> in the following manner.
>
> 1. Find the difference between the 2 rates that
>   establish the upper and lower limits of the range.
>   .10 — .09 = .01
>
> 2. Determine the difference between the subject rate
>   for which the PR factor is sought and the lower
>   rate.
>   .0975 — .09 = .0075
>
> 3. Divide the answer from Step 2 by the difference
>   found in Step 1.
>   .0075 ÷ .01 = .75
>   This indicates that the rate of 9¾% lies .75 of the
>   way between .09 and .10. In interpolation by
>   simple proportion it will be assumed that the PR
>   factor for 9¾% will also be a point .75 of the way
>   between the PR factors for 9% and 10%.
>
> 4. Locate the PR factors for 9% and 10% for 10
>   annual periods, and compute the difference (dis-

tance between them).

10% PR factor	.16275
9% PR factor	— .15582
Difference :	.00693

5. Find .75 of the difference: .75 x .00693 = .0051975

6. Add product found in Step 5 to PR factor at 9%, the lower limit of the range.

.15582 + .0051975 = .1610175, rounded to .16102

The same method of interpolation is used in problem solving, particularly in computing yield rates that fall between the tables.

EXTENSION TABLES

A special situation may require the computation of factors for time periods beyond those in the prepared tables in "Mini-Math." Extension can be accomplished as shown in the following outline:

Present Worth of 1

Extension is made directly, by multiplying factors for any two or more time periods whose sum equals the period for which a factor is sought.

Example: To find the PW 1 factor at 7% for period 75, select factors for any periods whose sum equals 75—say, periods 40 and 35.

PW 1 at 7% for period 40 is .06678.

PW 1 at 7% for period 35 is .09366.

Multiplying: .06678 x .09366 = .00625

Present Worth Of 1 Per Period

Extension is indirect. Steps involved are:

a. Compute PW 1 factor by extension.

b. Subtract factor in Step *a* from 1.0.

c. Divide difference by i (interest rate).

Example: Find PW 1/P factor at 7% for period 75 as follows:

a. Compute PW 1 to be .00625, as in prior example.

b. 1.0 — .00625 = .99375

c. .99375 ÷ .07 = 14.1964

Periodic Repayment

Extension is indirect. Follow these steps:

a. Compute PW 1 factor by extension.

b. Subtract factor in Step *a* from 1.0.

c. Divide i by the difference.

Example: PR factor at 7% for period 75 is found in this way:

a. PW 1 is .00625 (see examples above).

b. 1.0 — .00625 = .99375

c. .07 ÷ .99375 = .07044

Procedures illustrated and explained on the extension of the tables to a greater number of periods are also applicable to the extension of the tables to accommodate *monthly* intervals that cover a fractional portion of a year. For example, you need the *monthly* PW 1, PW 1/P, and PR factors at 7% for 20½ years. The monthly tables in "Mini-Math" list the factors for months 1 through 12, then years 1 through 30. The monthly factors for 20½ years, or 246 months, can be calculated by extension, as illustrated here:

PW 1 — Factor at 7% for 6 months is .96570.

Factor at 7% for 20 years (240 months) is .24760

PW 1, 7%, 246 months = .9657 x .2476

= .23911

PW 1/P — Factor at 7% for 246 months:

PW 1/P = (1.0 — .23911) ÷ .005833

= .76089 ÷ .005833

= 130.44

(For "i" use effective monthly interest rate of .005833, which corresponds to the nominal annual rate of .07, or 7%.)

PR — Factor at 7% for 246 months:

PR   = .005833 ÷ (1.0 — .23911)

= .005833 ÷ .76089

= .007666

Note that the PW 1 factor must be extended first before a calculation by extension can be made for either PW 1/P or PR.

Using the OAR Tables

The new "OAR Tables" in "Mini-Math" are derived from the compound interest and annuity tables. Variables built into the precomputed over-all rates include: desired equity yield rate; expected holding period before resale of the property; loan ratio, interest rate, and term; equity build-up through loan amortization; and anticipated percent of appreciation or depreciation within the holding period.

The two special sections in Part III explore, explain, and illustrate the use of both the standard compound interest factors and the convenient precomputed OAR's in the mortgage-equity technique of the income approach to value. To some appraisers, this technique may prove to be a new route to old objectives.

Mini-Math, Limited

The purpose of the shorthand method and streamlined approach is to place a compact, useable "how-to-do-it" manual in the hands of the appraiser—one that contains in the same volume the essential compound interest factors and precomputed mortgage-equity over-all rates required in most computations. Where there is brevity, there are also limitations:

1. Three tables do the work of six. This calls for some adjustment of factors and for division as well as multiplication in the use of factors.
2. Solving for rate or time may occasionally require going an alternate route, since FW 1, FW 1/P, and SF tables are omitted.
3. The number of tables tabulated by interest rate has been restricted. On

occasion a factor or an OAR may have to be computed by interpolation—for example, one at 6¼%.

4. One curtailment is that only monthly and annual compounding periods are given. In most problems dealing with quarterly or semi-annual intervals, there will usually be no significant difference, however, in going monthly or annual all the way.

5. Factors in "Mini-Math" are rounded to five decimal places. More complete tables give ten places. The difference in practical problem solving is usually negligible.

6. Factors are listed to 360 monthly periods and 50 annual periods. The tables must be extended to accommodate longer terms, if required.

7. The precomputed OAR tables are based on holding periods of 5, 10, and 15 years. Other time intervals between purchase and resale will involve interpolation or individual computation of rates.

8. Interpolation may be required between given percents of appreciation and depreciation in the OAR tables.

The two compound interest tables and the mortgage-equity over-all rates in "Mini-Math" are not appraisal answers. They are professional tools developed to assist the evaluator in finding answers—in solving maxi-problems.

PART 3, SECTION 1

Mini-Math Methods:
The Appraiser's Edge

There are three things one can do with any problem: ignore it, deplore it, or explore it. This calls for: folding the hands, wringing the hands, or rolling up the sleeves and doing something about it. We recommend the latter set of actions.

Parts I and II have dealt with theory; now, we shall get down to practice. If this text is considered a tool in the valuation of property, PART III is the cutting edge. Over 60 methods are outlined, explained, and illustrated in this "how-to-do-it" portion of the text. The methods presented in Section 1, and applied to procedures in Section 2, are given under nine general categories, arranged alphabetically:

- Bonds (pages 38 and 66)
- General Applications (pages 39 and 66)
- Growth of a Series of Periodic Deposits (pages 39 and 67)
- Growth of a Single Deposit or Investment (pages 39 and 68)
- Prepaid Interest (pages 39 and 69)
- Present Worth of Annuities, Leased Fees, Leasehold Interests, and Single Future Income Payments (Reversions) (pages 40 and 71)
- Real Estate Appraisal: Methods and Techniques of the Income Approach (pages 42 and 76)
- Special Section on Mortgage-Equity Technique (pages 45 and 80)
- Trust Deeds and Mortgages: Amortization, Analysis, and Discount (pages 57 and 94)

The student should relate the general explanations in Section 1 under each heading to the corresponding procedures outlined in Section 2, beginning on page 63. Discussions in Section 1 have been segregated purposely from the techniques outlined in Section 2. Thus the "Summary of Mini-Math Methods" (page 66) is as compact as possible and in immediate proximity to the compound interest tables themselves. The procedures and the tables are the portions of the text that the evaluator will be using in his appraisal problems.

BONDS

Valuation of a bond, discounted to a higher yield rate or selling at a premium, is computed by following the basic equation:

Value = Periodic Payment x PW 1/P + Reversion x PW 1

A bond is typically set up with semi-annual payments of interest only, the entire principal or face amount being due at maturity. The payment schedule consists of a level income stream (annuity) and a single lump sum terminal payment (reversion). If the bond is resold at a discount, it will generate a higher yield rate for the purchaser than the interest rate the bond bears. If it is sold at a higher price (premium) the yield rate to the purchaser will be less than the interest rate on the bond.

Certain type of bonds, such as improvement bonds, may be scheduled on an amortized basis of equal periodic payments, principal and interest included.

The basic concepts and procedures in discounting bonds to a yield rate different from the interest rate apply to valuing other investments that generate an income stream of similar structure. Such a category would include:

- Annuities
- Income property to which the mortgage-equity technique is applicable
- Leases
- Leased fees
- Mortgages and trust deeds

If bonds are given as total or partial consideration in the purchase of real estate, the appraiser discounts them to the indicated current market yield rate. This computation of "cash equivalent" is one step in the market approach to value—adjusting sales price for terms.

The assumption of annual payments in mini-math produces a value that is approximate, not precise, if interest payments on the bond are made semi-annually. When the exact figure is required, consult tables that list factors by semi-annual periods. Use the procedures outlined and illustrated under "Bonds" in Section 2 (page 66). There is, however, a possibility that the factors in the mini-math tables can be used in certain situations to give precise consideration to semi-annual payments. For example, consider discounting a 6%, 10 year bond with semi-annual interest payments, to a yield rate of 8%. Use the 4% PW 1 and PW 1/P tables, selecting factors for 20 periods. (A semi-annual rate of 4% corresponds to a nominal annual rate of 8%.) Problems related to bonds are of two types:

1. Computing *value* of a bond, when a yield rate higher or lower than the interest rate is specified.
2. Computing the *yield rate* on a bond, when a dollar value higher or lower than the face value is given.

In both cases, the fundamental equation is used. In computing *value* a single set of calculations is involved. However, in calculating *yield rate* it is a matter of "cut and try," requiring two or more sets of computations. These points are clarified in the procedures and illustrations beginning on page 66 in Section 2.

GENERAL APPLICATIONS

Procedures explained and illustrated under this heading (page 66) in Section 2 have applications to either financial or non-financial areas. Population growth, economic indices, etc., are cases in point.

GROWTH OF A SERIES OF PERIODIC DEPOSITS

The FW 1/P tables are prepared on the assumption that the deposit is made at the end of each period. If the deposit is made at the beginning of the period, the FW 1/P factor must be adjusted. An illustration will be the best explanation. To compute the growth of deposits made at the beginning of each period for 15 periods, subtract 1.0 from the FW 1/P factor for Period 16. Multiplication of the amount of periodic deposit by the adjusted factor will compute the future worth to which the series of deposits will grow by the end of 15 periods.

In mini-math a different type of adjustment is used, since PR — i substitutes for FW 1/P. This is explained and illustrated in Section 2 (see page 67). The student should give special attention to the time of deposit—whether it is at the end or at the beginning of the period.

Analysis of an amortized mortgage or trust deed will consider deposits (payments on principal) as being made at the *end* of the period. Usually, interest is not charged, paid, nor payable until the end of the payment interval (prepaid interest excepted). A real estate loan payment due on the first of July, for example, pays interest for the month of June. The portion of the payment applying to principal should be considered as having been made June 30—i.e., at the end of the period. Growth of an equity by loan amortization can be computed by finding the amount applied to principal the first period of the amortization schedule, then calculating its growth as though it were a periodic deposit made at the end of each period.

GROWTH OF A SINGLE DEPOSIT OR INVESTMENT

Calculations of future worth in mini-math are straightforward uses of the PW 1 factors as divisors. These computations demonstrate vividly the time value of money. An investor who does not realize how time affects yield may be short changing himself. The appraiser, too, must recognize this point. For details on procedures, see Section 2, page 68.

PREPAID INTEREST

Prepaid interest, like prepaid rent, is received before it has been earned. It is "cash in hand" and warrants no discount when the appraiser computes the cash equivalent of the sale. Advantages in this type of transaction are not all on the side of the purchaser and borrower. The seller and lender under the purchase money mortgage also has a substantial benefit. It is true that the motivation is usually income tax "breaks" for the buyer. However, the seller, who carries the loan, has the benefit of the earning power of unearned interest received before it is due.

In analyzing such a transaction, the appraiser should develop a complete payment schedule from the terms of the note. This may call for several calculations, such as computing the amount of a balloon payment. If interest has been prepaid, the face amount of the note has not decreased, but the future income stream has been diminished. Adjustment for this is made by the proper use of factors in the equation:

Value = Periodic Payment x PW 1/P + Reversion x PW 1

Reversion, in this case, is the terminal balloon payment.

Present worth to the seller of his total income stream is the sum of three items:

- Down payment
- Prepaid interest, undiscounted
- Mortgage or trust deed, with its remaining income stream discounted to the interest rate on the note.

Because prepaid interest is not discounted, present worth to the seller of the total income stream will exceed the sales price.

"Cash equivalent" of the sale will call for discounting the mortgage or trust deed to a yield rate which is higher than the interest rate on the note—a realistic rate derived from the current local private mortgage market. The presumption in calculating cash equivalent of the sale is that the seller of the property retains the down payment and the prepaid interest; he immediately resells the purchase money mortgage to another private investor at a discount.

The appraiser adjusts sales price for terms by discounting the mortgage or trust deed to a yield rate that would make the "paper" saleable in the private money market. "Cash equivalent" of the sale is the sum of:

- Down payment
- Prepaid interest, undiscounted
- Mortgage or trust deed, discounted to the required higher yield rate.

Procedures are illustrated in Section 2, beginning on page 69.

PRESENT WORTH OF ANNUITIES, LEASED FEES, LEASEHOLD INTERESTS AND SINGLE FUTURE INCOME PAYMENTS (REVERSIONS)

This category might be discussed and explained best by a definition of terms, as follows:

Annuity—Any investment which generates an annuity produces a measurable income stream of a specific duration. Annual income payments represent a return to the investor *of* his capital and a return *on* capital (yield or interest). The value or present worth of the annuity is computed by multiplying the amount of one periodic payment by the PW 1/P factor at the appropriate yield rate and for the given period of time.

Ordinary Annuity—The income payment is received at the end of the period. In valuing annuities such as leases in which payments are received monthly, quarterly, or semi-annually, compute the periodic payments on an annual basis and treat the income stream as an ordinary annuity. PW 1/P factors require no adjustment in valuing an ordinary lease.

Annuity Due—Payment is received at the beginning of the period (prepaid annual rent, for example). An easy adjustment of the PW 1/P factor is required, as shown in Procedure 2 under "Annuity" in the "Summary of Mini-Math Methods" (see page 72).

Deferred Annuity—If there is a specified time lag between the date of investment and the start of the annuity, adjustment must be made for the deferred return of capital and the deferred yield. This is another example of the time value of money. Two procedures for adjusting factors are illustrated and explained in the summary of methods.

Graduated Annuity—Instead of a level terminal series of income payments, the income stream consists of step-up and/or step-down segments. Calculate each level segment, after the initial one, as an annuity with a deferred start; add the separate valuations to find total present worth.

Leases—A lease might be considered as a short term sale, whereby the owner of the fee (the lessor) conveys to the tenant (lessee) the right to the use and occupancy of the property for a limited term at a stipulated rent.

Leased Fee—The owner's interest consists of his right to receive rent under the terms of the lease, plus the reversion of the property upon termination of the lease. The calculation of present worth involves valuing an income stream plus a single terminal sum (reversion). The basic equation is used:

Value = Periodic Payment x PW 1/P + Reversion x PW 1

Note the different procedures in Section 2 (page 73), depending on the relationship between contract and economic rent. *Economic rent* is the "fair" rent the property should command in the current market. *Contract rent* is the actual rent specified in the lease. Contract and economic rent may coincide or differ. The appraiser must determine this point in any given situation.

Leasehold Interest—(a.) If property is unimproved or if improvements have been erected by the lessor, the tenant has a leasehold interest only if economic rent exceeds contract rent. Present worth of the leasehold interest can be found by valuing the excess of economic rent over contract rent. (b.) When improvements are erected by the lessee, the tenant's leasehold interest is the difference between economic rent of the total property and contract rent of the land.

Sale-Leaseback—In this type of transaction, the purchaser of the property leases it back to the seller, usually for a long term, with renewal options. Annual rent is often computed as a fixed percent of the purchase price, allowing the buyer-lessor a complete recovery of capital and a reasonable yield on capital within the initial term of the lease.

Sandwich Lease—A leases to B, and B subleases to C. B holds the sandwich lease. B's interest can be found by subtracting the contract rent he pays to A from the contract rent he collects from C.

Single Future Income Payment (Reversion)—Concepts and procedures relate to any terminal sum or value receivable in the future. Possession and use of improved or unimproved property reverting to the lessor upon termination of the lease is an example.

Top Leasehold Interest—In the case of the "sandwich lease," if economic rent of the property exceeds contract rent paid by C to B, C has a top leasehold interest. The annual amount of this interest is measured by the difference, and can be valued at present worth. (A is the lessor; while B, in a dual position of lessee and sub-lessor, holds the sandwich lease; and C, the sub-lessee, has the top leasehold position.)

REAL ESTATE APPRAISAL:
METHODS AND TECHNIQUES OF THE INCOME APPROACH

One of the indicators of value can be derived by capitalizing the net income a property produces. Capitalization is a means of converting an income stream to a capital sum. Critical points of procedure to be determined by the appraiser in the income approach include selection of (1) proper method; (2) proper technique; and (3) proper yield rate.

Method refers primarily to the shape and duration of the income stream:

a. *Level perpetual* series of income payments. This method is applicable to land, which is considered as having an economic life in perpetuity. Since land is a non-wasting asset, *direct capitalization* of income provides for no amortization or recovery of capital. Computation is made by the formula: Value = Income ÷ Rate.

b. *Level terminal* series of income payments. *Annuity* and *sinking fund* procedures used in the three conventional residual techniques of valuing improved properties relate to this income stream structure, as does the *mortgage-equity technique.*

c. *Declining terminal* series of income payments. The *straight line* procedure may be applied to any of the residual techniques in the appraisal of improved income producing properties. Its use depends on the appraiser's analysis and judgment of the shape of the income stream.

d. *Single future* income payment. Examples are resale of nonproducing land, reversion of land in the property residual technique, and equity at the end of the holding period in the mortgage-equity technique.

If a traditional *residual technique* is to be used, its choice depends on the value which is known or which can best be estimated.

a. If land value is known, use the *building residual* technique. This is the preferred route to go in the conventional income approach.

b. If building value is known but data for determining land value is lacking, the *land residual* technique may be used. (In the case of vacant land, the appraiser may construct an hypothetical building in the appraisal process.)

c. If neither land nor improvement values are reasonably determinable, but future land value can be estimated, the *property residual* or *reversion* technique may be employed.

Rating the Rates and the Rents

Yield rates for capitalizing income from a real estate investment are derived by three principal methods: summation, band of investment, and market.

Here is an example of building a rate by summation:

"Safe" rate	.05
"Risk" rate	.02
Non-liquidity rate	.015

Money management   .005
                     _____
                      .09

This method is synthetic and subjective. Although it is not recommended, the presumption is that a rate taken from "the market" includes all these components.

The band of investment considers financing, loan rates and ratios, and equity investment. A capitalization rate developed by this means is a weighted average. For example, the purchaser arranges a first mortgage at 8% interest for 60% of the purchase price, and a second at 9% for 30% of total value. He pays 10% down and on this thin equity position, seeks a yield of 18%. Rate can be developed as follows:

	Percent of Value		Interest Rate		Yield
1st Mortgage	.60	x	.08	=	.048
2nd Mortgage	.30	x	.09	=	.027
Equity	.10	x	.18	=	.018
	1.00				.093

The fallacy is that no adjustment is made for loan amortization nor for appreciation or depreciation in property value.

Preferred method for deriving a yield rate is the market. Rates required to attract investment capital may be obtained from knowledgeable buyers, sellers, brokers, and lenders. The appraiser can derive rates by analyzing sales and relating market values to income. An over-all rate is computed by the equation:

Rate = Income ÷ Value

Calculation of the mortgage-equity over-all rate is discussed in the subsequent section. It is further explained and illustrated in the "Summary of Mini-Math Methods" (beginning on page 80). Perceptive market analysis will guide the appraiser in his computation of a rate or in his selection of a pre-computed over-all rate from the OAR tables in this text.

The appraiser should recognize the leverage effect of yield rates. A difference of one percent or less can be responsible for a variance of considerable magnitude in property valuation. A simple mistake in rate calculation or selection will produce a compound error in value conclusion.

Matters of judgement enter into rate selection. The appraiser must consider carefully both the *risk* element in the investment and the related *quality* of the income stream. It is axiomatic that the greater the risk, the higher the yield rate; and the higher the yield rate, the lower the value. For example, in the illustration of building a rate by the band of investment theory above, the holder of the first mortgage is in the most secure position. The lower interest rate of 8% is justified. The junior lien holder is less secure, and the higher 9% rate is warranted. In this case, the purchaser has a thin equity position and the greatest risk. If property values should drop by 10% before he has realized a significant amount of equity build-up through loan amortization, he is wiped out. To compensate for this high degree of risk, an anticipated yield rate of 18% is within reason.

Value of income property can be increased by raising either the quantity or the quality of the income stream. We will give simple illustrations by direct capitalization:

> Net income is $18,000. Property is leased to a new local business firm. Capitalization rate of 9% is used because of the degree of risk.
>
> Value = $18,000 ÷ .09, or $200,000
>
> Assume the income can be increased to $21,000 — same rate.
>
> Value = $21,000 ÷ .09, or $233,333
>
> Assume the property in the prior example is leased to a national AAA-1 chain store corporation at $18,000 net. Quantity of the income stream has not been increased, but the quality has been improved. Risk has been reduced. Yield rate can also be reduced, raising the value of the property. Assuming the market indicates an applicable rate of 7½%:
>
> Value = $18,000 ÷ .075, or $240,000

Appraisal policies related to total capitalization rates in an assessor's office differ from those of general practice in one respect. Instead of treating property taxes as an annual expense, the assessor builds a percentage allowance into the capitalization rate. For example, if the tax rate in an area is $9.00 per $100 of assessed value, and assessed value is 25% of appraised value, the tax increment is .09 x .25, or .0225 (2¼%). The rationale is that if taxes and tax rate are given, the value of the property has been pre-determined.

In the building residual and land residual techniques, note that a split capitalization rate is used: one for land, another for improvements. This calls for a reasonable estimate of the remaining economic life (REL) of the improvement. For example, take the case of an apartment house appraisal. Estimated REL is 40 years, yield rate of .08 is indicated, and tax allowance of .0225 has been determined. The total capitalization rate applied to land provides for no recovery of capital; it includes yield and taxes only. Capitalization rate for improvements also allows for yield and taxes. In addition it must include 100% recapture (amortization) of the value of the building during its remaining life—in this case, 1.00 ÷ 40, or .025 (2½%) per year.

Capitalization rate for land:

Yield (return on capital)	.08
Tax allowance	.0225
Total	.1025

Capitalization rate for improvements:

Yield (return on capital)	.08
Tax allowance	.0225
Amortization (return on capital)	.025
Total	.1275

Amortization is built into the PW 1/P factor. If the appraiser is using a residual technique with an annuity method, he provides for amortization (recovery of capital on the wasting asset) by selecting the proper factor. In the prior example, use the PW 1/P factor at 10¼% for 40 years in capitalizing income attributable to the improvement.

A point as critical as the selection of yield rate in the income approach is the appraiser's derivation of economic rents from the market. Reasonable, realistic deductions for vacancies, collection losses, and expenses will result in a valid estimate of the net income stream to be valued.

Procedures in Section 2 start with annual net income (beginning on page 76). Here is a reminder in outline form of steps to be followed in processing income to the point at which it can be capitalized:

- Gross Annual Income (Economic Rent)—Vacancy and Collection Loss Allowances = Effective Gross Income

- Effective Gross Income—Allowable Expenses (Fixed, Operating, and Reserves) = Net Annual Income before Recapture (Amortization)

A value indicator by the income approach will be as reliable as the appraiser's judgment and skill in gathering pertinent data and in processing it with the proper method, technique, and tools.

SINKING FUND

The purpose of a sinking fund is to build up a sum for the replacement of wasting assets or to pay off a debt. Future worth of the fund is specified. The sum to be calculated is the amount of periodic deposit, which will build up to the required total at a stated rate of compound interest within the given time period. Computations are explained in Section 2 under the heading "Growth of a Series of Periodic Deposits, (see page 67).

SPECIAL SECTION: MORTGAGE-EQUITY TECHNIQUE[1]

The mortgage-equity technique deserves to be treated in a category by itself, with more detailed discussion. This technique, now widely used in appraisals and feasibility studies, gives particular consideration to contemporary investors' major areas of concern: equity position, financing, loan constant, net income, limited holding period, and equity growth through both appreciation and loan amortization.

The procedures in Section 2 (beginning on page 80) give patterns for mortgage-equity computations which do not require algebraic equations, confusing symbols, or complex formulas. In their place, precomputed over-all rates and standard compound interest factors are used in step-by-step calculations. A review of a few of the basic mortgage-equity concepts may facilitate understanding and use of the methods outlined in the "Summary":

- Income property is usually purchased on a relatively "low" down payment and "high" loan. In recent years, the real estate market has not been a cash market.
- The investor uses leverage for two reasons: (1) hopefully, to maximize his projected gains; (2) as a safety measure, to minimize unexpected but possible losses.

---

[1] For a more detailed treatment of this subject, see Irvin Johnson, "Instant Mortgage-Equity Technique." This book contains over 40 mortgage-equity procedures and nearly 150,000 precomputed over-all rates, covering a wide range of variables. (Published for the Society of Real Estate Appraisers by D. C. Heath & Company, Lexington, Massachusetts, 1972.)

- The investor plans to hold the property for a limited time. Since deductible interest paid on the mortgage declines period by period and non-deductible payments on principal increase accordingly, a turnover point is reached, in spite of allowable depreciation. Because of income tax considerations, few investors project a holding period in excess of ten years before selling, refinancing, or exchanging the property.
- Within the holding period either appreciation, stability, or depreciation in market value is anticipated.
- Investor's equity at the time of purchase is his down payment.
- Investor's equity at the end of the holding period (or any point in time) is the resale value less the loan balance. (Note the graph "Profile of an Equity" on the facing page.)
- Even though a piece of property may depreciate in value within the holding period, the investor's equity may increase because of loan amortization.
- The income stream consists of an annuity and a reversion, representing both a return on capital and a recovery of original equity (capital investment).
- A portion of yield is received periodically as it is earned. The balance is deferred yield, received or receivable at the end of the holding period.
- Yield on equity is of greater significance to the investor than yield on purchase price. Most investors require a yield of from 12% to 20% on equity, depending on risk and loan ratio.

Divide, and Conquer the Problem

The "instant" mortgage-equity technique is based on the realistic concepts outlined and produces sophisticated results. However, the procedure, using precomputed over-all rates, is simplicity itself. It consists primarily of computing an indicator of value by use of the basic equation:

$$\text{Value} = \text{Income} \div \text{Rate}$$

In this case, "rate" is the mortgage-equity "over-all rate," rather than a pure yield rate. (See graph on the facing page)

One of the principal advantages of the mini-math version of mortgage-equity is that the over-all rates are precomputed. The appraiser has only to select the OAR that matches his data, in some cases adjusting by simple interpolation. The OAR tables are a breakthrough and a break for the appraiser in problems of income property valuation. The following variables are built into an over-all rate:

- The holding period between purchase and resale, refinancing, or exchange. The OAR tables adjust rates for holding periods of 5, 10 and 15 years. Easy interpolation can be made for intermediate periods of, for example, 7 or 8 years.
- Loan data
    Loan amortization term: 15, 20, 25, or 30 years
    Interest rate: 6% to 12%
    Payment interval: monthly or annual
    Loan ratio: 60%, 70%, 75%, 80%, 90%
    Loan amortization payments as a loan constant: 6% to 12% interest
    Loan balance at end of holding period

PROFILE OF AN EQUITY

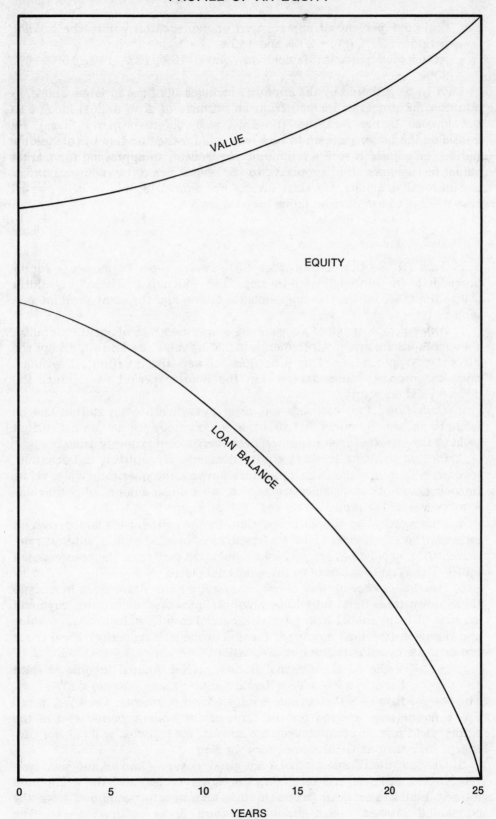

- Projected percent of appreciation or depreciation within the holding period: — 20%, 0%, + 20%, and +40%
- Anticipated percent of yield on equity: 10%, 12%, 14%, 15%, 16%, 20%

Data to be gathered by the appraiser includes all of the variables above. In addition, he processes income from an estimate of gross annual income to net income before recapture (possibly, also, before property taxes). He considers the income stream to be a level one for the duration of the holding period, or adjusts it to a level annuity equivalent. In appraising for market value he assumes the property to be encumbered by new maximum institutional financing. He then divides net annual income by the over-all rate selected to calculate an indicator of value.

Ways and Means

In Part III, Section 2 (see page 80), twelve types of mortgage-equity procedures are outlined, step-by-step, and illustrated. These procedures utilize the OAR tables, the supplemental tables, and the compound interest tables.

1. *Appreciation required* to generate a specified rate of yield on equity. Two methods are given. All elements, including value, are known, except the percent of appreciation. This procedure answers the question: How much must the property appreciate within the holding period to produce the desired yield on equity?

2. *Cash flow.* Two methods are given by which a computation can be made to answer the query: What is the dollar amount of net annual current yield to the investor, after expenses, debt service, and property taxes?

3. *Income required* to meet equity demands. By utilizing the equation, Income = Rate x Value, the procedure answers the question: When value, financing, and other variables are known, what dollar amount of net income would generate the projected rate of yield on equity?

4. *Interpolation* by simple proportion. By the methods explained, over-all rates can be adjusted to allow for variables in holding period, interest rate, percent of appreciation, etc., lying at points that vary from the precomputed tables. This is quite accurate to three decimal places.

5. *Investment analysis and check on computations.* Steps given in analysis break down these items into dollar amounts: purchase price; down payment; amount of loan; annual loan payment; annual cash flow; loan balance. value and reversion (terminal equity) at the end of the holding period. Final check can be made by substitution in the equation:

Value of the Original Equity = (Net Annual Income — Debt
Service) x PW 1/P + (Resale Value — Loan Balance) x PW 1

The "target figure" is the original equity (down payment). The PW 1/P and PW 1 factors are selected for the term of the holding period and at the equity yield rate. If computations are correct, the equation will balance out, except for a reasonable allowance for rounding.

6. *Over-all rate.* Three methods are given, covering known and unknown values, and utilizing market data, the OAR tables, and the compound interest tables. The OAR tables in this text were programmed from the compound interest tables, using Procedure 2, as outlined above. The

selection or derivation of an over-all rate is the key to valuation by the mortgage-equity technique.

7. *Rate of yield on equity.* Two procedures are given, the use of which will answer the question: When other variables, including value and income are known, what is the true yield rate on the original equity (down payment)?

8. *Rate of yield on equity investment in nonproducing property.* This procedure applies particularly to an investment in nonproducing land, held for appreciation. Besides the initial investment (down payment), the purchaser makes an additional series of periodic investments to cover such holding costs as property taxes and loan payments.

9. *Rate of yield on 100% equity.* Mortgage-equity implies a mortgage, as well as an equity. However, certain concepts and calculations are applicable to the analysis of cash transactions. Procedures outlined and illustrated cover stable, increasing, and decreasing market values.

10. *Reversion, dollar amount of.* Calculation deducts loan balance from projected property value at end of holding period. The supplemental tables facilitate this computation.

11. *Secondary financing, adjustment for, in calculating OAR.* Procedure explains and illustrates computations of rate and value on property encumbered by more than one mortgage. Such an analysis is particularly applicable to a feasibility study.

12. *Value of income property* as indicated by the mortgage-equity technique. This most important computation is made simply by dividing the over-all rate into net annual income (Value = Income ÷ Rate). The question is answered: What price can the investor pay for the property and realize his desired yield on equity?

In addition to these twelve principal procedures, six secondary, related ones are listed as a matter of cross reference:

1. Level annuity equivalent of a graduated or irregular income stream.
2. Loan constant.
3. Percent of loan paid off at any point in time.
4. Percent of loan unpaid at any point in time.
5. Present worth of an annuity.
6. Present worth of a reversion.

While the various procedures of the instant mortgage-equity technique are outlined step by step, usually without equations, they could all be given in equation form. The methods illustrated relate to this statement of valuation, a discounted cash flow technique by which the OAR tables in this book were derived:

$$\text{Value of the Equity} = (\text{Net Income} - \text{Loan Payments}) \times \text{PW 1/P}$$
$$+ (\text{Resale Value} - \text{Loan Balance}) \times \text{PW 1}$$

Example of Mortgage-Equity Technique

An illustration at this point will show how simple and fuctional the instant mortgage-equity technique is. The problem is to appraise an established five year old mobile home park. It is well located, properly designed and maintained, rated four star, and has a low vacancy factor. Assume you have reconstructed the owner's operating statement and have calculated net annual income before property taxes to be $138,400, generated by rent of the 300 mobile home spaces and by incidental income. Tax rate in the area is $10 per $100 of assessed valuation, and assessment ratio is 25% of market value. Therefore, you make a tax allowance of 2.5% of market value (.1 x .25 = .025). From local lending institutions you determine the current maximum conventional financing available to a purchaser: a 15 year loan for 70% of market value, monthly payments to amortize, 9% interest rate. From the market you find that the typical buyer would anticipate a yield of 12% on his 30% equity investment. You assume a holding period of 10 years, and 0% appreciation (stability in market value). You also project an annual level income stream of $138,400 net (before property taxes and loan payments) for the duration of the holding period.

Your problem is to value the property by the mortgage-equity technique. You turn to the proper OAR table and select the over-all rate: 10 year holding period, 12% equity yield, 70% loan ratio, 9% loan interest rate, 15 year loan term, 0% appreciation (page 151). The OAR you find to be .10080. To this you add the tax allowance of .025. Total capitalization rate is .1008 + .025, or .1258. Substituting in the basic equation (Value = Income ÷ Rate) you have:

Value = $138,400 ÷ .1258
      = $1,100,159, rounded to $1,100,000

Investment analysis and a final check on the calculations in the preceding problem can be made readily by simple arithmetic, the supplemental tables and the compound interest tables, as follows:

Down payment (original equity) = equity ratio x value:
  Since loan ratio is given as 70%, equity ratio is 100% less 70%, or 30%.
  .3 x $1,100,000 = $330,000
Original amount of loan = loan ratio x value:
  .7 x $1,100,000 = $770,000
Annual total of monthly loan payments = loan constant x amount of loan:
  .12171 x $770,000 = $93,717 (page 186)
Annual property tax allowance:
  .025 x $1,100,000 = $27,500
Annual cash flow = net income less loan payments and property taxes.
  $138,400 — ($93,717 + $27,500) = $17,183
Property value at end of 10 year holding period (0% appreciation):
  $1,100,000
Loan balance at end of holding period:
  .48861 x $770,000 = $376,230 (page 186)
Equity (reversion) at end of holding period = value less loan balance:
  $1,100,000 — $376,230 = $723,770

To summarize: This analysis, based on data and assumptions given in the problem, shows that the net income stream (after loan payments and property taxes) will consist of an annuity of $17,183 and a reversion of $723,770. The increase in equity from $330,000 (the down payment) to

$723,770 at the end of a ten year holding period, has resulted from loan amortization only, since 0% appreciation is assumed. The annuity and reversion together provide both a return *of* capital (the down payment) and a true 12% return *on* capital, giving full consideration to the time value of money and meeting an investor's dual requirements. The annuity of $17,183 is current yield. The $393,770 excess of the terminal equity over the original equity ($723,770 less $330,000) constitutes deferred yield.

Proof of the calculations and value conclusion can be demonstrated by reference to the definition of value which is particularly applicable to income producing property: value is the present worth of all expected future net benefits. In this illustration the future net benefits consist of:

- An annuity of $17,183 a year for 10 years.
- A reversion (single future income payment) of $723,770 at the end of ten years.

In other words, the original equity (down payment) of $330,000 is the present worth at a 12% yield rate of $17,183 a year for 10 years and $723,770 to be received at the end of 10 years:

Value of the Original Equity = Annuity x PW 1/P + Reversion x PW 1

Substituting: Value = ($17,183 x 5.65022) + ($723,770 x .32197)   (PW 1/P and PW 1, 12%, 10 years)

= $97,088 + $233,032

= $330,120

Our "target figure" is $330,000, the original equity. The slight difference of $120 is attributable to rounding.

Market Value vs. Investment Value

The appraiser recognizes the difference between a feasibility study and an appraisal for market value. The feasibility study may be an appraisal of investment value or value in use for a particular client. It considers such points as income tax position, possible unorthodox high leverage financing with two or more mortgages, etc. An appraisal for market value assumes the property to be encumbered by a new maximum institutional loan at current interest rates. It is also assumed that the buyer pays cash to the new loan, thereby automatically adjusting the market price to a cash equivalent. Market value is considered to be the value to persons in general, without being related to income tax brackets or unusual financing.

Appraisal by mortgage-equity can establish a band for decision making by the investor. The band may cover a range of possible values within which to negotiate a purchase price. Or, it may project a range of indicated yield on equity, based on assumptions, for example, of possible 20% depreciation or 20% appreciation within a holding period. In addition to telling the analyst the market value or investment value of the property and a possible rate of yield on equity, this technique may also point out properties that are not economic units. It may help the investor avoid mistakes and may set up criteria that will minimize losses as well as maximizing and retaining gains.

Variations on a Theme

The appraiser, using the mortgage-equity technique, should not be overwhelmed by the realization that there is an almost infinite number of possible combinations of variable factors. However, he should comprehend the effect of each type of variable on *value* and on the *rate of yield on equity*.

The influence on *value* will be illustrated by altering each of the following variables (making, however, only one change at a time): equity yield rate, holding period, loan ratio, loan term, interest rate and appreciation. Assume the following:

Equity yield rate:	12%
Holding period:	10 years
Loan ratio:	75%
Loan term:	20 years
Interest rate:	8%
Appreciation:	0%
Net annual income:	$150,000

Based on this data, the OAR is .09201 (See page 152)

Indicated value: $150,000 ÷ .09201 = $1,630,257

Note the change in OAR and consequently in value by altering each variable, making only one modification at a time in the given situation (all other data remaining constant):

Equity yield rate: 15%
OAR is now .10131 (page 158)
Value: $150,000 − .10131 = $1,480,604

Holding period: 5 years
OAR: .09056   (page 134)
Value: $150,000 ÷ .09056 = $1,656,360

Loan ratio: 60%
OAR: .09761   (page 151)
Value: $150,000 ÷ .09761 = $1,536,728

Loan term: 30 years
OAR: .09080   (page 152)
Value: $150,000 ÷ .0908 = $1,651,982

Interest rate: 7%
OAR: .08558   (page 152)
Value: $150,000 ÷ .08558 = $1,752,746

Appreciation: +40%
OAR: .06922   (page 152)
Value: $150,000 ÷ .06922 = $2,167,004

Note that all six variables affect value. Changes in holding period and loan term appear less critical than the other four components of the OAR.

In the preceding illustration, we consider as constants the net income of $150,000, OAR of .09201, and consequently value of $1,630,257. Note the effect on *equity yield rate*, as we change a few of the variables in the given data:

Loan ratio: Increasing from 75% to 90% raises equity
yield to 15% plus. (OAR, .09157 page 159)
Interest rate: Changing from 8% to 9% lowers
equity yield rate to about 10%. (OAR, .09235, page 149)
Appreciation: Projecting 20% appreciation raises
indicated equity yield to a little over 15%.

(OAR, .09146, page 158)

Variables in the mortgage-equity technique concern the investor and the appraiser. The investment analyst can, by changing variables he considers most meaningful, establish bands of value and ranges of equity yield for decision making. However, the appraiser, seeking market value, must determine a specific point within a band. Accurate data and reasonable assumptions, processed by precise procedures and good judgment, will be reflected in valid value conclusions.

The Traditional and the Contemporary

The time has come to question some traditional techniques of the income approach. Are the residual techniques realistic in today's investment market? Is the straight line, declining income method appropriate to the usual current valuation problem; or is it, for general use, becoming as out-dated as the buggy whip? Is it possible that appraisers have been coming up with approximately the right valuations, but by unrealistic procedures?

There are a few points of similarity between the mortgage-equity technique and the residual techniques of the income approach:

- The validity of each depends on a reasonably accurate projection and processing of annual income to the point at which it can be capitalized.
- Both the mortgage-equity and the residual techniques process income into an indicator of value.
- The mortgage-equity technique is more closely related to the property residual or reversion technique than to the building or land residual— even more closely allied to direct capitalization.

But there are more significant differences than similarities:

- The old "tried and true" residual techniques are all summation approaches: land value plus improvement value. Value by summation is not regarded as the best appraisal practice, if another technique can be used; for the value of the whole is not necessarily equal to the sum of its parts. A typical investor doesn't purchase land + improvements + personal property. He buys a total income producing package. The mortgage-equity technique is allied with the total property or unit appraisal concept.
- Mortgage-equity makes no segregation of income attributable to land and income attributable to improvements.
- Mortgage-equity does not assume that land is to be valued separately "as if vacant."
- It is not assumed that the subject property is "free and clear." It is assumed to be encumbered by new maximum institutional financing.
- There is no estimate of remaining economic life called for; hence, subjective judgment of depreciation is minimized.
- Projection of the size and shape of the income stream extends through a relatively short term holding period of possibly 10 years—not 40 or 50.
- The mortgage-equity technique assumes an annuity or converts a graduated annuity to a level annuity equivalent. It is not concerned with a questionable straight line declining or curvilinear declining concept.

- Recapture is provided for at the end of a realistically limited holding period, rather than being spread over 25 to 50 years.
- The mortgage-equity technique gives full consideration not only to current yield but also to deferred yield at the time of reversion — growth of equity resulting from both loan amortization and appreciation.
- The investor is concerned with two primary points: what he puts into an investment, and what he gets out of it. Mortgage-equity considers both.
- The mortgage-equity technique answers the investor's most meaningful question: "What is the yield on my equity, my actual cash investment?" The residual techniques all sidestep and ignore the issue.
- Calculation of value by mortgage-equity is a simple, one step computation: income divided by over-all rate.

The appraiser may not wish to dispense with the residual techniques. But neither should he ignore the mortgage-equity technique that speaks the investor's language and gives him the answers he seeks.

Questions on the Technique

A few "how about" or "what if" questions might be raised—and answered—concerning appraisal by the mortgage-equity technique:

1. How about the fact that equity increases with each periodic loan payment on principal? *ANSWER:* Equity growth is "locked in" until the time of reversion (resale, refinancing, or exchange). Therefore, it must be considered as *deferred yield.* Amounts applied to principal are not additional investments, but additional earnings from the income producing property. *Yield to maturity* on equity is computed on the original equity—the initial investment or down payment—and recognizes both current and deferred yield. In the example of mortgage-equity technique (pages 49-51), equity increased from $330,000 to $723,770; from an equity ratio of 30% to an equity ratio of 65.8%. The rate of yield, however, is computed on the original equity, the purchaser's actual investment of $330,000.

2. What if the investor doesn't intend to sell or refinance at the end of a projected holding period? How does his retaining the property indefinitely affect valuation by mortgage-equity? *ANSWER:* The appraisal, based on sound data and generally accepted market assumptions, would still be valid. The estimated value is still there at the end of a time period, regardless of the owner's disposition or retention of the property.

3. How about mortgage-equity and inflation? *ANSWER:* A projection of possible appreciation is made by percent and is translated into dollars, not purchasing power. If inflation continues for another 10 years, as it did from 1961 to 1971, appreciation of 35% would just keep up with it—no more. One of the prime reasons for investing in real estate is to provide a hedge against inflation. If an investor actually believes the property under consideration will *decline* in dollar value over a relatively short term, will he invest in it at all? In general, in dealing with economically feasible income property, well located, wouldn't it be more realistic to project appreciation of possibly 20% than stability or depreciation?

4. How is the mortgage-equity approach related to the market? *ANSWER:*

Yield rates and over-all rates are obtained from analysis of market sales. Economic rents are determined by the market. Financing data is found in the money market.

5. Can mortgage-equity be used in a mass appraisal program for purposes of assessment? If so, how? *ANSWER:* Yes, definitely. These specific steps are suggested:

(a) Develop over-all rates for each type of property in a specific area or comparable area from an analysis of market sales (see illustration and special form, page 88.) A note of caution: Be sure to use only verified sales, arms length transactions between knowledgeable buyers and sellers. *Adjust* sales prices to a cash equivalent, depending on terms. Also, subtract the value of excess land, if any, from total sales price before relating price to income.

(b) Obtain current financing data from lending institutions for the types of properties being appraised.

(c) Using the over-all rates developed in (a) above, loan data from (b), and realistic investor accepted projections of holding periods and appreciation, compute corresponding equity yield rates (see procedures, pages 86 to 89.)

(d) Now that an over-all rate has been developed into an equity yield rate, reverse the field. Find from interviews with investors, brokers, analysts, and other appraisers the required or desired rate of yield on equity that would attract money to a particular type of real estate investment market. Also, determine "typical" projections of holding periods and appreciation or depreciation. Translate the equity yield rates and projections you have discovered into over-all rates, by use of the OAR tables or the compound interest and annuity tables (see procedures, pages 84 to 86).

(e) Correlate over-all and equity yield rates from (a), (b), and (c) with rates from d.

(f) Once over-all rates have been developed for various types of income producing properties, test and substantiate them by comparison with other indicators of value. You are now ready to apply these mortgage-equity over-all rates to comparable properties in the area— comparable as to type of property (garden apartments, regional shopping centers, medical buildings, etc.), age, quality of construction, location, the general economy of the area (present and projected), etc.

Talking Terms

Following is a brief glossary of terms related to mortgage-equity:

Annuity. A level terminal annual income stream or its equivalent.

Appreciation. Increase in market value.

Cash flow. Net annual income after allowable expenses, property taxes, and loan payments.

Current yield. Cash flow.

Deferred yield. That portion of yield produced by appreciation and/or loan amortization, received at the end of a holding period (time of reversion). The dollar amount is found by adding loan balance to the original equity (down payment) and subtracting this sum from resale value.

Depreciation. Decrease in market value.

Equity. The difference between market value and principal amount of loan. Initially, it is the down payment. At the end of the holding period it is the net reversion (resale value less loan balance).

Equity ratio. Down payment as a percent of value (purchase price); e.g., if value is $100,000 and down payment is $30,000, equity ratio is .30 or 30% ($30,000 ÷ $100,000 = .30).

Equity yield rate. Current yield and deferred yield (yield to maturity) computed together as an annual percent of original equity (down payment).

Holding period. A limited time, usually not in excess of 10 years, between purchase and resale, refinancing, or exchange of the property.

Interest rate. The specified interest rate on the note, which is secured by a mortgage or trust deed. (Not to be mistaken for a yield rate.)

Loan amortization. Reduction of the principal amount of a loan, usually through equal periodic payments that include an increasing amount applied to principal and a decreasing amount of interest calculated on a declining loan balance.

Loan constant. Annual loan payment or payments as a percent of original principal. Found by dividing annual loan payment or payments by original principal. For example, a loan of $100,000, annual payments of $9,500, has a loan constant of .095 or 9½% ($9,500 ÷ $100,000 = .095).

Loan ratio. Original principal amount of loan as a percent of value; e.g., if value is $100,000 and loan is $70,000, loan ratio is .70 or 70% ($70,000 ÷ $100,000 = .70). Loan ratio and equity ratio should add up to 100%.

Loan term. Amortization period in years.

Mortgage or trust deed. Document that secures a loan on real estate.

Net annual income. Effective gross income less allowable expenses, but before loan payments and possibly property taxes.

Net spendable. Same as cash flow.

Reversion. The difference between resale value and loan balance at the end of a holding period.

Yield rate. A hoped for return on capital. (Not to be mistaken for a specified interest rate.)

Yield to maturity. Return *on* capital from annual cash flow and from that portion of the reversion which exceeds recovery *of* capital investment.

On Finding the Proper Table

Once the appraiser becomes familiar with the arrangement and scope of the OAR tables, he should be able to use them with ease. Sequence of variables is scheduled as follows:

First, by holding period:

All OAR's for 5 year holding periods are found on pages 130 through 147

OAR's for 10 years, pages 148 through 165

OAR's for 15 years, pages 166 through 183

Second, by equity yield rate: 10%, 12%, 14%, 15%, 16%, 20%

Third, by loan ratio: 60%, 70%, 75%, 80%, 90%

These three variables will lead you to the right page. For example, An OAR for a 10 year holding period, 15% equity yield, and 70% loan ratio will be found on page 157.

On each page, loan term in years and percent of appreciation or depreciation involve a vertical search to determine the pertinent line. A horizontal search by interest rate will take you across to the OAR, or to OAR's between which to interpolate. Referring to the example above, assuming a 25 year loan term, 20% appreciation, and 7% interest rate, you determine the OAR to be .08716.

An OAR is a tool. Most craftsmen in any line have neither the time, skill, nor necessity to make their own tools, yet they may be very proficient in using them. An appraiser is a craftsman, and the OAR tables provide him with a set of ready made tools of the trade.

The alert appraiser on the now frontier understands and is skilled in the mortgage-equity technique. He is able to talk the investor's language. His concepts are contemporary and realistic. He realizes, for example, that it is possible to have a mortgage rate of 9%, an equity yield rate of 15%, and at the same time an over-all rate of 7.76%.

It is not necessary, of course, to agree with all we have said on mortgage-equity; just consider it food for thought. Think the process through, and relate to the challenge of change as you explore new routes to old objectives.

TRUST DEEDS AND MORTGAGES:
AMORTIZATION, ANALYSIS, AND DISCOUNT

Every appraiser really should earn the professional designation of TDM or MM (Trust Deed Mechanic or Mortgage Mechanic). By proper procedures, the compound interest factors can be used to tear a mortgage apart, analyze it, put it back together, or compute its cash equivalent. For procedures and illustrations of the various points discussed here, see Section 2, page 94.

An appraiser should be as adept in loan analysis as a sophisticated lender, investor, borrower, or broker. Expertise in this area is essential to one important step in the market approach—adjusting sales price for terms. Six conditions must be considered for each sale analyzed:

1. Sale in the open market.
2. Neither party takes advantage of the exigencies of the other.
3. Reasonable time allowed to find a buyer.
4. Reasonable knowledge of the property's uses—present and potential—by both buyer and seller.
5. No collusion and no "love and affection" consideration between parties.
6. *Consideration in cash or its equivalent*, when a non-cash consideration is involved.

Few sales are made for all cash. The appraiser must search out terms in his sales analysis and convert non-cash items (usually trust deeds or mortgages carried by the seller) to their cash equivalent. By cash equivalent we mean the price the "paper" would bring if offered for sale in the mortgage market.

Frequently, the appraiser comes up with incomplete data on a note. He must then compute the remainder of the terms, such as the periodic payment to amortize within a given time, amount of a balloon payment, length of time it takes to pay off a loan with a specified periodic payment, principal balance at any point on time, etc. "Mini-Math" provides the ways and means.

Basic concepts essential to an understanding of discounting trust deeds or mortgages in computing the cash equivalent of a sale are as follows:

1. The initial step in analyzing the mortgage is the preparation of a payment schedule so that the size, shape, and duration of the income stream are delineated.

2. It is not necessary to segregate principal and interest for purposes of determining present worth or cash equivalent. The quantity to be processed is the entire income stream, not the principal sum only.

3. The first phase in discounting (compiling the complete payment schedule) might be thought of as *capitalization in reverse.* Instead of converting an income stream to a capital sum, you start with a capital sum (face value of the note) and process it into an income stream to be discounted.

4. Yield rates must be obtained from the current local mortgage market. Rates to be found are those which would make the subject trust deed or mortgage saleable on the open market to a third party, usually a private investor in the discounted mortgage market.

5. Present worth or cash equivalent may be found by this equation: Value = Periodic Payment x PW 1/P + Balloon Payment x PW 1

6. Discounting the face value of a trust deed by any given dollar amount or percent "off the top" disregards all variable factors of the note except the principal sum. This is a "broad brush" approach that can mean anything or nothing. It is a questionable discount of principal only.

7. Discounting a trust deed or mortgage to a *true yield rate,* as indicated by the mortgage market, automatically considers and *adjusts for all variable factors* in the note: principal amount, stated interest rate, term of the loan, prepaid interest removed from the income stream, periodic payment, balloon payment, and the specified higher yield rate the purchaser of the trust deed requires. This approach is a precise discount of the entire income stream.

8. A "high" interest rate specified on a note generates a larger income stream than a "low" interest rate on a note for the same principal amount. Consequently, the higher the stipulated interest rate, the less the dollar amount of discount to a greater yield rate, and vice versa.

9. Cash equivalent of the sales price in a prepaid interest transaction is the sum of: down payment, prepaid interest, and discounted trust deed. (Prepaid interest warrants no discount, since it is cash in hand, received before it is earned.)

10. Cash equivalent of the sales price in a transaction where there is no prepaid interest is the sum of the down payment and the mortgage or trust deed discounted to make it marketable.

11. A computation of the cash equivalent of the subject property or of comparable properties is not an appraisal. It is merely one step in the market approach to value: adjusting the sales price for terms only.

The discreet appraiser will not get cash-equivalent-happy and discount every mortgage he encounters "just because it's there." Following is an outline that may help in answering the question of when to discount or not to discount:

I. Types of trust deeds or mortgages usually discounted:
   A. Purchase money trust deeds carried by the seller under any one or more of the following conditions:
      1. If the loan ratio or security is such that the loan could not be made by a lending institution.
      2. If written at an interest rate significantly above or below the going market interest rate.
      3. If of a "junior" nature.
      4. If there is a subordination clause.
      5. If interest is prepaid.
   B. Purchase money mortgages or trust deeds carried by lending institutions on a new loan made to finance the resale of existing property, if seller pays "points."
   C. Existing "low" interest rate institutional loan assumed by the buyer, if the market shows the purchaser paid a premium price to assume the loan.
II. Types of trust deeds or mortgages normally not discounted:
   A. Purchase money mortgages carried by the seller, if of such a nature that the loan could have been made by a lending institution.
   B. Purchase money loans made by lending institutions on new construction. (Points paid by the developer are considered costs of production. Usually, no discount in purchase price is given for cash.)
   C. Existing institutional loans bearing an interest rate lower than the current rate, if the market indicates the buyer assuming the loan is paying no premium.

Trust deeds and mortgages are similar in that they are both negotiable instruments which serve as security for promissory notes. Space limitations in this book do not permit an exploration in depth of the significant differences between the two types of documents. Both lending practice and legislation throughout the country are increasing the use of the trust deed, with its advantages of the third party (trustee), 90 day reinstatement period, and possible 110 day foreclosure without court action.

The difference between a "first" and a "second" trust deed or mortgage is the date of recording, and consequently the order of priority. In some regions the "all inclusive" or "wrap-around" trust deed has begun to replace junior liens and contracts of sale. If a first trust deed contains a subordination clause, it automatically becomes a "second" upon further encumbrance permitted by the first lender. The appraiser must consider this point in discounting to cash equivalent.

There are a number of reasons why the seller of a parcel of real estate will agree to "carry" the loan himself:

- In many cases it is the only way of financing the property and "closing the deal." It helps the owner make the sale.
- Terms of the loan usually provide the seller with a form of annuity and a higher interest rate than on guaranteed savings.
- The seller may be able to report and pay his long term capital gains income tax in installments.

If the seller of the property wants to "cash out" the loan he is carrying, he must in nearly every case sell the trust deed or mortgage to a private investor at a discount. The only motivation for the new purchaser of the trust deed is a higher yield rate—a rate that exceeds the interest rate the note bears.

Payment schedules are prepared in many ways: periodic payments of interest only, with the entire principal amount due in a lump sum on maturity; periodic payments that amortize a portion of the loan, and a balloon payment for the balance of the principal; equal periodic payments of principal plus interest to amortize; equal periodic payments, including interest and principal until amortized.

Complete amortization by equal periodic payments, including principal and interest, is a common pattern. From each succeeding payment an increasing amount applies to principal and a decreasing amount to interest, since interest is computed each period on a declining balance. Progression of equity growth through loan amortization and the decline of principal balance are both curvilinear, as shown in the following graph. Note that in the case of a 6% loan running for 30 years, the first half of the principal amount is paid off in about 21 years, and the last half in 9 years.

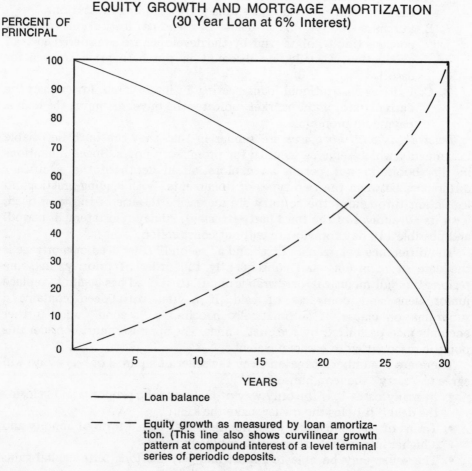

EQUITY GROWTH AND MORTGAGE AMORTIZATION
(30 Year Loan at 6% Interest)

PERCENT OF
PRINCIPAL

YEARS

——————— Loan balance

— — — Equity growth as measured by loan amortization. (This line also shows curvilinear growth
pattern at compound interest of a level terminal
series of periodic deposits.

In adjusting sales price for terms, the appraiser may have to discount certain other intangibles; for example:

1. *Bonds.* A case in point was a recent local sale in which the total consideration was $1,800,000 in 5% municipal bonds, issued and given for the purchase of 470 acres as a new college site. At the time the transaction was concluded, the bonds were not marketable at a yield rate of 5%, but could have been sold on the open market if discounted to yield 5¾% to 6¼%, depending on the term to maturity. Rates were obtained from securities dealers, and the bonds discounted accordingly. Cash equivalent of the sale was computed to be $1,648,500. The discount was realistic and precise.

2. *Promissory notes, unsecured.* If the purchaser-borrower is a triple A national corporation, an unsecured note is more advantageous to the seller-lender than a first trust deed or mortgage. The reason is that all the assets of the corporation stand back of the promise to pay, which affords a greater degree of security than just the subject property alone. Our experience has indicated that a discount to a yield rate of ½% to 1½% above the prime rate at the time of sale is a reasonable approach.

There are two ways to discount a trust deed or mortgage, as noted under "basic concepts." The point bears emphasis: (1.) The simple, wrong way—this method merely takes a percent or dollar amount off the face value (principal amount) of the note. (2.) The correct, precise, not too difficult way—in this procedure, the total income stream is discounted to a true yield rate.

For example, take a note secured by a purchase money first trust deed or mortgage, in which these terms are given:

>Principal amount: $250,000
>Interest rate: 7%
>Repayment schedule:
>>$25,000 per year for 15 years
>>$61,532 balloon payment at the end of 15 years (in addition to final regular 15th annual payment)

The problem is to discount the trust deed to its "cash equivalent" so that you can adjust sales price for terms.

1. The incorrect way is to discount the face value by some percent between 10% and 60%—say, 35% "pulled out of the air." The simple computation is:

>.35 x $250,000 = $87,500 discount

$250,000	face value
− 87,500	discount
$162,500	discounted value

It's easy, but probably wrong. This calculation disregards the interest rate on the note, periodic payments, balloon payment, and term of the loan. In other words, it has not considered the size, shape, and duration of the income stream; nor the time value of money.

2. The proper procedure finds the applicable yield rate that would make the note marketable, outlines the payment schedule (income stream), and discounts it to a true yield rate. Each variable—interest rate, periodic payment, balloon payment, term, and required higher yield rate—has been considered. A thorough study of the market possibly indicates a true yield rate of 12%. The appraiser notes that the income stream consists of an

annuity of $25,000 a year for 15 years and a reversion of $61,532 at the end of 15 years. He selects factors at 12% for 15 periods, and makes his computations in this manner:

$25,000 x 6.81086 = $170,272	(PW 1/P, 12%, 15 years)
61,532 x .18270 = 11,242	(PW 1, 12%, 15 years)
$181,514	cash equivalent of TD

Calculations have followed the basic formula:

Value = Periodic Payment x PW 1/P + Balloon Payment x PW 1

Yield rates on trust deeds or mortgages are as significant to an investor as are yield rates on equity, bonds, savings accounts, or any other type of investment. An investor isn't particularly interested in a discount of 25, 30, 40, 50 percent. But he is seeking a yield rate of 10, 12, 15, or 20 percent. A 1971 Survey of the private money market in Southern California indicated yield rates of 12% in the resale of well secured first trust deeds and 18% on second trust deeds. These are considered only as central points; deviation above or below is a matter of judgment in each specific case.

Suggestions for Solving Problems

"Mini-Math" is here to help the appraiser in his quest for value. Here is a list of suggestions, applicable to the solution of a typical, practical problem:

1. Determine the class or category of the subject to be analyzed.
2. Gather and outline the known data: size, shape, quality and duration of the income stream; present worth or future worth; yield or interest rate; etc.
3. Spell out the specific question or questions to be answered. What are the unknowns?
4. If you are dealing with a lengthy, complex problem, break it up into a number of smaller, component problems.
5. Arrange the individual segments of the total problem in logical sequence.
6. Consult Part III, Section 2 to find the applicable procedure in the "Summary of Mini-Math Methods" (page 63) for each separate part of the problem and for the whole problem.
7. Study the suggested solution of a similar problem.
8. Select, list, and label the proper factors from the "Compound Interest and Annuity Tables," the "OAR Tables," and the "Supplemental Tables," adjusting factors as required.
9. Follow the procedures outlined, step by step, relating factors to the data given in order to find the unknown for which you are solving.
10. Look again at the problem and your solution. Ask yourself, "Is it a reasonable answer?"

Summary of Mini-Math Methods

READY REFERENCE ROSTER

BONDS

Present worth of a bond, offered at a specified yield rate above or below the coupon rate:
Procedure:
    a. Multiply periodic interest payment by PW 1/P at determined yield rate. (Assume annual interest payments.)
    b. Multiply face amount of bond by PW 1.
    c. Add a and b.
Problem: A 5% general obligation municipal bond for $10,000, interest paid annually, runs 12 years to maturity. Discount the bond to yield 6%.
Solution:
    a. Annual interest payment is .05 x $10,000, or $500.
        $500 x 8.3838 = $4,192 (PW 1/P, 6%, 12 years)
    b. $10,000 x .49697 = 4,970 (PW 1, 6%, 12 years)
    c. $9,162

Rate of yield on bond, offered at a specified dollar discount or premium:
Procedure:
    a. Estimate, by "cut and try," one rate above and one below the rate sought.
    b. Apply PW 1/P to interest payments, and PW 1 to undiscounted value of bond at each rate estimated in a.
    c. Interpolate, to find true yield rate. (The target figure on which to "zero in" is the discounted price offered.)
Problem: A 4% state bond for $5,000, interest paid annually, runs 15 years to maturity and is offered at $4,000. Compute the yield rate.
Solution:
    a. Try 7% and 5%. (Annual interest: .04 x $5,000 = $200.)
    b. At 7%: $200 x 9.10791 = $1,822 (PW 1/P, 7%, 15 years)
               $5,000 x   .36245 =   1,812 (PW 1, 7%, 15 years)
                                   $3,634

      At 5%: $200 x 10.37966 = $2,076 (PW 1/P, 5%, 15 years)
               $5,000 x   .48102 =   2,405 (PW 1, 5%, 15 years)
                                   $4,481

    c. By interpolation: About 6.1%

GENERAL APPLICATIONS

Conversion of simple percent of increase to an annual compound rate:
Procedure:
    a. Express percent of increase as a decimal and add 1.0.
    b. Divide 1.0 by sum from a.
    c. Locate quotient from b in PW 1 tables, interpolating if necessary.
Problem: A comprehensive study of land value appreciation in California shows the statewide average increase from 1945 to 1965 to be 475%. What was the annual rate, compounded?
Solution:

a. 4.75 + 1.0 = 5.75
b. 1.0 ÷ 5.75 = .1739
c. At 9%, PW 1 factor for 20 years is .17843.
At 10%, PW 1 factor for 20 years is .14864.
By interpolation: About 9.15%, compounded annually.

Rate of growth, expressed as an annual percent, compounded:
Procedure:
a. Divide amount for first year of period to be checked by final year's figure.
b. Locate quotient from a in PW 1 tables, interpolating if required.

Problem: In 1961 the average annual Consumer Price Index for the United States was 89.6. In 1971 it stood at 121.3 (1967 = 100.0). What is the annual rate of inflation for this 10 year period as measured by the CPI?
Solution:
a. 89.6 ÷ 121.3 = .73866
b. At 3%, PW 1 factor for 10 years is .74409
At 4%, PW 1 factor for 10 years is .67556
By interpolation: About 3.1%, compounded annually.

Time required to double a sum at any rate, compounded:
Procedure:
1. Find first entry in PW 1 tables approximating .50.
2. (Alternate) Divide .72 by the given rate.

Problem 1: If the rate of inflation, as measured by the Consumer Price Index, should average 5% annually, in how many years would prices double?
Solution 1:
PW 1 factor at 5% for 14 years is .50507.
PW 1 factor at 5% for 15 years is .48102.
Indicated time is a little more than 14 years.

Problem 2: In how many years will the value of an investment double at 8% compounded annually?
Solution 2:
.72 ÷ .08 = 9 years
(Check: PW 1 factor at 8% for 9 years is .50025.)

GROWTH OF A SERIES OF PERIODIC DEPOSITS

Amount of periodic deposit required, which will grow to a specified future sum:
Procedure:
Multiply the sum by (PR − i).
(This procedure is applicable to the computation of sinking fund requirements.)

Problem: A level series of deposits, made at the end of each year for 8 years in an account paying 5% compounded annually, has grown to $23,873. Determine the amount of annual deposit.

Solution:

    .15472 — .05 = .10472 (PR, 5%, 8 years.)
    $23,873 x .10472 = $2,500

Amount to which a series of uniform periodic deposits will grow at compound interest:

Procedure:

1. If deposit is made at end of period, divide periodic deposit by (PR — i).
2. If deposit is made at the beginning of the period:
    a. Divide the periodic deposit by (PR — i), using the PR factor for the period following the final deposit.
    b. Subtract the amount of one periodic deposit from the quotient computed in a.

Problem: A deposit of $1,500 is made annually for 10 years in a savings account paying 5% compounded annually. To what sum would the account grow?

Solution 1 (deposits made at end of period):

    .1295 — .05 = .0795 (PR, 5%, 10 years.)
    $1,500 ÷ .0795 = $18,868

Solution 2 (deposits made at beginning of period):

    a. .12039 — .05 = .07039 (PR, 5%, 11 years.)
       $1,500 ÷ .07039 = $21,310
    b. $21,310 — $1,500 = $19,810

GROWTH OF A SINGLE DEPOSIT OR INVESTMENT

Amount of single deposit or investment required when future worth is given:

Procedure:

Multiply future worth by PW 1.

Problem: Bare land lying in the direction of urban growth has an estimated value of $8,000 per acre 5 years hence, when it is anticipated residential subdivision is due. The land is producing no income. Required yield rate is 8% and allowance for property taxes is 2%. What price per acre could an investor feasibly pay for the property?

Solution:

Total capitalization rate: .08 + .02 = .10
$8,000 x .62092 = $4,967 per acre (PW 1, 10%, 5 years)

Amount to which a single deposit or investment will grow at compound interest:

Procedure:

Divide amount of deposit or investment by PW 1.

Problem: Don Shure has purchased land at $3,600 an acre, and anticipates appreciation at the rate of 9% a year for the next 12 years. What is the expected sales price (future worth) at the end of the 12 year holding period?

Solution:

    $3,600 ÷ .35553 = $10,125 per acre (PW 1, 9%, 12 years)

Rate of interest (or yield) when time, amount of single deposit or investment, and future worth are known:

Procedure:

    a. Divide original deposit or investment by future worth.

    b. Locate quotient from a in PW 1 tables, interpolating if necessary.

Problem: Property purchased 15 years ago for $25,000 is now valued at $91,000. Compute the rate of increase, compounded annually.

Solution:

    a. $25,000 ÷ $91,000 = .274725

    b. Inspection of the PW 1 tables for 15 periods shows the factor at 9% to be .27454. Indicated rate is slightly less than 9%.

Time required to reach a specified future worth of a single deposit or investment at a given rate:

Procedure:

    a. Divide original deposit or investment by future worth.

    b. Locate quotient from a in PW 1 tables.

Problem: Hira Hall purchased a shopping center for $1,750,000. He anticipates appreciation in market value at the rate of 7% annually and plans to sell when he can expect a price of $2,500,000. What is the estimated holding period?

Solution:

    a. $1,750,000 ÷ $2,500,000 = .70

    b. Inspection of the PW 1 tables at 7% shows factors of .71299 for 5 years and .66634 for 6 years. Indicated time is slightly more than 5 years.

PREPAID INTEREST

Cash equivalent of a real estate sale in which a portion of interest on the loan has been prepaid:

Procedure:

    a. Compile complete loan repayment schedule.

    b. Discount the trust deed (mortgage) to a yield rate indicated by the mortgage resale market.

    c. Add: down payment, prepaid interest, and discounted trust deed.

Problem: Tony Dean purchased acreage for $225,000 on the following terms:

    Down payment: $10,000

    Note and first trust deed carried by the seller:

        Principal amount: $215,000

        Interest rate: 7%

        Prepaid interest: $75,250, applied to years 1 through 5

        No additional payment of any kind until end of year 2

        Interest payments, years 2 through 6, applied to years 6 through 10

        Principal payments of $10,000 annually, years 6 through 10

        Equal annual payments of $30,000, including principal and interest, years 11 through 15

        Principal balance of $58,900 due as a balloon payment, end of year

15 (in addition to $30,000 regular payment for year 15)

Find the cash equivalent of the sales price, discounting the trust deed to yield a true 10%. (The assumption is that the seller of the property retains down payment and prepaid interest and immediately resells the note and trust deed to a private investor, who purchases at a discounted price that will yield 10% and return his capital investment.)

Solution:

a. Loan Repayment Schedule

Period	Interest Earned	Interest Paid	Periods Applied to	Principal Paid	Principal Balance	Total Paid
0	0	75,250	1-5	10,000	215,000	85,250
1	15,050	0	—	0	215,000	0
2	15,050	15,050	6	0	215,000	15,050
3	15,050	14,350	7	0	215,000	14,350
4	15,050	13,650	8	0	215,000	13,650
5	15,050	12,950	9	0	215,000	12,950
6	15,050	12,250	10	10,000	205,000	22,250
7	14,350	0	—	10,000	195,000	10,000
8	13,650	0	—	10,000	185,000	10,000
9	12,950	0	—	10,000	175,000	10,000
10	12,250	0	—	10,000	165,000	10,000
11-15	—	—	11-15	106,100	58,900	30,000P/P
15	—	—	—	58,900	0	58,900

b. Trust Deed Discounted to Yield 10%

Period(s)	Payments x PW or PW 1/P	= Discounted Worth
2	$15,050 x .82645	= $12,438.07 (PW 1, 10%, 2 yrs.)
3	14,350 x .75131	= 10,781.30 (PW 1, 10%, 3 yrs.)
4	13,650 x .68301	= 9,323.09 (PW 1, 10%, 4 yrs.)
5	12,950 x .62092	= 8,040.91 (PW 1, 10%, 5 yrs.)
6	22,250 x .56447	= 12,559.46 (PW 1, 10%, 6 yrs.)
7-10	10,000 x 1.7893	= 17,893.00 (PW 1/P, 10%, 10 yrs. minus PW 1/P, 10%, 6 yrs.)
11-15	30,000 x 1.4615	= 43,845.00 (PW 1/P, 10%, 15 yrs. minus PW 1/P, 10%, 10 yrs.)
15	58,900 x .23939	= 14,100.07 (PW 1, 10%, 15 yrs.)
		$128,980.90

c. Down payment: $10,000
   Prepaid interest: 75,250
   Discounted trust deed: 128,980
   Cash Equivalent of Sales Price: $214,230

Present worth of the seller's total income stream on a prepaid interest sale:

Procedure:

a. Compile complete loan repayment schedule.

b. Discount the trust deed (mortgage) to a yield rate identical to the interest rate on the note.

c. Add: down payment, prepaid interest, and discounted trust deed.

Problem: Compute present worth of seller's income stream, using data

from the preceding illustration.
Solution:
    a. Use payment schedule in preceding problem.
    b. Trust Deed Discounted to Yield 7%

Periods	Payments	x	PW or PW 1/P	= Discounted Worth
2	$15,050	x	.87344	= $13,145.27 (PW 1, 7%, 2 yrs.)
3	14,350	x	.81630	= 11,713.91 (PW 1, 7%, 3 yrs.)
4	13,650	x	.76290	= 10,413.59 (PW 1, 7%, 4 yrs.)
5	12,950	x	.71300	= 9,233.35 (PW 1, 7%, 5 yrs.)
6	22,250	x	.66634	= 14,826.07 (PW 1, 7%, 6 yrs.)
7-10	10,000	x	2.25704	= 22,570.40 (PW 1/P, 7%, 10 yrs. minus PW 1/P, 7%, 6 yrs.)
11-15	30,000	x	2.08433	= 62,529.90 (PW 1/P, 15 yrs. minus PW 1/P, 7%, 10 yrs.)
15	58,900	x	.36245	= 21,348.31 (PW 1, 7%, 15 yrs.)
				$165,780.80

    c. Down payment: $10,000
       Prepaid interest: 75,250
       Present worth of trust deed: 165,780

       Present Worth of Income Stream: $251,030

PRESENT WORTH OF ANNUITIES, LEASED FEES, LEASEHOLD INTERESTS, AND SINGLE FUTURE INCOME PAYMENTS (REVERSIONS)

Annuity (any level, terminal series of income payments):
    Procedure:
        1. If payment is made, or is assumed to be made, at the end of each period:
            Multiply periodic income payment by the PW 1/P.
        2. If payment is made at the beginning of each period:
            a. Add 1.0 to the PW 1/P factor for the next-to-the-final period.
            b. Multiply the periodic income payment by the adjusted factor computed in a.

Problem 1: Find the present worth of an annuity of $7,500 for 12 years at a yield rate of 9%, assuming payment to be made at the end of each year.
Solution:
    $7,500 x 7.16073 = $53,705 (PW 1/P, 9%, 12 years)

Problem 2: A lease calls for annual net rental payments of $7,500 at the beginning of each year for 12 years. Find present worth at a yield rate of 9%.
Solution:
    a. 6.80519 + 1.0 = 7.80519 (PW 1/P, 9%, 11 years)
    b. $7,500 x 7.80519 = $58,539

Annuity with a deferred start:
  Procedure:
      1. a. Subtract PW 1/P factor for period immediately preceding start
          from factor for final period.
        b. Multiply periodic income payment by the difference (adjusted
          factor from a.)
      2. (Alternate)
        a. Multiply PW 1/P factor, selected as though there were no deferred
          start, by the PW 1 factor for period immediately preceding start.
        b. Multiply periodic income payment by the adjusted factor from a.
  Problem: An annuity of $15,000 per year runs for 15 years, starting 5
years hence. Compute present worth at a rate of 7%.
  Solution 1:
      a. 10.59401 − 4.10020 = 6.49381 (PW 1/P, 7%, 20 years, and 5 years)
      b. $15,000 x 6.49381 = $97,407
  Solution 2:
      a. 9.10791 x .71299 = 6.49385 (PW 1/P, 7%, 15 years;
                                  PW 1, 7%, 5 years)
      b. $15,000 x 6.49385 = $97,408
      (Slight difference is due to rounding factors.)

Annuity with a graduated (step-up or step-down) schedule:
  Procedure:
      a. Multiply periodic payment in first level series of payments by the PW
         1/P factor for the final period in the first series.
      b. Subtract factor in a from factor for final period in next level series of
         payments. (Use same method in adjusting PW 1/P factors for each
         additional series of payments.)
      c. Multiply adjusted factor(s) from b by periodic payment(s).
      d. Add a and c.
  Problem: A 15 year lease specifies $4,000 per year the first 3 years,
$5,000 the next 7 years, and $6,000 per year for the final 5 years. What is
the present worth at a 10% yield rate?
  Solution:
      a. $4,000 x 2.48685 = $9,947.40 (PW 1/P, 10%, 3 years)
      b. Adjusted factor for years 4-10:
        6.14457 − 2.48685 = 3.65772 (PW 1/P, 10%, 10 years, 3 years)
        Adjusted factor for years 11-15:
        7.60608 − 6.14457 = 1.46151 (PW 1/P, 10%, 15 years, 10 years)
      c. $5,000 x 3.65772 = $18,288.60
        $6,000 x 1.46151 =   8,769.06
      d. Years 1-3: $9,947.40
        Years 4-10:   18,288.60
        Years 11-15:   8,769.06
                    ——————
                $37,005.06

Leased fee:
  Procedure:
      1. If economic rent equals or exceeds contract rent:
        a. Multiply annual periodic payment by PW 1/P, adjusting factors for

a graduated annuity as required.
   b. Add estimated improvement value (if any) at end of lease to
      assumed land value.
   c. Multiply sum from b by PW 1 factor for final period.
   d. Add a and c.
2. If contract rent exceeds economic rent:
   a. Separate income into two streams: economic rent, and excess rent.
   b. Value each stream separately by the PW 1/P factors, using a
      "normal" yield rate for the economic rent and a higher "risk" rate
      for the excess.
   c. Multiply assumed land value plus terminal improvement value (if
      any) by PW 1 factor for final period.
   d. Add b and c.

Problem 1: Five years ago property was leased for 25 years at $1,500 per
month net. Economic rent and contract rent are now considered to be
equal, although contract rent is likely to be "low" in the future. Assumed
land value is $95,000. Replacement cost of improvements new is
computed at $100,000, and it is estimated that the building will have a
value of 30% of RCN upon expiration of the lease. What is the indicated
value of the leased fee at a yield rate of 8½%?

Solution:
   a. $25 - 5 = 20$ years remaining $1,500 x 12 = $18,000 annual rent
      $18,000 x 9.46334 = $170,340 (PW 1/P, 8½%, 20 years)
   b. Reversion:
      Improvements: .30 x $100,000   = $30,000
      Land: = 95,000
                                        _____
                                         $125,000
   c. $125,000 x .19562 = $24,453 (PW 1, 8½%, 20 years)
   d. $170,340 + $24,453 = $194,793

Problem 2: A ground lease on a parcel valued at $50,000 runs for 10 years
at annual contract rent of $5,000 net. Economic rent is $4,000 per
annum. Compute present worth of the leased fee at a yield rate of 8% on
economic rent and 12% on the excess.
Solution:
   a. Contract rent: $5,000
      Economic rent: − 4,000
                          _____
      Excess rent: $1,000
   b. $ 4,000 x 6.71008 = $26,840 (PW 1/P, 8%, 10 years)
        1,000 x 5.65022 =   5,650 (PW 1/P, 12%, 10 years)
   c. $50,000 x   .46319 = 23,160 (PW 1, 8%, 10 years)
                           _____
   d. $55,650
Note that present worth of economic rent only plus present worth of
the reversion equals land value of $50,000:
      $26,840 + $23,160 = $50,000

Leasehold interests:
   Procedure:
      1. When improvements, if any, are erected by lessor, and economic rent

exceeds contract rent:
  a. Subtract annual contract rent from annual economic rent.
  b. Multiply the difference by the PW 1/P at a determined "risk" rate.
2. When improvements are erected by lessee:
  a. Subtract annual contract rent of land from economic rent of total
     improved property.
  b. Multiply the difference by the PW 1/P at a determined yield rate.
Problem 1: A commercial building is leased for 20 years at $600 per
month. Economic rent is $750 a month for the first 8 years and $900 a
month for the remainder of the lease. At a yield rate of 10%, determine
the present worth of the leasehold interest.
Solution:
  a. Contract rent: $600 x 12 = $7,200
     Economic rent:
     Years 1-8:   750 x 12 = 9,000
     Years 9-20: 900 x 12 = 10,800
     Leasehold interest:
     Years 1-8: $9,000 − 7,200 = $1,800
     Years 9-20: 10,800 − 7,200 = 3,600
  b. $1,800 x 5.33493 = $9,603 (PW 1/P, 10%, 8 years)
       3,600 x 3.17863 = 11,443 (PW 1/P, 10%, 20 years, minus 8 years)
                        ─────────
                        $21,046

Problem 2: Ground lease runs 40 years at $500 a month net. Building,
erected by lessee, becomes property of lessor on expiration of the lease.
Economic rent of land and improvements is estimated to be $950 a month
for the first 25 years and $1,200 a month thereafter. Find present worth
of the leasehold at 9%.
Solution:
  a. Contract rent of land: $500 x 12 = $6,000
     Economic rent of land and improvements:
     Years 1-25:   950 x 12 = 11,400
     Years 26-40: 1,200 x 12 = 14,400
     Leasehold interest:
     Years 1-25: $11,400 − 6,000 = $5,400
     Years 26-40:   14,400 − 6,000 = 8,400
  b. $5,400 x 9.82258 = $53,042 (PW 1/P, 9%, 25 years)
       8,400 x .93478 =   7,852 (PW 1/P, 9%, 40 years,
                          ─────────
                          $60,894   minus 25 years)

Level annuity equivalent of a graduated or irregular income stream:
  Procedure:
  a. Compute the present worth of the total income stream at the given
     yield rate.
  b. Multiply a by the periodic repayment factor at the given rate, for the
     total term.
Problem: Net annual income from a shopping center is projected to be
$300,000 a year for the first 3 years, $360,000 a year for the next 3
years, then $400,000 per year for the final 4 years of a 10 year holding

period. Compute the level annuity equivalent of the entire graduated income stream, using a 12% yield rate.

Solution:

a. $300,000 x 2.40183   = $ 720,549 (PW 1/P, 12%, 3 years)

   360,000 x (4.11141 − 2.40183) =   615,449 (PW 1/P, 12%, 6 years minus 3 years)

   400,000 x (5.65022 − 4.11141) =   615,524 (PW 1/P, 12%, 10 years minus 6 years)

$1,951,522

b. $1,951,522 x .176984 = $345,388 (PR, 12%, 10 years)
   PROOF: $345,388 x 5.65022 = $1,951,518 (PW 1/P, 12%, 10 years)

NOTE: The level annuity equivalent is the amount to be capitalized by the mortgage-equity technique. For example: In this problem assume the specifications considered are 12% equity yield, 10 year holding period, 20% appreciation; 70% loan ratio, 9% interest rate, 20 year loan term. OAR is .08863 (see page 151).

Value = $345,388 ÷ .08863
      = $3,896,965, say $3,900,000

Sale and leaseback (calculating annual rent):

Procedure:

Multiply total property value by the PR factor at the agreed rate for the term of the lease.

Problem: A corporation erects a building at a cost of $1,500,000 on a site costing $400,000. Property is then sold to an investor for $1,900,000 on a leaseback arrangement. A straight net lease for 25 years is set up on annual payments that will give the purchaser a complete recovery of capital within 25 years and return 7½% yield on the declining principal balance. The lessee has an option to renew the lease for an additional 25 years at a reduced rental of 3% of total property value. Compute the annual rental agreed upon for the first 25 years.

Solution:

$1,900,000 x .08971 = $170,450 (PR, 7½%, 25 years)

NOTES: Rental per annum first 25 years is 8.97% of property value. Leasehold interest may have substantial worth upon renewal of lease.

Sandwich lease:

Procedure:

a. Subtract contract rent paid to lessor from contract rent paid to sub-lessor.

b. Multiply a by the PW 1/P at a determined "risk" rate.

Problem: Contract rent paid to A, the lessor, by lessee B is $6,500 net per year for 10 years. Sub-lessee C pays $8,000 contract rent to sub-lessor B. At a yield rate of 10%, find present worth to B of the sandwich lease.

Solution:

a. $8,000 − $6,500 = $1,500

b. $1,500 x 6.14457 = $9,217 (PW 1/P, 10%, 10 years)

Single future income payment (reversion):
Procedure:
   Multiply payment by PW 1.
   Problem: A parcel of ground has an estimated value of $300,000. Using a yield rate of 6½%, what is the present worth of the reversion at the end of a 50 year lease?
   Solution:
      $300,000 x .04291 = $12,873 (PW 1, 6½%, 50 years)

Top leasehold interest:
Procedure:
      a. Subtract contract rent paid to sub-lessor from economic rent.
      b. Multiply a by the PW 1/P at a determined "risk" rate.
   Problem: In the preceding sandwich lease example, economic rent is $9,000 a year for 3 years and $10,500 a year for the next 7 years. Compute the top leasehold interest of C at 12%.
   Solution:
      a. Top leasehold interest:
         Years 1-3: $9,000 − 8,000 = $1,000
         Years 4-10:   10,500 − 8,000 =   2,500
      b. $1,000 x 2.40183 = $2,402 (PW 1/P, 12%, 3 years)
           2,500 x 3.24839 =   8,121 (PW 1/P, 12%, 10 years − 3 years)
                              $10,523

REAL ESTATE APPRAISAL: METHODS AND TECHNIQUES
OF THE INCOME APPROACH

Building residual technique:
Procedure:
   1. Annuity method:
      a. Multiply land value by yield rate, giving income attributable to land.
      b. Subtract income to land from net annual income; difference is income attributable to building.
      c. Multiply income to building by PW 1/P at yield rate for term of remaining economic life of improvements; product is indicated value of building.
      d. Add land and building values.
   2. Sinking fund method:
      a. Multiply land value by yield rate, giving income attributable to land.
      b. Subtract income to land from net annual income; difference is income attributable to building.
      c. Add yield rate and (PR − i) at a "safe" rate; say 4%.
      d. Divide income to building by total capitalization rate from c; quotient is indicated value of building.

e. Add land and building values.
3. Straight line method:
   a. Multiply land value by yield rate, giving income attributable to land.
   b. Subtract income to land from net annual income; difference is income attributable to building.
   c. Divide 1.0 by years of remaining economic life to determine amortization rate; add yield rate. Result is the total capitalization rate to be applied to building.
   d. Divide income to building by total capitalization rate from c; quotient is indicated value of building.
   e. Add land and building values.

NOTE: In the methods and techniques of the income approach, as outlined and illustrated, the flow to be capitalized is given as net annual income before amortization. Property taxes have been included with other allowable expenses. However, the appraiser in the assessor's office will not deduct property taxes as an expense but will include a percentage allowance in the total capitalization rate.

Problem: Annual net income from commercial property is estimated to be $22,500 before recapture of capital investment in improvements. Land value is considered to be $80,000. Using a yield rate of 8% and a remaining economic life of 25 years, compute indicated building value and total property value, using three methods of building residual technique.
Solution 1 (Annuity Method):
   a. Income to land: .08 x $80,000 = $6,400
   b. Income to building: $22,500 − $6,400 = $16,100
   c. Building value: $16,100 x 10.67478 = $171,864 (PW 1/P, 8%, 25 years)
   d. $80,000 + $171,864 = $251,864
Solution 2 (Sinking Fund Method):
   a. Income to land: .08 x $80,000 = $6,400
   b. Income to building: $22,500 − $6,400 = $16,100
   c. Yield rate: .08
      (PR − i) at 4%, 25 yrs.: .024 (PR, 4%, 25 years, less .04)
      Capitalization rate: .104

   d. Building value: $16,100 ÷ .104 = $154,808
   e. $80,000 + $154,808 = $234,808
Solution 3 (Straight Line Method):
   a. Income to land: .08 x $80,000 = $6,400
   b. Income to building: $22,500 − $6,400 = $16,100
   c. Yield rate: = .08
      Amortization rate: 1.0 ÷ 25 = .04
      Capitalization rate: = .12
   d. Building value: $16,100 ÷ .12 = $134,167
   e. $80,000 + $134,167 = $214,167
NOTE: Method to be used depends principally on the appraiser's opinion of the shape of the income stream. Both the annuity and sinking fund methods assume a level terminal series of income payments. The straight

line method assumes a straight line declining terminal income stream.

Direct capitalization of land:
Procedure:
   Divide net annual income by yield rate.
Problem: A ground lease for 15 years produces net annual income of
$15,000. It is assumed that there will be a level perpetual income stream
provided by this commercial lot. Capitalize it at a yield rate of 9%.
Solution:
   $15,000 ÷ .09 = $166,667
(This procedure, applied to improved property, is known as the "broker's
method.")

Land residual technique:
Procedure:
   1. Annuity Method:
      a. Multiply building value by PR factor at yield rate for term of
         remaining economic life, giving income attributable to building.
      b. Subtract income to building from net annual income; difference is
         income attributable to land.
      c. Divide income to land by the yield rate; the quotient is the
         indicated land value.
      d. Add building and land values.
   2. Sinking Fund Method:
      a. Add yield rate to (PR − i) at a "safe" rate; suggest 4%.
      b. Multiply building value by capitalization rate from a; product is
         income attributable to building.
      c. Subtract income to building from net annual income; difference is
         income attributable to land.
      d. Divide income to land by the yield rate; the quotient is the
         indicated land value.
      e. Add building and land values.
   3. Straight Line Method:
      a. Divide 1.0 by years of remaining economic life to determine
         amortization rate; add yield rate. Result is the total capitalization
         rate to be applied to building.
      b. Multiply building value by capitalization rate from a; product is
         income attributable to building.
      c. Subtract income to building from net annual income; difference is
         income attributable to land.
      d. Divide income to land by the yield rate; the quotient is the
         indicated land value.
      e. Add building and land values.
Problem: Value of an apartment building is estimated to be $120,000.
Yearly net income before recapture is $16,000. Remaining economic life
is 40 years. Find land value and total property value at a yield rate of
8½%. Use three methods of the land residual technique.
Solution 1 (Annuity Method):
   a. Income to building: $120,000 x .088382 = $10,606 (PR, 8½%, 40
      years)

b. Income to land: $16,000 — $10,606 = $5,394
c. Indicated land value $5,394 ÷ .085 = $63,459
d. $120,000 + $63,459 = $183,459

Solution 2 (Sinking Fund Method):

a. Yield rate: .085
   (PR — i) at 4%, 40 yrs.:   .0105   (PR, 4%, 40 years, less .04)
                               _____

   Capitalization rate: .0955

b. Income to building: $120,000 x .0955 = $11,460
c. Income to land: $16,000 — $11,460 = $4,540
d. Indicated land value: $4,540 ÷ .085 = $53,412
e. $120,000 + $53,412 = $173,412

Solution 3 (Straight Line Method):

a. Yield rate: = .085
   Amortization rate: 1.0 ÷ 40   = .025
                                        _____

   Capitalization rate: .11
b. Income to building: $120,000 x .11 = $13,200
c. Income to land: $16,000 — $13,200 = $2,800
d. Indicated land value: $2,800 ÷ .085 = $32,941
e. $120,000 + $32,941 = $152,941

Property residual (reversion) technique:

Procedure:

1. Annuity method:
   a. Multiply net annual income by PW 1/P at yield rate for period of remaining economic life of improvements; product is present worth of the total level terminal income stream.
   b. Multiply assumed future land value by PW 1 at yield rate for final period; product is present worth of the land reversion.
   c. Add a and b.
2. Sinking fund method:
   a. Add yield rate and (PR — i) for remaining economic life at a "safe" rate (4%); the sum is the capitalization rate.
   b. Divide net annual income by capitalization rate; the quotient is present worth of the total level terminal income stream.
   c. Multiply assumed future land value by PW 1 at yield rate for final period; product is present worth of the land reversion.
   d. Add b and c.
3. Straight line method:
   a. Divide years of remaining economic life into 1.0 to find amortization rate; add yield rate. Result is capitalization rate.
   b. Divide net annual income by capitalization rate; the quotient is present worth of the total straight line declining terminal income stream.
   c. Multiply assumed future land value by PW 1 at yield rate for final period; product is present worth of the land reversion.
   d. Add b and c.

Problem: Assumed future land value is $60,000; estimated net annual income before recapture, $18,500; remaining economic life, 20 years;

yield rate, 8%. Estimate value of the total property, using three methods of the property residual (reversion) technique.

Solution 1 (Annuity Method):

    a. $18,500 x 9.818 = $181,633 (PW 1/P, 8%, 10 years)

    b. $60,000 x .21455 = $12,873 (PW 1, 8%, 20 years)

    c. $181,633 + $12,873 = $194,506

Solution 2 (Sinking Fund Method):

    a. Yield rate: .08

       (PR -i) at 4%, 20 yrs.:   .0336 (PR, 4%, 20 yrs., — .04)

       Capitalization rate: .1136

    b. $18,500 ÷ .1136 = $162,852

    c. $60,000 x .21455 = $12,873 (PW 1, 8%, 20 years)

    d. $162,852 + $12,873 = $175,725

Solution 3 (Straight Line):

    a. Yield rate: = .08

       Amortization rate: 1.0 ÷ 20   = .05

       Capitalization rate: .13

    b. $18,500 ÷ .13 = $142,308

    c. $60,000 x .21455 = $12,873 (PW 1, 8%, 20 years)

    d. $142,308 + $12,873 = $155,181

SINKING FUND:

For an explanation of computations, see "Growth of a Series of Periodic Deposits," page 67.

SPECIAL SECTION: MORTGAGE-EQUITY TECHNIQUE[1]

Appreciation required to generate a specified rate of yield on equity:

    Procedure:

      1. From the OAR tables, when property value and/or over-all rate are known:

        a. Compute over-all rate by dividing property value into net annual income.

        b. Find percent of appreciation in OAR tables by search and interpolation.

      2. From the compound interest and annuity tables (alternate procedure):

STEPS IN COMPUTATION	FACTOR SELECTION	
	Rate	Term
a. Multiply loan ratio by loan constant.	—	—
b. Subtract a from OAR.	—	—
c. Multiply b by PW 1/P.	Equity Yield	Holding Period
d. Multiply loan ratio by percent of loan unpaid at end of holding period.	—	—

---

[1] For a more detailed treatment of the methods involved in this technique, see Irvin Johnson, "Instant Mortgage-Equity Technique." (D. C. Heath & Company: Lexington, Massachusetts. 1972.)

	FACTOR SELECTION	
STEPS IN COMPUTATION	Rate	Term
e. Multiply d by PW 1	Equity Yield	Holding Period
f. Add equity ratio to e	–	–
g. Subtract c from f	–	–
h. Divide g by PW 1	Equity Yield	Holding Period
i. Subtract 1.0 from h. Difference is plus or minus percent of appreciation.	–	–

Problem 1: Given the following:

Loan data:

Loan ratio:	80%
Interest rate:	9%
Term:	20 years
Holding period	15 years
Anticipated equity yield:	10%
Property value:	$400,000
Net annual income:	$ 31,800

What percent of appreciation would be required in order to generate a yield of 10% on equity?

Solution (Procedure 1):

a. OAR = $31,800 ÷ $400,000
   = .0795

b. From the OAR tables:
   10% equity yield, 15 year holding period, 80% loan ratio.
   9% interest rate, 20 year loan term:
   OAR at 40% appreciation: .07952
   Appreciation of 40% would thus be required to generate a yield of 10% on equity under this set of variables.

Problem 2: Income property under consideration by an investor can be financed on a 25 year loan, 8% interest rate, for 60% of market value. Market analysis shows that comparable property in the area is bought and sold on an overall rate of .0856. Based on this data, compute the percent of appreciation required to produce a yield of 12% on equity within a 10 year holding period.

Solution (Procedure 2):

a. .6 x .09262 = .0556
b. .0856 — .0556 = .03
c. .03 x 5.65 = .1695 (PW 1/P, 12%, 10 years)
d. .6 x .80763 = .48458
e. .48458 x .322 = .156 (PW 1, 12%, 10 years)
f. .4 + .156 = .556
g. .556 — .1695 = .3865
h. .3865 ÷ .322 = 1.2 (PW 1, 12%, 10 years)
i. 1.2 — 1.0 = .2, or 20%

Cash Flow:

Procedure:

1. Dollar amount of annual cash flow:
   a. Multiply original principal amount of loan by the loan constant

(from supplemental tables).
  b. Subtract a from net annual income.
  2. Annual cash flow as a percent of property value:
    a. Multiply given loan ratio by loan constant (from supplemental tables).
    b. Subtract a from over-all rate.

Problem 1: Property valued at $800,000 can be financed on a 20 year loan at 8% for 70% of value. The purchaser anticipates a 10 year holding period, 0% appreciation, and 14% yield on equity. Net annual income is $80,816. Compute the annual cash flow.
Solution (Procedure 1):
  a. Original principal amount of loan:
      .70 x $800,000 = $560,000
        $560,000 x .10037 = $56,207 (see page 186.)
  b. $80,816 − 56,207 = $24,609

Problem 2: Given (as in preceding problem):
  Loan data:

Loan ratio:	70%	
Interest rate:	8%	
Loan term:	20 years	
Holding period:		10 years
Projected appreciation:		0%
Anticipated yield on equity:		14%

Calculate annual cash flow as a percent of property value (after allowable expenses and debt service).
Solution (Procedure 2):
  a. .7 x .10037 = .07026 (Loan Constant, page 186.)
  b. OAR: .10102 (OAR, page 154)
      .10102 − .07026
      or 3.076%

NOTES: In the preceding problem (Procedure 1), $24,609 is 3.076% of $800,000. Conversely, .03076 x $800,000 = $24,608. If Loan Constant x Loan Ratio is less than the OAR, there will be a positive "cash flow." If it is greater than the OAR, there will be a negative "cash flow."

Income required to meet equity demands:
Procedure:
  Multiply value by over-all rate.
Problem: Property valued at $650,000 can be financed at 8½% for 25 years and for 75% of value. The prospective investor projects 20% appreciation within a 5 year holding period. What net annual income before debt service would be required in order to produce a yield of 15% on equity?
Solution:
  From the OAR tables: (See page 140)
    At 8%: .06871
    At 9%: .07589
  Interpolate to mid point for OAR at 8½%
    .06871 + .07589 = .1446

.1446 ÷ 2 = .0723

$650,000 x .0723 = $46,995

NOTE: The simplest way to interpolate to a midpoint is to add the two rates or factors and divide by 2.

Interpolation by simple proportion:

Procedure:

To calculate an over-all rate from the prepared tables in solving a problem whose variables do not correspond to the precomputed tables:

a. Bracket the differing variable between lower and higher corresponding variables in the OAR tables.

b. Compute the over-all rate through interpolation by simple proportion. (See also the preceding problem and solution. Refer to pages 32-33.)

Problem: Given the following:

Loan data:

Loan ratio:	75%
Interest rate:	9%
Loan term:	20 years

Projected appreciation: 0%

Anticipated yield on equity: 12%

Calculate the OAR, assuming a holding period of 8 years.

Solution:

(For a holding period of 8 years, the OAR will lie between the OAR's for 5 year and 10 year holding periods, at a point to be determined.)

a. OAR, 5 year holding period: .09765 (page 134)

OAR, 10 year holding period: .09860 (page 152)

b. 10 years — 5 years = 5 years

8 years — 5 years = 3 years

3 ÷ 5 = .6 or 60%

The OAR for 8 years is, by proportion, 60% of the distance between the OAR's for 5 and 10 years.

This distance is: .09860 — .09765 = .00095

.00095 x .6 = .00057

The OAR for an 8 year holding period: .09765 + .00057 = .09822

NOTE: The appraiser can interpolate for varying holding periods, interest rates, term of the loan, loan ratios, percent of appreciation or depreciation, and equity yield rates. The procedure follows the same basic format in all cases. Interpolation by simple proportion is approximate, not precise. However, it is accurate enough for the major portion of practical applications. For example, if the OAR in this problem were computed with accuracy from the compound interest tables (see procedure on pages 84-86) it would be calculated to be .09825, compared to .09822 as found by interpolation. If these two over-all rates were each used to capitalize net annual income of $200,000, the indicated values would be $2,035,623 and $2,036,245 respectively. The difference of $622 is so slight in relation to total value as to be absorbed entirely by rounding either figure to a reasonable sum.

Investment analysis and check on computations:
Procedure (using OAR, supplemental, and compound interest tables):
    a. Multiply the annual "cash flow" by the PW 1/P at equity yield rate for term of the holding period.
    b. Multiply the reversion by the PW 1 at equity yield rate for term of the holding period.
    c. Add a and b. Compare sum with the original equity (down payment , which is the "target figure."

Problem: Appraisal of a mobile home park by the mortgage-equity technique has been based on the following data: loan terms, 9% interest rate, 20 year amortization, 70% loan ratio; 10 year holding period; 10% projected appreciation; 14% anticipated equity yield. Net annual income is estimated to be $200,000. The OAR, selected from the tables and adjusted by interpolation is .10192, indicating a value of $1,962,300. Check the validity of calculations by computing the present worth of the income stream and the reversion.

Solution:
    a. Equity (down payment):
      .3 x $1,962,300 = $588,690
    Principal amount of loan:
      .7 x $1,962,300 = $1,373,610
    Annual debt service:
      .108 x $1,373,610 = $148,350 (Loan Constant, page 186)
    Cash flow:
      $200,000 − $148,350 = $51,650
    PW of cash flow:
      $51,650 x 5.21612 = $269,412 (PW 1/P, 14%, 10 years)
    b. Value at end of holding period:
      1.1 x $1,962,300 = $2,158,530
    Loan balance at end of holding period:
      .71026 x $1,373,610 = $975,620 (See page 186)
    Amount of reversion:
      $2,158,530 − $975,620 = $1,182,910
    PW of reversion:
      $1,182,910 x .27 = $319,386 (PW 1, 14%, 10 years)
    c. $269,412 + $319,386 = $588,798
    Target figure is $588,690, indicating an insignificant differential of $108 attributable to "rounding."

Level annuity equivalent of a graduated or irregular income stream:
For an explanation of procedures, see "Present Worth of Annuities," page 71.

Loan Constant:
See procedures under "Trust Deeds and Mortgages," page 97; also see "Loan Constant" in supplemental tables.

Over-All Rate:
Procedure:
    1. If value is not known:

Select the rate from the OAR tables, interpolating if necessary.

2. If value is not known (alternate procedure):

Steps in Computation	Factor Selection		
	Rate	Term	Period
a. Multiply loan ratio by loan constant	Interest	Total	Monthly or Annual
b. Multiply step a by PW 1/P.	Interest	Total less Holding Period	Monthly ÷ 12 or Annual
c. Express projected resale price as a percent of purchase price and subtract step b.	—	—	—
d. Multiply step a by PW 1/P	Equity Yield	Holding Period	Annual
e. Multiply step c by PW 1	Equity Yield	Holding Period	Annual
f. Subtract step e from step d.	—	—	—
g. Add equity ratio to step f.	—	—	—
h. Divide step g by PW 1/P. Quotient is over-all rate.	Equity Yield	Holding Period.	Annual

3. If value is *known:* Divide net annual income by property value
(R = I ÷ V).

Problem 1: Given the following:

Loan data:

    Loan ratio: 80%

    Interest rate: 8½%

    Term: 20 years

Holding period: 10 years

Anticipated depreciation: 20%

Required equity yield: 10%

What is the indicated over-all rate, based on these data and assumptions?

Solution (Procedure 1):

From the OAR tables, 10% equity yield, 10 year holding period, 80% loan ratio, 20 year term 20% depreciation:

    OAR at 8%:   .09726

    OAR at 9%:   .10438

By interpolation: .10082 over-all rate

Problem 2: Given the following data:

Loan Specifications:

    Loan ratio: 80%

    Interest rate: 9%

    Loan term: 30 years, monthly payments

Holding period: 10 years

Anticipated appreciation: 20%

Required equity yield: 14%

Compute the OAR.

Solution (Procedure 2):

  a. .8 x .09656 = .077248 (Loan Constant, page 186)

  b. .077248 x (111.144954 ÷ 12) = .715477 (PW 1/P, 9%, 240 months)

    c. $1.2 - .715477 = .484523$
    d. $.077248 \times 5.216116 = .40293$ (PW 1/P, 14%, 10 years)
    e. $.484523 \times .269744 = .1307$ (PW 1, 14%, 10 years)
    f. $.40293 - .1307 = .27223$
    g. $.2 + .27223 = .47223$
    h. $.47223 \div 5.216116 = .09053$ (PW 1/P, 14%, 10 years)
    (Compare answer with precomputed OAR, page 155)

Problem 3: Property was sold for $750,000. Net annual income is $61,725. What is the over-all rate?
Solution (Procedure 3):
    OAR = $61,725 ÷ $750,000
        = .0823

Percent of loan paid off at any point in time:
See procedure under "Trust Deeds and Mortgages," page 101.

Percent of loan unpaid at any point in time:
See procedure under "Trust Deeds and Mortgages," page 100; see also "Supplemental Tables," pages 185-186.

Present worth of an annuity:
See procedures under "Present Worth of Annuities," page 71.

Present worth of a reversion:
See procedure under "Present Worth of Annuities . . . and Single Future Income Payments (Reversions)," page 76.

Rate of yield on equity:
Procedure:
    1. Using OAR tables:
        a. Compute over-all rate by dividing property value into net income. (Rate = Income ÷ Value)
        b. Find rate in OAR tables by search and interpolation.
    2. Using compound interest tables:
        (Equity yield rate derived from an over-all rate and loan data)
        a. Multiply the loan ratio by the loan constant.
        b. Subtract a from the over-all rate.
        c. Multiply the loan ratio by the percent of loan remaining unpaid at the end of the holding period.
        d. Subtract c from estimated value at end of holding period expressed as a percent of purchase price.
        e. Make the following considerations:
            Step b computes the annuity.
            Step d gives the reversion
            Value (the "target figure") is the equity ratio.
        Use the following equation in a dual "cut and try" operation to bracket the equity yield rate:
            Value = Annuity x PW 1/P + Reversion x PW 1
            (Select PW 1/P and PW 1 factors at estimated equity yield rates

for term of holding period.)
f. "Zero in" on equity yield rate by interpolation.
Problem 1: Given the following:
Loan data:

Loan ratio:	75%
Interest rate:	9%
Term:	20 years

Holding period:	10 years
Anticipated appreciation:	0%
Property value:	$650,000
Net income after property taxes:	$ 70,000

What is the equity yield rate?
Solution (Procedure 1):
  a. OAR = $70,000 ÷ $650,000 = .1077
  b. From the tables: OAR, 10 year holding period, 75% loan ratio (see page 158), 9% interest rate, 20 year term:
    At 15% Equity Yield: .10778 OAR
  Actual OAR of .1077 indicates equity yield is about 15%.

Problem 2: You are deriving equity yield rates from the market on comparable apartment houses in a given area of the city. Your analysis of sales and rents indicates an over-all rate of .1038. Data from lending institutions shows that residential income properties of this age, quality and type, and in this location would support a new maximum loan for 75% of appraised value at 9% interest rate for a term of 25 years. Based on these data and on a projected holding period of 10 years, compute equity yield rates:
  1. Assuming 0% appreciation within the holding period.
  2. Assuming 10% depreciation.
Solution (1) Assuming 0% appreciation (Procedure 2):
  a. .75   x .10071 = .0755 (Loan constant from supplemental tables)
  b. .1038 − .0755 = .0283
  c. .75   x .8274 = .62055 (% loan balance, supplemental tables)
  d. 1.0 −.62055 = .37945
  e. Try 15%
      .0283 x 5.01877 = .14203 (PW 1/P, 15%, 10 years)
      .37945 x .24718 = .09379 (PW 1, 15%, 10 years)
                        .23582

  Try 13%
      .0283 x 5.42624 = .15356 (PW 1/P, 13%, 10 years)
      .37945 x .29459 = .11178 (PW 1, 13%, 10 years)
                        .26534

  "Target figure" is .25, the equity ratio. By interpolation between .23582 and .26534, equity yield rate is computed to be 14%, assuming 0% appreciation during the 10 year holding period.

  Solution (2) Assuming 10% depreciation (Procedure 2):
    a. .75 x .10071 = .0755
    b. .1038 − .0755 = .0283
    c. .75 x .8274 = .62055

d. $.90 - .62055 = .27945$

e. Try 12%:

   $.0283 \times 5.6502 = .1599$ (PW 1/P, 12%, 10 years)

   $.2795 \times .32197 = \underline{.0900}$ (PW 1, 12%, 10 years)

   $\underline{.2499}$

Since computed .2499 is so close to the target figure of .25, there is no need for an additional estimate of rate, nor for bracketing and interpolation. Equity yield rate is 12%, assuming 10% depreciation in value during the 10 year holding period.

The format that follows was developed by Richard Laquess, Senior Appraiser, under the auspices of Edwin B. Shriner, CAE, Assessor of Ventura County, California. The example demonstrates the use of a mortgage-equity work sheet in the appraisal of a shopping center. The over-all rate, developed from five comparable sales and related to current financing terms applicable to the subject property, is translated into terms of rate of yield on equity. Net annual income of $250,000 before property taxes is capitalized by a rate of .123 (including OAR of .098 and tax allowance of .025). Indicated value of the subject property is $2,032,500. Over-all rates pertinent to other categories of income producing property—apartments, commercial buildings, mobile home parks, etc.—can be derived from the market by the same procedure. The appraiser can convert these rates into equity yield rates by the OAR or compound interest tables and use the rates with validity in the appraisal of other comparable properties.

OAR from Market

Sale Number & Date	I 8/71	II 9/71	III 7/70	IV 12/70	V 5/68
Assessor's parcel no.	185-0-200-34	094-0-155-40	300-0-121-05	212-0-075-17	618-0-011-09
Location	Thousand Oaks	Camarillo	Simi	Ventura	Oxnard
Adjusted price	$419,500	$1,215,000	$3,490,000	$1,700,000	$1,210,000
Gross income	$58,100	$152,380	$492,780	$243,700	$189,000
Eff. Gr. @2–4% vac.	2% $56,940	2% $149,330	3% $478,000	2% $238,826	4% $181,440
Expenses or ratio*	28% $37,330	$143,000	$71,646	30%	
Net income	$41,000	$112,000	$335,000	$167,180	$127,000
Comparability	Good	Good	Good	Good	Fair
OAR	.098	.092	.096	.098	.105

*Includes property taxes.

OAR from Mortgage-Equity Technique

Interest, 9%; Loan Ratio, 75%; Term, 20 Years; Holding Period, 10 Years

Equity yield rate = 12% with no change in value
Equity yield rate = 15% with 20% app.
  Indicated OAR .098

Selected OAR, .098 + tax, .025 = capitalization rate, .123
Net income,** $250,000 ÷ capitalization rate, .123
Indicated value, $2,032,500

** Before property taxes.

Rate of yield on equity investment in non-producing property held for appreciation:
  Procedure:
    a. Compute average annual expense payment.
    b. Estimate equity at anticipated time of resale (future worth) by subtracting loan balance from expected sales price.
    c. Estimate two yield rates: one above and one below the true yield rate to be determined.
    d. Let "future worth" represent equity (target figure) at time of resale. At each yield rate from step c, solve equation:
      Future worth = (Original cash investment ÷ PW 1) + [Annual Expense ÷ (PR – i)]
    e. Compare final equity (the target figure) with the two future worth values from step d. Interpolate to find indicated yield rate.
  Problem: An investor is considering a syndicate proposal to purchase non-producing acreage, zoned commercial. Plans are to hold the parcel for a period of 5 years in anticipation of appreciation, then resell. Terms of the proposed purchase are as follows:
    Sales price: $1,500,000
    Down payment: $500,000
    First trust deed, carried by seller:
      Principal: $1,000,000
      Interest rate: 7%
      Payment schedule:
        Annual interest payments of $70,000 for 12 years
        Principal amount of $1,000,000 due as a balloon payment at the end of 12 years.
  Annual property taxes are estimated at $30,000. If the client invests $10,000, his pro-rata share (1/50 or 2%) of the yearly "call" for payment of taxes and interest would amount to $2,000. Compute the yield rate if the land is held for 5 years and is sold for $2,500,000. How would the yield rate be affected if the holding period were extended to 7 years, all other data remaining the same?
  Solution:
    a. Annual call: $2,000 (given)
    b. Equity at time of resale: $2,500,000 – $1,000,000 = $1,500,000
      1/50 or 2% interest = .02 x $1,500,000 = $30,000
    c. If holding period is 5 years, try 12% and 10%; if 7 years, try 5% and 4½%.
    d, e. Holding period of 5 years:

Try 12% (use 12% PW 1 and PR factors for 5 years):
   Future worth = ($10,000 ÷ .56743) + [$2,000 ÷ (.27741 − .12)]
                 = $17,623 + ($2,000 ÷ .15741)
                 = $17,623 + 12,706
                 = $30,329
Try 10% (use 10% PW 1 and PR factors for 5 years):
   Future worth = ($10,000 ÷ .62092) + [$2,000 ÷ (.26380 − .10)]
                 = $16,105 + ($2,000 ÷ .1638)
                 = $16,105 + 12,210
                 = $28,315
By interpolation: About 11.67% yield on equity
Holding period of 7 years:
Try 5% (use 5% PW 1 and PR factors for 7 years):
   Future worth = ($10,000 ÷ .71068) + [$2,000 ÷ (.17282 − .05)]
                 = $14,071 + ($2,000 ÷ .12282)
                 = $14,071 + 16,284
                 = $30,355
Try 4½% (use 4½% PW 1 and PR factors for 7 years):
   Future worth = ($10,000 ÷ .73483) + [$2,000 ÷ (.1697−.045)]
                 = $13,609 + ($2,000 ÷ .1247)
                 = $13,609 + 16,039
                 = $29,648
By interpolation: About 4¾% yield on equity.
NOTE: Time value of money illustrated above.

Rate of yield on 100% equity:
Procedure:
   1. If neither appreciation nor depreciation is assumed within a holding
      period:
      Divide net annual income by value.
      (NOTE: In this case, the over-all rate and the equity yield rate
      coincide.)
   2. If either appreciation or depreciation is projected within a holding
      period:
      a. Estimate two yield rates: one above and one below the true yield
         rate sought.
      b. Multiply net annual income by PW 1/P, making two calculations,
         using two rates from a, for the term of the holding period.
      c. Multiply estimated value at end of holding period by PW 1 at each
         rate from a.
      d. At each rate, add computations from b and c.
      e. Use original value (equity) as a target figure and interpolate.
         (NOTE: This procedure is an example of the use of the basic
         equation: Value = Annuity x PW 1/P + Reversion x PW 1.
         Net annual income is the annuity. Value at the end of the holding
         period is the reversion.)
Problem 1: An investor pays $600,000 cash for a commercial building.
Net annual income is $54,000. Stability of both value and income are
projected for a 10 year holding period. What is the rate of yield on the
purchaser's 100% equity position?

Solution (Procedure 1):
   $54,000 ÷ $600,000 = .09, or 9%
   (Over-all rate and equity yield rate correspond.)
   PROOF: Use the equation:
   Value = Annuity x PW 1/P + Reversion x PW 1
      $54,000 x 6.41766 = $346,554 (PW 1/P, 9%, 10 years)
      $600,000 x .42241 = $\underline{253,446}$ (PW 1, 9%, 10 years)
                          $600,000

Problem 2: An apartment complex, purchased for $1,500,000 cash, generates net annual income of $127,500. A holding period of 12 years is anticipated, during which time net income is expected to remain stable. Compute the rate of yield on equity, assuming:
   A. Depreciation of 20% within the 12 year holding period.
   B. Appreciation of 30%, within the 12 year holding period.
Solution (Procedure 2):

Assuming 20% depreciation:
a. Try 7% and 8%.
b. At 7%:
      $127,500 x 7.94269 = $1,012,693 (PW 1/P, 7%, 12 years)
   At 8%:
      $127,500 x 7.53608 = $960,850 (PW 1/P, 8%, 12 years)
c. Estimated value at end of holding period:
      .8 x $1,500,000 = $1,200,000
   At 7%:
      $1,200,000 x .44401 = $532,812 (PW 1, 7%, 12 years)
   At 8%:
      $1,200,000 x .39711 = $476,532 (PW 1, 8%, 12 years)
d. At 7%:
      $1,012,693 + $532,812 = $1,545,505
   At 8%:
      $960,850 + $476,532 = $1,437,382
e. Target figure is the original value or original 100% equity, or $1,500,000
   By interpolation, equity yield rate is about 7.42%.

Assuming 30% appreciation:
a. Try 9% and 10%
b. At 9%:
      $127,500 x 7.16073 = $912,993 (PW 1/P, 9%, 12 years)
   At 10%:
      $127,500 x 6.81369 = $868,745 (PW 1/P, 10%, 12 years)
c. Estimated value at end of holding period:
      1.3 x $1,500,000 = $1,950,000
   At 9%:
      $1,950,000 x .35553 = $693,284 (PW 1, 9%, 12 years)
   At 10%:
      $1,950,000 x .31863 = $621,329 (PW 1, 10%, 12 years)
d. At 9%:
      $912,993 + $693,284 = $1,606,277

At 10%:

$868,745 + $621,329 = $1,490,074

e. Target figure, $1,500,000

By interpolation, equity yield rate is about 9.9%.

(NOTE: If depreciation is anticipated, over-all rate exceeds equity yield rate; if appreciation is projected, equity yield rate exceeds over-all rate. Over-all rate is the rate of current yield; equity yield rate is yield to maturity.)

Reversion, dollar amount of:

Procedure:

a. Calculate estimated property value at end of holding period.

b. Compute loan balance at end of holding period.

c. Subtract b from a.

Problem: A shopping center acquired for $4,500,000 is expected to appreciate 25% within a 10 year projected holding period. The center is financed on a 70% loan for 20 years at 8% interest. What is the amount of anticipated reversion at the end of 10 years?

Solution:

a. At 25% appreciation, property would be worth 125% of original purchase price: 1.25 x $4,500,000 = $5,625,000

b. Original loan (70% loan ratio): .7 x $4,500,000 = $3,150,000

Loan balance at end of 10 years: .68941 x $3,150,000 = $2,171,642 (see page 186)

c. Reversion: $5,625,000 − 2,171,642 = $3,453,358

Secondary financing, adjustment for, in calculating OAR:

Procedure:

a. Add the loan ratios for all mortgages or trust deeds on the property.

b. Compute each loan ratio separately as a percent of a.

c. Determine the combined interest rate as a weighted average.

d. Find the combined loan constant by calculating the weighted average.

e. Interpolate in the Supplemental Loan Constant Tables to find the term.

f. Using the weighted average loan interest rate from c and the weighted average loan term from e, find the OAR in the precomputed tables by search, bracket, and interpolation.

Problem: Income property being analyzed is encumbered by a first trust deed, which secures a loan for 60% of value at 9% for 30 years. The seller will carry a second trust deed for 30% of value at 12% interest for 15 years. Assume 0% appreciation during a 10 year holding period. Net annual income is $75,000. The prospective purchaser anticipates a yield rate of 20% on his thin equity position. Based on this data, compute the mortgage-equity OAR and the indicated property value.

Solution:

a. Loan ratio of 1st. T.D.:   .60

Loan ratio of 2nd. T.D.:   .30

Combined loan ratio: .90

b. .60 ÷ .90 = .6667
.30 ÷ .90 = .3333
c. .6667 x .09 = .06
.3333 x .12 = .04
$$\overline{.10}$$

Weighted average interest rate: .10
d. .6667 x .09656 =   .06438 (see page 186)
.3333 x .14402 =   .048
Weighted average loan constant: .11238
e. Loan constant, 10%, 20 years: .11580 (see page 186)
Loan constant, 10%, 25 years: .10905 (see page 186)
By interpolation, loan constant computed in Step d indicates loan
term of 22½ years.
f. OAR, 20% equity yield, 90% loan ratio, 10 year holding period,
0% appreciation, 10% interest rate:
    20 year loan term: .11488 (see page 165)
    25 year loan term: .11279 (see page 165)
$$\overline{.22767}$$

OAR, 22½ years: .1138, by interpolation
Value: $75,000 ÷ .1138 = $659,000
Check and proof (See supplemental tables):
Equity: .10 x $659,000 = $65,900
1st TD: .60 x $659,000 = 395,400
2nd TD: .30 x $659,000 = 197,700
Annual payments on 1st TD: .09656 x $395,400 = $38,180
Annual payments on 2nd TD: .14402 x $197,700 =   28,473
$$\overline{\$66,653}$$

Cash flow: $75,000 − $66,653 = $8,347
Loan balance, 1st TD, end of 10 years:
        .8943 x $395,400   = $353,606
Loan balance, 2nd TD, end of 10 years:
        .53954 x $197,700   =   106,667
$$\overline{\$460,273}$$

Reversion:
    $659,000 − $460,273 = $198,727
Value of Original Equity = Annuity x PW 1/P + Reversion x PW 1
Substituting (use PW 1/P, PW 1, 20%, 10 years):
Value = ($8,347 x 4.1925) + ($198,727 x .16151)
      = $34,995 + $32.096
      = $67,091
Target figure is $65,900, the down payment. Computations by
weighted averages and interpolation are approximate and usually
close enough for practical purposes, though not precise.

Value of income property as indicated by the mortgage-equity technique:
Procedure:
Divide net annual income by OAR. (Value = Income ÷ Rate)
NOTE: Tax allowance can be added to OAR without distortion.

Problem: Apartment house data given and assumed:
  Loan specifications:
      Loan ratio   75%
      Interest rate: 8%
      Term: 25 years
  Holding period: 10 years
  Anticipated appreciation: 20%
  Required equity yield rate: 15%
  Tax allowance: 2.7%
  Net annual income before property taxes: $31,200
Estimate value by the mortgage-equity technique.
  Solution:
      OAR (from the tables):   .09001
      Tax allowance: .027
                               ———————
                               .11701
      $31,200 ÷ .11701 = $266,644, say $266,600

TRUST DEEDS AND MORTGAGES:
AMORTIZATION, ANALYSIS, AND DISCOUNT

Adjusting sales price for loans assumed or carried at a rate above or below the "going" rate:
  Procedure:
      a. Multiply periodic payment by PW 1/P at "going" rate.
      b. If loan involved in sale is at a rate *below* the "going" rate, subtract product found in a from the actual loan balance, and adjust sales price *down*.
         If loan in sale is at a rate *above* the "going" interest rate, subtract actual loan balance from product computed in a and adjust sales price *up*.
         (See special note below.)
Problem 1: Ranch property is sold for $250,000 on these terms: Down payment, $80,647. Existing first trust deed assumed has 15 years to run; principal balance is $169,353; annual payments to amortize are $17,437, including 6% interest. If the current going rate on such trust deeds is 8½%, determine the cash value of the trust deed at 8½%, and the additional amount the purchaser might have been justified in paying in order to assume the 6% loan.
Solution:
      a. $17,437 x 8.30424 = $144,801 (PW 1/P, 8½%, 15 years)
      b. $169,353 − $144,801 = $24,552
SPECIAL NOTE: Since $17,437 per year for 15 years repays $169,353 at 6% or $144,801 at 8½%, the purchaser could pay up to $24,550 more for the property if he can assume the "low" interest rate loan than if one were carried at the "going" rate of 8½%. However, the appraiser must check carefully to see if and to what extent the market is recognizing this point. If sales analysis shows this matter was given full consideration, the sales price should be adjusted downward to reflect it:

Nominal sales price: $250,000

Less premium paid for 6% loan assumption: 24,550

Adjusted sales price: $225,450

To look at it another way, annual payments to amortize a loan of $169,353 at 8½% in 15 years is: $169,353 x .12042 = $20,393 (PR, 8½%, 15 years). The annual dollar savings, if the 6% loan is assumed, would be: $20,393 − $17,437 = $2,956. Present worth of $2,956 a year for 15 years is $2,956 x 8.30424 = $24,550, rounded (PW 1/P, 8½%, 15 years).

Problem 2: Sales price of income property is $150,000. Buyer pays $50,000 down and seller carries $100,000 at 10% with annual payments of $14,676 to amortize in 12 years. Again, on the basis of a current going rate of 8½%, what additional amount of sales price might have been warranted if the note had been written at 8½% instead of 10%?

    a. $14,676 x 7.34469 = $107,791 (PW 1/P, 8½%, 12 years)

    b. $107,791 − $100,000 = $7,800, rounded

An adjustment to $157,800 might be reasonably assumed, but see special note above on market recognition.

Amortization, preparation of complete schedule:

Procedure:

    a. Compute periodic payment to amortize, by multiplying principal by PR.

    b. Multiply periodic payments by PW 1 factors in reverse order for the entire schedule, the products being the amount applied to principal for each period.

    c. Subtract each principal amount computed in b from the periodic payment. The difference is the interest for each period.

    d. Subtract each principal amount computed in b from the prior loan balance. The difference is the remaining loan balance.

Problem: Prepare an amortization schedule for a loan of $6,000 at 8%, with 10 equal annual payments. Give complete breakdown of principal, interest, and loan balance for each period.

Solution:

    a. Annual payment: $6,000 x .14903 = $894.18 (PR, 8%, 10 years)

    b, c and d.

Period	Total Payment	PW 1		Principal	Interest	Loan Balance
1	$894.18	x .46319	=	$414.18	$480.00	$5,585.82
2	894.18	x .50025	=	447.31	446.87	5,138.51
3	894.18	x .54027	=	483.10	411.08	4,655.41
4	894.18	x .58349	=	521.75	372.43	4,133.66
5	894.18	x .63017	=	563.49	330.69	3,570.17
6	894.18	x .68058	=	608.56	285.62	2,961.61
7	894.18	x .73503	=	657.25	236.93	2,304.36
8	894.18	x .79383	=	709.83	184.35	1,594.53
9	894.18	x .85734	=	766.62	127.56	827.91
10	894.14	x .92593	=	827.91	66.23	0
				$6,000.00		

Check: Find loan balances for Periods 1 through 9 by multiplying total payment for each period by PW 1/P factors for periods remaining unpaid. Rounding will account for slight differences.

Period	Total Payment		PW 1/P		Loan Balance
1	$894.18	x	6.24689	=	$5,585.84
2	894.18	x	5.74664	=	5,138.53
3	894.18	x	5.20637	=	4,655.43
4	894.18	x	4.62288	=	4,133.69
5	894.18	x	3.99271	=	3,570.20
6	894.18	x	3.31213	=	2,961.64
7	894.18	x	2.57710	=	2,304.39
8	894.18	x	1.78326	=	1,594.56
9	894.18	x	.92593	=	827.95

Balloon payment (in addition to final regular payment):
Procedure:
1. a. Multiply periodic payment by PW 1/P for final period.
   b. Subtract product computed in a from original principal.
   c. Divide difference by PW 1 for final period.
2. (Alternate, for fully amortized loan schedule only):
   Multiply periodic payment by PW 1/P for number of periods remaining unpaid.

Problem 1: On a loan of $60,000 at 8% for 10 years, monthly payments are $625, with the unpaid balance due at the end of 10 years. Compute the balloon payment.
Solution: (Method 1)
   a. $625 x 82.42148 = $51,514 (PW 1/P, 8%, 120 months)
   b. $60,000 — $51,514 = $8,486
   c. $8,486 ÷ .45052 = $18,836 (PW 1, 8%, 120 months)
   NOTE: Balloon payment of $18,836 will be in addition to the regular payment of $625 for month 120.

Problem 2: A note for $200,000, secured by a first trust deed, carries an interest rate of 7½%. Annual payments are specified to be $19,618, which would amortize the loan in 20 years. However, terms require that the unpaid principal balance be paid as a balloon at the end of 12 years. Find this amount.
Solution: (Method 2)

   $19,618 x 5.8573 = $114,909 (PW 1/P, 7½%, 8 years remaining)
   (Balloon payment of $114,909 is in addition to regular payment of $19,618 for year 12.)

Cash equivalent of a prepaid interest sale:
Procedure:
   a. Compile complete loan repayment schedule.
   b. Discount the trust deed (mortgage) to a yield rate indicated by the mortgage resale market.
   c. Add down payment, prepaid interest, and discounted trust deed.
Problem: Find the cash equivalent of a prepaid interest land sale for which

these terms are given:
    Sales price: $650,000
    Down payment: $50,000
    First trust deed carried by the seller:
        Principal amount: $600,000
        Interest rate: 7%
        Prepaid interest: $126,000, applied to years 1-3
        Annual payments: $75,000, years 4-10, principal and interest
        Balloon payment: $314,400 at the end of 10 years
Assume the seller retains the down payment and prepaid interest, and sells
the trust deed discounted to yield 10%.
Solution:

a. Year(s)	Interest Paid	Principal Paid	Total Paid
0	$126,000	$ 50,000	$176,000
4-10	—	—	75,000 P/P
10	0	314,400	314,400

b. Trust deed discounted to yield 10%:
    $ 75,000 x 3.65772 = $274,329 (PW 1/P, 10%, 10 yrs. — 3 yrs.)
    $314,400 x .38554 = 121,214 (PW 1, 10%, 10 yrs.)

Discounted TD:	$395,543
c. Down payment:	50,000
Prepaid interest:	126,000
Cash Equivalent:	$571,543

Loan constant: (See "Supplemental Tables, " page 186.)
    Procedure:
        1. Annual PR factor as a percent, or
        2. Monthly PR factor multiplied by 12, or
        3. Annual loan payment divided by original principal, or
        4. Any stipulated percent in excess of the annual interest rate.
    Illustrations:
        1. On a 7% loan for 15 years with annual payments, the PR factor is
           .1098. Therefore, the loan constant is .1098, or 10.98%.
        2. If a loan is made at 7½% with monthly payments for 30 years, the
           loan constant is 12 x .006992, or .0839 (8.39%).
        3. On a loan of $75,000, annual payments of $7,000 until paid, the
           loan constant is $7,000 ÷ $75,000, or .0933 (9.33%).
        4. An 8% loan might be set up with a loan constant of 9.5% to
           amortize. On a loan of $100,000 annual payments would be $9,500,
           including principal and interest.

Payment to amortize a loan:
    Procedure:
        Multiply the principal amount by the PR factor.
    Problem: What annual payment would amortize a loan of $10,000 at 10%
    in 8 years?
    Solution:
        $10,000 x .18744 = $1,874.40 (PR, 10%, 8 years)

Payment to amortize a loan with a specified balloon payment:
   Procedure:
   a. Divide principal into two sums: balloon payment and balance to be
       amortized.
   b. Multiply amount to be amortized by PR.
   c. Compute interest for one period on amount of balloon payment.
   d. Add b and c.

Problem: A note and trust deed at 7½% call for annual payments to
amortize a loan of $300,000 in 9 years, except that $100,000 (plus the
last year's interest) will be paid as a balloon payment at the end of year
10. What is the amount of annual payment years 1 through 9, and the
total amount of the final payment?
Solution:
   a. $300,000 — $100,000 = $200,000 to be amortized
   b. $200,000 x .15677 = $31,354 (PR, 7½%, 9 years)
   c. $100,000 x .075 = $7,500
   d. $31,354 + $7,500 = $38,854 per year for 9 years
       Final payment is $100,000 principal plus $7,500 interest for year 10,
       or $107,500.

**Payment to amortize a specified percent of principal in a stipulated period of
time:**
   Procedure:
   a. Multiply percent to be amortized by (PR — i).
   b. Add "i" to product computed in a.
   c. Multiply original principal by b.

Problem: A deposit receipt specifies that the seller will carry a note and
trust deed for $625,000 at 8% with equal annual payments for 15 years.
During this period 60% of the principal is to be amortized, all interest
kept current, and the remaining 40% to be paid in full at the end of the
term. What periodic payment is required?
Solution:
   a. .11683 — .08 = .03683 (PR, 8%, 15 years)
       .03683 x .60 = .022098
   b. .022098 + .08 = .102098
   c. $625,000 x .102098 = $63,811.25
       (This annual amount would pay all interest and amortize $375,000
       in 15 years, leaving $250,000 due and payable.)

Present worth of a trust deed discounted to interest rate of note:
   Procedure:
   a. Multiply periodic payment by PW 1/P at interest rate.
   b. Multiply balloon payment by PW 1.
   c. Add a and b.

Problem: A note and trust deed for $75,000 at 7% specify annual
payments of $8,870 for 10 years and a balloon payment of $25,000 at the
end of 10 years. Find the present worth of the total income stream
generated by the note at a 7% yield rate.
Solution:
   a. $ 8,870 x 7.02358 = $62,299 (PW 1/P, 7%, 10 years)

b. 25,000 x .50835 =   12,709 (PW 1, 7%, 10 years)

c. $75,000 (rounded)

Present worth of a trust deed discounted to a specified yield rate which is higher or lower than the interest rate:
Procedure:
a. Determine yield rate as indicated by the mortgage market.
b. Multiply periodic payment by PW 1/P.
c. Multiply balloon payment by PW 1.
d. Add b and c.
Problem: Discount the trust deed in the preceding problem to yield 12%.
Solution:
a. Use 12%.
b. $ 8,870 x 5.65022 = $50,117 (PW 1/P, 12%, 10 years)
c. 25,000 x .322   =   8,050 (PW 1, 12%, 10 years)
d. $58,167

Present worth of the seller's total income stream on a prepaid interest sale:
Procedure:
a. Compile complete loan repayment schedule.
b. Discount the trust deed (mortgage) to the interest rate stipulated on the note.
c. Add: down payment, prepaid interest, and discounted trust deed.
Problem: Compute present worth of the seller's income stream in the problem on cash equivalent of a prepaid interest sale, page 96, using 7% yield rate, corresponding to the interest rate on the note.
Solution:
a. Payment schedule, same as in "cash equivalent" problem.
b. Trust deed discounted to yield 7%:
   $ 75,000 x 4.39926 = $329,945 (PW 1/P, 7%, 10 years — 3 years)
   $314,400 x .50835 = 159,825 (PW 1, 7%, 10 years)

   Present worth TD: $489,770
c. Down payment: 50,000
   Prepaid interest: 126,000
                         $665,770

Principal, amount applied to, from any periodic payment in an amortized loan schedule:
Procedure:
   Multiply periodic payment by PW 1 for the number of periods remaining unpaid, including the period to be checked.
Problem: On a 30 year loan of $240,000 at 7½% with annual payments of $20,321 to amortize, what amount is applied to principal from the 17th annual payment?
Solution:
   Since 16 payments have been made, 14 remain unpaid.
   $20,321 x .36331 = $7,383 (PW 1, 7½%, 14 years)

Principal, amount applied to, from first periodic payment on an amortized

loan:
   Procedure:
      1. Multiply periodic payment by PW 1 for final period.
      2. (Alternate) Multiply principal by (PR — i).
   Problem: On a loan of $90,000 at 8% for 15 years, annual payments of
   $10,515, what amount is applied to principal the first period?
   Solution 1:
      $10,515 x .31524 = $3,315 (PW 1, 8%, 15 years)
   Solution 2:
      $90,000 x (.11683 — .08) = $3,315 (PR, 8%, 15 years — .08)

Principal amount of loan when other terms are known:
   Procedure:
      Multiply periodic payment by PW 1/P.
   Problem: Annual payments to amortize a loan at 8% in 20 years are
   $5,092.50. What is the original principal amount of the loan?
   Solution:
      $5,092.50 x 9.81815 = $50,000, rounded (PW 1/P, 8%, 20 years)

Principal balance unpaid, amount of, at any time on an amortized loan:
   Procedure:
      Multiply the periodic payment by PW 1/P for the number of periods
      remaining unpaid in the full schedule.
   Problem: On a 25 year loan of $150,000 at 8½%, annual payments of
   $14,657, what is the principal balance remaining unpaid after 10 years?
   Solution:
      $14,657 x 8.30424 = $121,715 (PW 1/P, 8½%, 15 years)

Principal balance unpaid, percent of, at any time on an amortized loan:
   Procedure:
      Multiply the PR factor for the full term by the PW 1/P factor for the
      number of periods remaining unpaid. (See also supplemental tables for
      precomputed loan balance percentages.)
   Problem: Calculate the percent of principal unpaid at the end of 10 years
   on a 9% loan with monthly payments to amortize in 25 years.
   Solution:
      PR factor at 9% for 300 months: .00839
      PW 1/P factor at 9% for 180 months: 98.59341
      .00839 x 98.59341 = .827, or 82.7%

Principal paid off, amount of, at any time on an amortized loan:
   Procedure:
      a. Multiply periodic payment by PW 1/P for number of periods
         remaining unpaid.
      b. Subtract product from original principal.
   Problem: Annual payments to amortize a loan of $80,000 at 8½% in 15
   years amount to $9,634. What has been applied to principal by the end of
   12 years?
   Solution:
      a. $ 9,634 x 2.55402 = $24,605 (PW 1/P, 8½%, 3 years)

b. $80,000 — $24,605 = $55,395

Principal paid off, percent of, at any time on an amortized loan:
Procedure:
   a. Multiply the PR factor for the full term by the PW 1/P factor for the
      number of periods remaining unpaid.
   b. Subtract a from 1.0.
Problem: On a loan at 8% with monthly payments to amortize in 20
years, what percent of principal has been paid off at the end of 15 years?
Solution:
   a. PR, 8%, 240 months: .00837
      PW 1/P, 8%, 60 months: 49.31843
      .00837 x 49.31843 = .413
   b. 1.0 — .413 = .587, or 58.7%

Rate of interest (true rate) on a loan with "points" paid by the borrower:
Procedure:
   a. Subtract initial "point" charge in dollars from amount of loan.
   b. Divide periodic payment by the remainder.
   c. Locate quotient in PR tables.
   d. Interpolate, if necessary.
Problem: A borrower pays 6 "points" on a loan of $35,000 at 7% for 20
years. What is the true interest rate?
Solution:
   a. $35,000 x .06 = $2,100 "point" charge
      $35,000 — $2,100 = $32,900 net loan proceeds
   b. $35,000 x .09439 = $3,304 annual payment (PR, 7%, 20 years)
      $3,304 ÷ $32,900 = .10043
   c,d. By inspection of the PR tables for 20 years, and by interpolation,
        rate is determined to be about 7.83%.

Rate of interest on an amortized loan:
Procedure:
   a. Divide periodic payment by original principal.
   b. Locate quotient in PR tables.
   c. Interpolate, if necessary.
Problem: Annual payments to amortize a loan of $37,000 in 15 years are
$4,192. What is the rate of interest?
Solution:
   a. $4,192 ÷ $37,000 = .1132973
   b. By inspection of the tables, 7½% (PR, 7½%, 15 years)

Time required to amortize a loan:
Procedure:
   a. Divide periodic payment by original prinicpal.
   b. Locate first entry of this amount or less in PR tables.
Problem: A loan of $45,000 at 8% specifies $5,000 per year until paid. In
what year will the loan be amortized?
Solution:
   a. $5,000 ÷ $45,000 = .1111

    b. An inspection of PR factors at 8% indicates year 17, the final payment being less than $5,000.

Time required to amortize a loan when the loan constant is known:
Procedure:
1. If monthly payments to amortize:
   a. Divide the loan constant, expressed as a decimal, by 12.
   b. Locate the factor computed in a in the monthly PR tables, interpolating if necessary.
2. If annual payments to amortize:
   Locate the loan constant, expressed as a percent, in the annual PR tables.

Problem 1: A loan written at 8% interest, calls for monthly payments to amortize and a loan constant of 9.262%. What is the term of the loan?
Solution (Procedure 1):
    a. .09262 ÷ 12 = .07718
    b. From the tables: 25 years (PR, 8%, 300 months)

Problem 2: The loan constant to amortize a 10% loan, annual payments, is 13.6%. Calculate the time to amortize.
Solution (Procedure 2):
    Loan constant, as a decimal: .136
    Tables indicate 14 years (PR, 10%, 14 years)

Yield rate on a trust deed discounted a specified dollar amount or percent from face value:
Procedure:
1. If loan is written on a fully amortized schedule:
   a. Divide discounted present worth by periodic payment.
   b. Locate quotient in PW 1/P tables.
   c. Interpolate.
2. If loan has periodic payment and balloon payment:
   a. Estimate two yield rates: one above and one below the true yield rate sought.
   b. Using two rates from a, multiply periodic payment by PW 1/P.
   c. Multiply balloon by PW 1, using same two rates.
   d. At each rate, add computations from b and c.
   e. Use discounted value of trust deed as a target figure and interpolate.

Problem 1: A note and second trust deed for $7,500 at 10% run for 10 years, annual payments of $1,220 to amortize. If the trust deed is sold at a 40% discount from face value, what would the yield rate be to the new beneficiary?
Solution: (Method 1)
    a. $7,500 x .60 = $4,500, discounted value
       $4,500 ÷ $1,220 = 3.6885
    b. PW 1/P, 10 years, 20% = 4.19247
       PW 1/P, 10 years, 25% = 3.57050
    c. By interpolation: About 24% yield rate

Problem 2: A note, secured by a trust deed, is written on the following terms: principal, $350,000; interest rate, 7%; annual payments of $30,000 for 12 years; principal balance of $251,600 due at the end of 12 years. The trust deed is offered for sale at $284,500. At this discounted worth, what is the yield?

Solution: (Method 2)

a. Try 12% and 9%.

b. At 12%: $30,000 x 6.19437 = $185,831 (PW 1/P, 12%, 12 years)
   At   9%: $30,000 x 7.16073 = $214,822 (PW 1/P, 9%, 12 years)

c. At 12%: $251,600 x .25668 = $ 64,581 (PW 1, 12%, 12 years)
   At   9%: $251,600 x .35553 = $ 89,451 (PW 1, 9%, 12 years)

d. At 12%: $185,831 + $64,581 = $250,412
   At   9%: $214,822 + $89,451 = $304,273

e. Target figure: $284,500
   By interpolation: About 10% yield rate

Ending the Endless

So, there you have it—mini-math! Perhaps it is not quite so "mini" as its name implies. The serious student and the professional appraiser will find the mathematics of compound interest to be a rewarding, challenging, continuing study. For while there is a last letter in the alphabet, and the "last word" is sometimes spoken, there is no last number. It's up to the individual to "turn the tables." They are your tools.

COMPOUND INTEREST
AND ANNUITY TABLES

$$3\% - 25\%$$

Monthly Periods: 1 — 360 Months (30 Years)

Annual Periods: 1 — 50 Years

PW 1   = Present Worth of 1 (Reversion)

PW 1/P   = Present Worth of 1 Per Period (Inwood Coefficient; Annuity)

PR   = Periodic Repayment (Partial Payment; Amortization)

(In most cases, the fifth digit of the decimal has been rounded upward.)

To find factors for other tables:

Future Worth (Amount) of 1   = 1.0 ÷ PW 1

Future Worth (Amount) of 1 Per Period   = 1.0 ÷ (PR − i)

Sinking Fund   = PR − i

Note: "i" represents effective interest rate.

MONTHLY COMPOUND INTEREST AND ANNUITY TABLES

3% Nominal Annual Rate
0.25% Effective Monthly Rate

4% Nominal Annual Rate
0.333% Effective Monthly Rate

Months	PW 1	PW 1/P	PR		PW 1	PW 1/P	PR	Months
1	.99751	.99751	1.00250		.99668	.99668	1.00333	1
2	.99502	1.99253	.50188		.99337	1.99004	.50250	2
3	.99254	2.98506	.33500		.99007	2.98011	.33556	3
4	.99006	3.97512	.25157		.98678	3.96689	.25209	4
5	.98759	4.96272	.20150		.98350	4.95039	.20201	5
6	.98513	5.94785	.16813		.98023	5.93062	.16862	6
7	.98267	6.93052	.14429		.97698	6.90759	.14477	7
8	.98022	7.91075	.12641		.97373	7.88132	.12688	8
9	.97778	8.88852	.11251		.97049	8.85182	.11297	9
10	.97534	9.86386	.10138		.96727	9.81909	.10184	10
11	.97291	10.83677	.09228		.96406	10.78314	.09274	11
12	.97048	11.80725	.08470		.96085	11.74399	.08515	12
				Years				
12	.97048	11.80725	.08470	1	.96085	11.74399	.08515	12
24	.94184	23.26598	.04298	2	.92324	23.02825	.04343	24
36	.91403	34.38647	.02908	3	.88710	33.87077	.02953	36
48	.88705	45.17870	.02214	4	.85237	44.28883	.02258	48
60	.86087	55.65236	.01797	5	.81900	54.29907	.01842	60
72	.83546	65.81686	.01520	6	.78694	63.91744	.01565	72
84	.81080	75.68132	.01321	7	.75614	73.15928	.01367	84
96	.78686	85.25460	.01173	8	.72654	82.03933	.01219	96
108	.76364	94.54530	.01058	9	.69809	90.57176	.01104	108
120	.74110	103.56175	.00966	10	.67077	98.77018	.01013	120
132	.71922	112.31206	.00891	11	.64451	106.64765	.00938	132
144	.69799	120.80407	.00828	12	.61928	114.21674	.00876	144
156	.67739	129.04541	.00775	13	.59504	121.48954	.00823	156
168	.65739	137.04349	.00730	14	.57174	128.47762	.00778	168
180	.63799	144.80547	.00691	15	.54936	135.19215	.00740	180
192	.61915	152.33834	.00657	16	.52785	141.64382	.00706	192
204	.60088	159.64885	.00627	17	.50719	147.84294	.00677	204
216	.58314	166.74357	.00600	18	.48734	153.79938	.00650	216
228	.56593	173.62886	.00576	19	.46826	159.52264	.00627	228
240	.54922	180.31091	.00555	20	.44993	165.02186	.00606	240
252	.53301	186.79573	.00535	21	.43231	170.30580	.00587	252
264	.51728	193.08912	.00518	22	.41539	175.38290	.00570	264
276	.50201	199.19674	.00502	23	.39913	180.26124	.00555	276
288	.48719	205.12408	.00488	24	.38351	184.94861	.00541	288
300	.47281	210.87645	.00474	25	.36849	189.45248	.00528	300
312	.45885	216.45903	.00462	26	.35407	193.78005	.00516	312
324	.44531	221.87682	.00451	27	.34021	197.93820	.00505	324
336	.43216	227.13468	.00440	28	.32689	201.93358	.00495	336
348	.41941	232.23734	.00431	29	.31409	205.77255	.00486	348
360	.40703	237.18938	.00422	30	.30180	209.46124	.00478	360

MONTHLY COMPOUND INTEREST AND ANNUITY TABLES

4½% Nominal Annual Rate
0.375% Effective Monthly Rate

5% Nominal Annual Rate
0.4166% Effective Monthly Rate

Months	PW 1	PW 1/P	PR	PW 1	PW 1/P	PR	Months
1	.99626	.99626	1.00375	.99585	.99585	1.00417	1
2	.99254	1.98881	.50282	.99172	1.98757	.50313	2
3	.98883	2.97764	.33584	.98760	2.97517	.33612	3
4	.98514	3.96278	.25235	.98351	3.95868	.25261	4
5	.98146	4.94424	.20226	.97943	4.93810	.20251	5
6	.97779	5.92203	.16886	.97536	5.91346	.16911	6
7	.97414	6.89617	.14501	.97131	6.88478	.14525	7
8	.97050	7.86667	.12712	.96728	7.85206	.12736	8
9	.96687	8.83354	.11321	.96327	8.81533	.11344	9
10	.96326	9.79681	.10208	.95927	9.77460	.10231	10
11	.95966	10.75647	.09297	.95529	10.72989	.09320	11
12	.95608	11.71255	.08538	.95133	11.68122	.08561	12

Years

Months	PW 1	PW 1/P	PR	Years	PW 1	PW 1/P	PR	Months
12	.95608	11.71255	.08538	1	.95133	11.68122	.08561	12
24	.91409	22.91066	.04365	2	.90503	22.79390	.04387	24
36	.87394	33.61692	.02975	3	.86098	33.36570	.02997	36
48	.83555	43.85294	.02280	4	.81907	43.42296	.02303	48
60	.79885	53.63938	.01864	5	.77921	52.99071	.01887	60
72	.76377	62.99598	.01588	6	.74128	62.09278	.01611	72
84	.73022	71.94161	.01390	7	.70520	70.75184	.01414	84
96	.69815	80.49434	.01242	8	.67088	78.98944	.01266	96
108	.66748	88.67141	.01128	9	.63823	86.82611	.01152	108
120	.63817	96.48932	.01037	10	.60716	94.28135	.01061	120
132	.61014	103.96386	.00962	11	.57761	101.37373	.00987	132
144	.58334	111.11010	.00900	12	.54950	108.12092	.00925	144
156	.55772	117.94247	.00848	13	.52275	114.53970	.00873	156
168	.53322	124.47474	.00804	14	.49731	120.64608	.00829	168
180	.50980	130.72010	.00765	15	.47310	126.45524	.00791	180
192	.48741	136.69115	.00732	16	.45008	131.98167	.00758	192
204	.46600	142.39995	.00702	17	.42817	137.23911	.00729	204
216	.44553	147.85799	.00676	18	.40733	142.24066	.00703	216
228	.42596	153.07632	.00653	19	.38751	146.99878	.00680	228
240	.40726	158.06544	.00633	20	.36865	151.52531	.00660	240
252	.38937	162.83543	.00614	21	.35070	155.83153	.00642	252
264	.37227	167.39591	.00598	22	.33363	159.92816	.00625	264
276	.35592	171.75608	.00582	23	.31739	163.82540	.00611	276
288	.34028	175.92475	.00569	24	.30195	167.53295	.00597	288
300	.32534	179.91032	.00556	25	.28725	171.06005	.00585	300
312	.31105	183.72084	.00544	26	.27327	174.41548	.00573	312
324	.29739	187.36399	.00534	27	.25997	177.60759	.00563	324
336	.28432	190.84713	.00524	28	.24732	180.64434	.00554	336
348	.27184	194.17728	.00515	29	.23528	183.53328	.00545	348
360	.25990	197.36116	.00507	30	.22383	186.28162	.00537	360

MONTHLY COMPOUND INTEREST AND ANNUITY TABLES

5½% Nominal Annual Rate
0.45833% Effective Monthly Rate

6% Nominal Annual Rate
0.5% Effective Monthly Rate

Months	PW 1	PW 1/P	PR		PW 1	PW 1/P	PR	Months
1	.99544	.99544	1.00458		.99503	.99503	1.00500	1
2	.99090	1.98633	.50344		.99008	1.98510	.50375	2
3	.98638	2.97271	.33640		.98515	2.97025	.33667	3
4	.98188	3.95458	.25287		.98025	3.95050	.25313	4
5	.97740	4.93198	.20276		.97537	4.92587	.20301	5
6	.97294	5.90491	.16935		.97052	5.89638	.16960	6
7	.96850	6.87341	.14549		.96569	6.86207	.14573	7
8	.96408	7.83749	.12759		.96089	7.82296	.12783	8
9	.95968	8.79717	.11367		.95611	8.77906	.11391	9
10	.95530	9.75247	.10254		.95135	9.73041	.10277	10
11	.95094	10.70341	.09343		.94662	10.67703	.09366	11
12	.94660	11.65002	.08584		.94191	11.61893	.08607	12

Years

Months	PW 1	PW 1/P	PR	Years	PW 1	PW 1/P	PR	Months
12	.94660	11.65002	.08584	1	.94191	11.61893	.08607	12
24	.89606	22.67797	.04410	2	.88719	22.56287	.04432	24
36	.84821	33.11708	.03020	3	.83565	32.87102	.03042	36
48	.80292	42.99878	.02326	4	.78710	42.58032	.02349	48
60	.76005	52.35284	.01910	5	.74137	51.72556	.01933	60
72	.71947	61.20743	.01634	6	.69830	60.33951	.01657	72
84	.68105	69.58922	.01437	7	.65774	68.45304	.01461	84
96	.64468	77.52345	.01290	8	.61952	76.09522	.01314	96
108	.61026	85.03404	.01176	9	.58353	83.29342	.01201	108
120	.57768	92.14358	.01085	10	.54963	90.07345	.01110	120
132	.54683	98.87351	.01012	11	.51770	96.45960	.01037	132
144	.51763	105.24408	.00950	12	.48763	102.47474	.00976	144
156	.48999	111.27450	.00899	13	.45930	108.14044	.00925	156
168	.46383	116.98291	.00855	14	.43262	113.47699	.00881	168
180	.43906	122.38652	.00817	15	.40748	118.50352	.00844	180
192	.41562	127.50160	.00784	16	.38381	123.23803	.00812	192
204	.39343	132.34355	.00756	17	.36151	127.69749	.00783	204
216	.37242	136.92696	.00730	18	.34051	131.89788	.00758	216
228	.35253	141.26564	.00708	19	.32073	135.85425	.00736	228
240	.33371	145.37265	.00688	20	.30210	139.58077	.00717	240
252	.31589	149.26036	.00670	21	.28455	143.09081	.00699	252
264	.29902	152.94049	.00654	22	.26802	146.39693	.00683	264
276	.28306	156.42411	.00639	23	.25245	149.51098	.00669	276
288	.26794	159.72172	.00626	24	.23778	152.44412	.00656	288
300	.25364	162.84325	.00614	25	.22397	155.20686	.00644	300
312	.24009	165.79810	.00603	26	.21095	157.80911	.00634	312
324	.22727	168.59518	.00593	27	.19870	160.26017	.00624	324
336	.21514	171.24290	.00584	28	.18716	162.56884	.00615	336
348	.20365	173.74925	.00576	29	.17628	164.74339	.00607	348
360	.19278	176.12176	.00568	30	.16604	166.79161	.00600	360

MONTHLY COMPOUND INTEREST AND ANNUITY TABLES

6½% Nominal Annual Rate
0.54167% Effective Monthly Rate

7% Nominal Annual Rate
0.5833% Effective Monthly Rate

Months	PW 1	PW 1/P	PR		PW 1	PW 1/P	PR	Months
1	.99461	.99461	1.00542		.99420	.99420	1.00583	1
2	.98925	1.98387	.50407		.98844	1.98264	.50438	2
3	.98392	2.96779	.33695		.98270	2.96534	.33723	3
4	.97862	3.94642	.25340		.97700	3.94234	.25366	4
5	.97335	4.91977	.20326		.97134	4.91368	.20352	5
6	.96811	5.88787	.16984		.96570	5.87938	.17009	6
7	.96289	6.85077	.14597		.96010	6.83948	.14621	7
8	.95770	7.80847	.12807		.95454	7.79402	.12831	8
9	.95255	8.76101	.11414		.94900	8.74302	.11438	9
10	.94741	9.70843	.10300		.94350	9.68651	.10324	10
11	.94231	10.65074	.09389		.93802	10.62454	.09412	11
12	.93723	11.58797	.08630		.93258	11.55712	.08653	12

				Years				
12	.93723	11.58797	.08630	1	.93258	11.55712	.08653	12
24	.87840	22.44858	.04455	2	.86971	22.33510	.04477	24
36	.82327	32.62749	.03065	3	.81108	32.38646	.03088	36
48	.77159	42.16749	.02372	4	.75640	41.76020	.02395	48
60	.72316	51.10868	.01957	5	.70541	50.50199	.01980	60
72	.67777	59.48865	.01681	6	.65785	58.65444	.01705	72
84	.63523	67.34262	.01485	7	.61350	66.25729	.01509	84
96	.59536	74.70362	.01339	8	.57214	73.34757	.01364	96
108	.55799	81.60258	.01226	9	.53357	79.95985	.01251	108
120	.52296	88.06850	.01136	10	.49760	86.12635	.01161	120
132	.49014	94.12857	.01063	11	.46405	91.87713	.01089	132
144	.45937	99.80826	.01002	12	.43277	97.24022	.01029	144
156	.43054	105.13145	.00951	13	.40359	102.24174	.00978	156
168	.40351	110.12051	.00908	14	.37638	106.90607	.00936	168
180	.37819	114.79641	.00871	15	.35101	111.25596	.00899	180
192	.35445	119.17882	.00839	16	.32734	115.31259	.00867	192
204	.33220	123.28615	.00811	17	.30528	119.09573	.00840	204
216	.31135	127.13568	.00787	18	.28469	122.62383	.00816	216
228	.29181	130.74357	.00765	19	.26550	125.91408	.00794	228
240	.27349	134.12500	.00746	20	.24760	128.98251	.00775	240
252	.25632	137.29419	.00729	21	.23091	131.84407	.00759	252
264	.24023	140.26446	.00713	22	.21534	134.51272	.00744	264
276	.22516	143.04828	.00699	23	.20083	137.00146	.00730	276
288	.21102	145.65737	.00687	24	.18729	139.32242	.00718	288
300	.19778	148.10270	.00675	25	.17466	141.48690	.00707	300
312	.18536	150.39453	.00665	26	.16289	143.50547	.00697	312
324	.17373	152.54251	.00656	27	.15190	145.38795	.00688	324
336	.16282	154.55566	.00647	28	.14166	147.14352	.00680	336
348	.15260	156.44246	.00639	29	.13211	148.78073	.00672	348
360	.14303	158.21082	.00632	30	.12321	150.30757	.00665	360

MONTHLY COMPOUND INTEREST AND ANNUITY TABLES

7½% Nominal Annual Rate
0.625% Effective Monthly Rate

8% Nominal Annual Rate
0.667% Effective Monthly Rate

Months	PW 1	PW 1/P	PR		PW 1	PW 1/P	PR	Months
1	.99379	.99379	1.00625		.99338	.99338	1.00667	1
2	.98762	1.98141	.50469		.98680	1.98018	.50501	2
3	.98148	2.96289	.33751		.98026	2.96044	.33779	3
4	.97539	3.93827	.25392		.97377	3.93421	.25418	4
5	.96933	4.90760	.20377		.96732	4.90154	.20402	5
6	.96331	5.87091	.17033		.96092	5.86245	.17058	6
7	.95732	6.82823	.14645		.95455	6.81701	.14669	7
8	.95138	7.77961	.12854		.94823	7.76524	.12878	8
9	.94547	8.72508	.11461		.94195	8.70719	.11485	9
10	.93960	9.66467	.10347		.93571	9.64290	.10370	10
11	.93376	10.59843	.09436		.92952	10.57242	.09459	11
12	.92796	11.52639	.08676		.92336	11.49578	.08699	12

Years

Months	PW 1	PW 1/P	PR		PW 1	PW 1/P	PR	Months
12	.92796	11.52639	.08676	1	.92336	11.49578	.08699	12
24	.86111	22.22242	.04500	2	.85260	22.11054	.04523	24
36	.79908	32.14791	.03111	3	.78726	31.91181	.03134	36
48	.74151	41.35837	.02418	4	.72692	40.96191	.02441	48
60	.68809	49.90531	.02004	5	.67121	49.31843	.02028	60
72	.63852	57.83652	.01729	6	.61977	57.03452	.01753	72
84	.59252	65.19638	.01534	7	.57227	64.15926	.01559	84
96	.54984	72.02602	.01389	8	.52841	70.73797	.01414	96
108	.51023	78.36367	.01276	9	.48792	76.81250	.01302	108
120	.47347	84.24474	.01187	10	.45052	82.42148	.01213	120
132	.43936	89.70215	.01115	11	.41600	87.60060	.01142	132
144	.40771	94.76640	.01055	12	.38412	92.38280	.01083	144
156	.37834	99.46583	.01006	13	.35468	96.79850	.01033	156
168	.35108	103.82671	.00963	14	.32750	100.87578	.00991	168
180	.32579	107.87343	.00927	15	.30240	104.64059	.00956	180
192	.30232	111.62862	.00896	16	.27922	108.11687	.00925	192
204	.28054	115.11329	.00869	17	.25782	111.32673	.00898	204
216	.26033	118.34693	.00845	18	.23806	114.29060	.00875	216
228	.24158	121.34762	.00824	19	.21982	117.02731	.00855	228
240	.22417	124.13213	.00806	20	.20297	119.55429	.00837	240
252	.20803	126.71605	.00789	21	.18742	121.88761	.00821	252
264	.19304	129.11383	.00775	22	.17305	124.04210	.00806	264
276	.17913	131.33886	.00762	23	.15979	126.03148	.00794	276
288	.16623	133.40361	.00750	24	.14754	127.86839	.00782	288
300	.15425	135.31961	.00739	25	.13624	129.56452	.00772	300
312	.14314	137.09759	.00730	26	.12580	131.13067	.00763	312
324	.13283	138.74748	.00721	27	.11616	132.57679	.00754	324
336	.12326	140.27851	.00713	28	.10725	133.91208	.00747	336
348	.11438	141.69924	.00706	29	.09903	135.14503	.00740	348
360	.10614	143.01763	.00699	30	.09144	136.28349	.00734	360

MONTHLY COMPOUND INTEREST AND ANNUITY TABLES

8½% Nominal Annual Rate
0.70833% Effective Monthly Rate

9% Nominal Annual Rate
0.75% Effective Monthly Rate

Months	PW 1	PW 1/P	PR	PW 1	PW 1/P	PR	Months
1	.99297	.99297	1.00708	.99256	.99256	1.00750	1
2	.98598	1.97895	.50532	.98517	1.97772	.50563	2
3	.97905	2.95800	.33807	.97783	2.95556	.33835	3
4	.97216	3.93016	.25444	.97055	3.92611	.25471	4
5	.96532	4.89548	.20427	.96333	4.88944	.20452	5
6	.95853	5.85402	.17082	.95616	5.84560	.17107	6
7	.95179	6.80581	.14693	.94904	6.79464	.14718	7
8	.94510	7.75091	.12902	.94198	7.73661	.12926	8
9	.93845	8.68936	.11508	.93496	8.67158	.11532	9
10	.93185	9.62121	.10394	.92800	9.59958	.10417	10
11	.92530	10.54650	.09482	.92110	10.52068	.09505	11
12	.91879	11.46529	.08722	.91424	11.43491	.08745	12

Years

Months	PW 1	PW 1/P	PR	Years	PW 1	PW 1/P	PR	Months
12	.91879	11.46529	.08722	1	.91424	11.43491	.08745	12
24	.84417	21.99945	.04546	2	.83583	21.88915	.04569	24
36	.77561	31.67811	.03157	3	.76415	31.44681	.03180	36
48	.71262	40.57074	.02465	4	.69861	40.18478	.02489	48
60	.65475	48.74118	.02052	5	.63870	48.17337	.02076	60
72	.60158	56.24808	.01778	6	.58392	55.47685	.01803	72
84	.55272	63.14532	.01584	7	.53385	62.15397	.01609	84
96	.50783	69.48243	.01439	8	.48806	68.25844	.01465	96
108	.46659	75.30488	.01328	9	.44621	73.83938	.01354	108
120	.42870	80.65447	.01240	10	.40794	78.94169	.01267	120
132	.39388	85.56961	.01169	11	.37295	83.60642	.01196	132
144	.36189	90.08558	.01110	12	.34097	87.87109	.01138	144
156	.33250	94.23480	.01061	13	.31173	91.77002	.01090	156
168	.30550	98.04705	.01020	14	.28499	95.33456	.01049	168
180	.28069	101.54969	.00985	15	.26055	98.59341	.01014	180
192	.25789	104.76788	.00955	16	.23820	101.57277	.00985	192
204	.23695	107.72471	.00928	17	.21778	104.29661	.00959	204
216	.21771	110.44141	.00906	18	.19910	106.78686	.00937	216
228	.20003	112.93748	.00886	19	.18202	109.06353	.00917	228
240	.18378	115.23084	.00868	20	.16641	111.14495	.00900	240
252	.16886	117.33795	.00852	21	.15214	113.04787	.00885	252
264	.15514	119.27393	.00839	22	.13909	114.78759	.00871	264
276	.14254	121.05269	.00826	23	.12716	116.37811	.00859	276
288	.13097	122.68699	.00815	24	.11626	117.83222	.00849	288
300	.12033	124.18857	.00805	25	.10629	119.16162	.00839	300
312	.11056	125.56820	.00797	26	.09717	120.37701	.00831	312
324	.10158	126.83579	.00789	27	.08884	121.48817	.00823	324
336	.09333	128.00043	.00781	28	.08122	122.50404	.00816	336
348	.08575	129.07049	.00775	29	.07425	123.43278	.00810	348
360	.07879	130.05364	.00769	30	.06789	124.28187	.00805	360

MONTHLY COMPOUND INTEREST AND ANNUITY TABLES

10% Nominal Annual Rate
0.8333% Effective Monthly Rate

11% Nominal Annual Rate
0.91667% Effective Monthly Rate

Months	PW 1	PW 1/P	PR		PW 1	PW 1/P	PR	Months
1	.99174	.99174	1.00833		.99092	.99092	1.00917	1
2	.98354	1.97528	.50626		.98192	1.97283	.50689	2
3	.97541	2.95069	.33891		.97300	2.94583	.33946	3
4	.96735	3.91804	.25523		.96416	3.90999	.25576	4
5	.95936	4.87739	.20503		.95540	4.86539	.20553	5
6	.95143	5.82882	.17156		.94672	5.81211	.17206	6
7	.94356	6.77238	.14766		.93812	6.75023	.14814	7
8	.93577	7.70815	.12973		.92960	7.67984	.13021	8
9	.92803	8.63618	.11579		.92116	8.60099	.11627	9
10	.92036	9.55654	.10464		.91279	9.51378	.10511	10
11	.91276	10.46930	.09552		.90450	10.41828	.09599	11
12	.90521	11.37451	.08792		.89628	11.31457	.08838	12

Months	PW 1	PW 1/P	PR	Year	PW 1	PW 1/P	PR	Months
12	.90521	11.37451	.08792	1	.89628	11.31457	.08838	12
24	.81941	21.67086	.04615	2	.80332	21.45562	.04661	24
36	.74174	30.99124	.03227	3	.72001	30.54487	.03274	36
48	.67143	39.42816	.02536	4	.64533	38.69142	.02585	48
60	.60779	47.06537	.02125	5	.57840	45.99303	.02174	60
72	.55018	53.97867	.01853	6	.51841	52.53735	.01904	72
84	.49803	60.23667	.01660	7	.46464	58.40290	.01712	84
96	.45082	65.90149	.01518	8	.41645	63.66010	.01571	96
108	.40809	71.02936	.01408	9	.37326	68.37204	.01463	108
120	.36941	75.67116	.01322	10	.33454	72.59528	.01378	120
132	.33439	79.87299	.01252	11	.29985	76.38049	.01309	132
144	.30270	83.67653	.01195	12	.26875	79.77311	.01254	144
156	.27400	87.11954	.01148	13	.24087	82.81386	.01208	156
168	.24803	90.23620	.01108	14	.21589	85.53923	.01169	168
180	.22452	93.05744	.01075	15	.19350	87.98194	.01137	180
192	.20324	95.61126	.01046	16	.17343	90.17129	.01109	192
204	.18398	97.92301	.01021	17	.15544	92.13358	.01086	204
216	.16654	100.01563	.01000	18	.13932	93.89234	.01065	216
228	.15075	101.90990	.00981	19	.12487	95.46869	.01048	228
240	.13646	103.62462	.00965	20	.11192	96.88154	.01032	240
252	.12353	105.17680	.00951	21	.10031	98.14786	.01019	252
264	.11182	106.58186	.00938	22	.08991	99.28284	.01007	264
276	.10122	107.85373	.00927	23	.08058	100.30010	.00997	276
288	.09163	109.00505	.00918	24	.07223	101.21185	.00988	288
300	.08294	110.04723	.00909	25	.06473	102.02904	.00980	300
312	.07508	110.99063	.00901	26	.05802	102.76148	.00973	312
324	.06796	111.84461	.00894	27	.05200	103.41795	.00967	324
336	.06152	112.61764	.00888	28	.04661	104.00633	.00962	336
348	.05569	113.31739	.00883	29	.04178	104.53369	.00957	348
360	.05041	113.95082	.00878	30	.03744	105.00635	.00952	360

MONTHLY COMPOUND INTEREST AND ANNUITY TABLES

12% Nominal Annual Rate
1.00% Effective Monthly Rate

13% Nominal Annual Rate
1.0833% Effective Monthly Rate

Months	PW 1	PW 1/P	PR		PW 1	PW 1/P	PR	Months
1	.99010	.99010	1.01000		.98928	.98928	1.01083	1
2	.98030	1.97040	.50751		.97868	1.96796	.50814	2
3	.97059	2.94099	.34002		.96819	2.93616	.34058	3
4	.96098	3.90197	.25628		.95782	3.89397	.25681	4
5	.95147	4.85343	.20604		.94755	4.84152	.20655	5
6	.94205	5.79548	.17255		.93740	5.77892	.17304	6
7	.93272	6.72820	.14863		.92735	6.70626	.14912	7
8	.92348	7.65168	.13069		.91741	7.62367	.13117	8
9	.91434	8.56602	.11674		.90758	8.53125	.11722	9
10	.90529	9.47131	.10558		.89785	9.42910	.10606	10
11	.89632	10.36763	.09646		.88823	10.31733	.09693	11
12	.88745	11.25508	.08885		.87871	11.19604	.08932	12
				Years				
12	.88745	11.25508	.08885	1	.87871	11.19604	.08932	12
24	.78757	21.24339	.04707	2	.77213	21.03411	.04754	24
36	.69893	30.10751	.03322	3	.67848	29.67892	.03370	36
48	.62026	37.97396	.02634	4	.59619	37.27519	.02683	48
60	.55045	44.95504	.02225	5	.52387	43.95011	.02275	60
72	.48850	51.15039	.01955	6	.46033	49.81542	.02008	72
84	.43352	56.64845	.01765	7	.40450	54.96933	.01819	84
96	.38472	61.52770	.01625	8	.35544	59.49812	.01681	96
108	.34142	65.85779	.01519	9	.31233	63.47760	.01576	108
120	.30300	69.70052	.01435	10	.27444	66.97442	.01493	120
132	.26889	73.11075	.01368	11	.24116	70.04710	.01428	132
144	.23863	76.13716	.01314	12	.21191	72.74710	.01375	144
156	.21177	78.82294	.01269	13	.18620	75.11961	.01331	156
168	.18794	81.20643	.01232	14	.16362	77.20436	.01295	168
180	.16678	83.32166	.01200	15	.14377	79.03625	.01265	180
192	.14801	85.19882	.01174	16	.12634	80.64595	.01240	192
204	.13135	86.86471	.01151	17	.11101	82.06041	.01219	204
216	.11657	88.34310	.01132	18	.09755	83.30331	.01201	216
228	.10345	89.65509	.01116	19	.08572	84.39545	.01185	228
240	.09181	90.81942	.01101	20	.07532	85.35513	.01172	240
252	.08147	91.85270	.01089	21	.06618	86.19841	.01160	252
264	.07230	92.76968	.01078	22	.05816	86.93941	.01150	264
276	.06417	93.58346	.01069	23	.05110	87.59053	.01142	276
288	.05694	94.30565	.01061	24	.04490	88.16268	.01134	288
300	.05053	94.94655	.01053	25	.03946	88.66543	.01128	300
312	.04485	95.51532	.01047	26	.03467	89.10720	.01122	312
324	.03980	96.02008	.01042	27	.03047	89.49539	.01118	324
336	.03532	96.46802	.01037	28	.02677	89.83650	.01113	336
348	.03135	96.86555	.01033	29	.02352	90.13623	.01110	348
360	.02782	97.21833	.01029	30	.02067	90.39961	.01106	360

MONTHLY COMPOUND INTEREST AND ANNUITY TABLES

14% Nominal Annual Rate
1.1667% Effective Monthly Rate

15% Nominal Annual Rate
1.25% Effective Monthly Rate

Months	PW 1	PW 1/P	PR		PW 1	PW 1/P	PR	Months
1	.98847	.98847	1.01167		.98765	.98765	1.10250	1
2	.97707	1.96554	.50877		.97546	1.96312	.50940	2
3	.96580	2.93134	.34114		.96342	2.92653	.34170	3
4	.95466	3.88600	.25734		.95152	3.87806	.25786	4
5	.94365	4.82966	.20706		.93978	4.81784	.20756	5
6	.93277	5.76243	.17354		.92818	5.74601	.17404	6
7	.92202	6.68444	.14960		.91672	6.66273	.15009	7
8	.91138	7.59582	.13165		.90540	7.56812	.13213	8
9	.90087	8.49670	.11769		.89422	8.46235	.11817	9
10	.89048	9.38718	.10653		.88318	9.34553	.10700	10
11	.88021	10.26739	.09740		.87228	10.21780	.09787	11
12	.87006	11.13746	.08979		.86151	11.07931	.09026	12

Months	PW 1	PW 1/P	PR	Years	PW 1	PW 1/P	PR	Months
12	.87006	11.13746	.08979	1	.86151	11.07931	.09026	12
24	.75701	20.82774	.04801	2	.74220	20.62424	.04849	24
36	.65865	29.25890	.03418	3	.63941	28.84727	.03467	36
48	.57306	36.59455	.02733	4	.55086	35.93148	.02783	48
60	.49860	42.97702	.02327	5	.47457	42.03459	.02379	60
72	.43382	48.53017	.02061	6	.40884	47.29247	.02115	72
84	.37745	53.36176	.01874	7	.35222	51.82219	.01930	84
96	.32840	57.56555	.01737	8	.30344	55.72457	.01795	96
108	.28573	61.22311	.01634	9	.26142	59.08651	.01693	108
120	.24860	64.40542	.01553	10	.22521	61.98285	.01613	120
132	.21630	67.17423	.01489	11	.19402	64.47807	.01551	132
144	.18820	69.58327	.01437	12	.16715	66.62772	.01501	144
156	.16374	71.67928	.01395	13	.14400	68.47967	.01460	156
168	.14247	73.50295	.01361	14	.12406	70.07514	.01427	168
180	.12395	75.08965	.01332	15	.10688	71.44964	.01400	180
192	.10785	76.47019	.01308	16	.09208	72.63379	.01377	192
204	.09383	77.67134	.01288	17	.07933	73.65395	.01358	204
216	.08164	78.71641	.01271	18	.06834	74.53282	.01342	216
228	.07103	79.62570	.01256	19	.05888	75.28998	.01328	228
240	.06180	80.41683	.01244	20	.05072	75.94228	.01317	240
252	.05377	81.10516	.01233	21	.04370	76.50424	.01307	252
264	.04679	81.70406	.01224	22	.03765	76.98837	.01299	264
276	.04071	82.22514	.01216	23	.03243	77.40546	.01292	276
288	.03542	82.67851	.01210	24	.02794	77.76478	.01286	288
300	.03082	83.07297	.01204	25	.02407	78.07434	.01281	300
312	.02681	83.41617	.01199	26	.02074	78.34102	.01277	312
324	.02333	83.71478	.01195	27	.01787	78.57078	.01273	324
336	.02030	83.97459	.01191	28	.01539	78.76871	.01270	336
348	.01766	84.20064	.01188	29	.01326	78.93924	.01267	348
360	.01537	84.39732	.01185	30	.01142	79.08614	.01265	360

MONTHLY COMPOUND INTEREST AND ANNUITY TABLES

16% Nominal Annual Rate	18% Nominal Annual Rate
1.333% Effective Monthly Rate	1.50% Effective Monthly Rate

Months	PW 1	PW 1/P	PR		PW 1	PW 1/P	PR	Months
1	.98684	.98684	1.01333		.98522	.98522	1.01500	1
2	.97386	1.96070	.51002		.97066	1.95588	.51128	2
3	.96104	2.92174	.34226		.95632	2.91220	.34338	3
4	.94840	3.87014	.25839		.94218	3.85439	.25945	4
5	.93592	4.80606	.20807		.92826	4.78265	.20909	5
6	.92360	5.72967	.17453		.91454	5.69719	.17553	6
7	.91145	6.64112	.15058		.90103	6.59821	.15156	7
8	.89946	7.54058	.13262		.88771	7.48593	.13359	8
9	.88762	8.42820	.11865		.87459	8.36052	.11961	9
10	.87595	9.30414	.10748		.86167	9.22219	.10844	10
11	.86442	10.16856	.09834		.84893	10.07112	.09930	11
12	.85305	11.02161	.09073		.83639	10.90751	.09168	12

				Years				
12	.85305	11.02161	.09073	1	.83639	10.90751	.09168	12
24	.72769	20.42354	.04896	2	.69954	20.03041	.04993	24
36	.62075	28.44381	.03516	3	.58509	27.66068	.03615	36
48	.52953	35.28547	.02834	4	.48936	34.04255	.02938	48
60	.45171	41.12171	.02432	5	.40930	39.38027	.02539	60
72	.38533	46.10028	.02169	6	.34233	43.84467	.02281	72
84	.32870	50.34724	.01986	7	.28632	47.57863	.02102	84
96	.28040	53.97008	.01853	8	.23948	50.70168	.01972	96
108	.23919	57.06052	.01753	9	.20029	53.31375	.01876	108
120	.20404	59.69682	.01675	10	.16752	55.49845	.01802	120
132	.17406	61.94569	.01614	11	.14011	57.32571	.01745	132
144	.14848	63.86409	.01566	12	.11719	58.85401	.01699	144
156	.12666	65.50056	.01527	13	.09802	60.13226	.01663	156
168	.10805	66.89655	.01495	14	.08198	61.20137	.01634	168
180	.09217	68.08739	.01469	15	.06857	62.09556	.01611	180
192	.07862	69.10323	.01447	16	.05735	62.84345	.01591	192
204	.06707	69.96979	.01429	17	.04797	63.46898	.01576	204
216	.05721	70.70900	.01414	18	.04012	63.99216	.01563	216
228	.04881	71.33959	.01402	19	.03355	64.42974	.01552	228
240	.04163	71.87750	.01391	20	.02806	64.79573	.01543	240
252	.03552	72.33637	.01383	21	.02347	65.10184	.01536	252
264	.03030	72.72780	.01375	22	.01963	65.35787	.01530	264
276	.02584	73.06171	.01369	23	.01642	65.57200	.01525	276
288	.02205	73.34655	.01364	24	.01373	65.75110	.01521	288
300	.01881	73.58953	.01359	25	.01149	65.90090	.01518	300
312	.01604	73.79681	.01355	26	.00961	66.02619	.01515	312
324	.01369	73.97362	.01352	27	.00804	66.13098	.01512	324
336	.01167	74.12445	.01349	28	.00672	66.21863	.01510	336
348	.00996	74.25312	.01347	29	.00562	66.29193	.01509	348
360	.00850	74.36288	.01345	30	.00470	66.35324	.01507	360

MONTHLY COMPOUND INTEREST AND ANNUITY TABLES

20% Nominal Annual Rate
1.667% Effective Monthly Rate

25% Nominal Annual Rate
2.083% Effective Monthly Rate

Months	PW 1	PW 1/P	PR		PW 1	PW 1/P	PR	Months
1	.98361	.98361	1.01667		.97959	.97959	1.02083	1
2	.96748	1.95109	.51254		.95960	1.93919	.51568	2
3	.95162	2.90271	.34451		.94002	2.87921	.34732	3
4	.93602	3.83873	.26050		.92083	3.80004	.26316	4
5	.92068	4.75941	.21011		.90204	4.70208	.21267	5
6	.90558	5.66499	.17652		.88363	5.58571	.17903	6
7	.89074	6.55573	.15254		.86560	6.45131	.15501	7
8	.87614	7.43187	.13456		.84793	7.29924	.13700	8
9	.86177	8.29364	.12058		.83063	8.12987	.12300	9
10	.84765	9.14128	.10940		.81368	8.94355	.11181	10
11	.83375	9.97503	.10025		.79707	9.74062	.10266	11
12	.82008	10.79511	.09264		.78080	10.52142	.09505	12

Months	PW 1	PW 1/P	PR	Years	PW 1	PW 1/P	PR	Months
12	.82008	10.79511	.09264	1	.78080	10.52142	.09505	12
24	.67253	19.64799	.05090	2	.60965	18.73659	.05337	24
36	.55153	26.90806	.03717	3	.47602	25.15102	.03976	36
48	.45230	32.86192	.03043	4	.37168	30.15943	.03316	48
60	.37092	37.74456	.02650	5	.29021	34.07001	.02935	60
72	.30419	41.74873	.02395	6	.22660	37.12342	.02694	72
84	.24946	45.03247	.02221	7	.17693	39.50752	.02531	84
96	.20458	47.72541	.02095	8	.13815	41.36904	.02417	96
108	.16777	49.93383	.02003	9	.10786	42.82252	.02335	108
120	.13759	51.74492	.01933	10	.08422	43.95741	.02275	120
132	.11283	53.23017	.01879	11	.06576	44.84353	.02230	132
144	.09253	54.44818	.01837	12	.05135	45.53541	.02196	144
156	.07588	55.44706	.01804	13	.04009	46.07564	.02170	156
168	.06223	56.26622	.01777	14	.03130	46.49745	.02151	168
180	.05103	56.93799	.01756	15	.02444	46.82681	.02136	180
192	.04185	57.48891	.01740	16	.01908	47.08397	.02124	192
204	.03432	57.94070	.01726	17	.01490	47.28476	.02115	204
216	.02815	58.31121	.01715	18	.01164	47.44154	.02108	216
228	.02308	58.61505	.01706	19	.00908	47.56395	.02103	228
240	.01893	58.86423	.01699	20	.00709	47.65953	.02098	240
252	.01552	59.06858	.01693	21	.00554	47.73416	.02095	252
264	.01273	59.23616	.01688	22	.00432	47.79243	.02093	264
276	.01044	59.37359	.01684	23	.00338	47.83793	.02091	276
288	.00856	59.48629	.01681	24	.00264	47.87346	.02089	288
300	.00702	59.57872	.01679	25	.00206	47.90119	.02088	300
312	.00576	59.65451	.01676	26	.00161	47.92285	.02087	312
324	.00472	59.71667	.01675	27	.00126	47.93976	.02086	324
336	.00387	59.76765	.01673	28	.00098	47.95297	.02086	336
348	.00318	59.80945	.01672	29	.00077	47.96328	.02085	348
360	.00260	59.84374	.01671	30	.00060	47.97133	.02085	360

ANNUAL COMPOUND INTEREST AND ANNUITY TABLES

		3%				4%		
Period	PW 1	PW 1/P	PR	PW 1	PW 1/P	PR	Period
1	.97087	.97087	1.03000	.96154	.96154	1.04000	1
2	.94260	1.91347	.52261	.92456	1.88609	.53020	2
3	.91514	2.82861	.35353	.88900	2.77509	.36035	3
4	.88849	3.71710	.26903	.85480	3.62990	.27549	4
5	.86261	4.57971	.21835	.82193	4.45182	.22463	5
6	.83748	5.41719	.18460	.79031	5.24214	.19076	6
7	.81309	6.23028	.16051	.75992	6.00205	.16661	7
8	.78941	7.01969	.14246	.73069	6.73274	.14853	8
9	.76642	7.78611	.12843	.70259	7.43533	.13449	9
10	.74409	8.53020	.11723	.67556	8.11090	.12329	10
11	.72242	9.25262	.10808	.64958	8.76048	.11415	11
12	.70138	9.95400	.10046	.62460	9.38507	.10655	12
13	.68095	10.63496	.09403	.60057	9.98565	.10014	13
14	.66112	11.29607	.08853	.57748	10.56312	.09467	14
15	.64186	11.93794	.08377	.55526	11.11839	.08994	15
16	.62317	12.56110	.07961	.53391	11.65230	.08582	16
17	.60502	13.16612	.07595	.51337	12.16567	.08220	17
18	.58739	13.75351	.07271	.49363	12.65930	.07899	18
19	.57029	14.32380	.06981	.47464	13.13394	.07614	19
20	.55368	14.87747	.06722	.45639	13.59033	.07358	20
21	.53755	15.41502	.06487	.43883	14.02916	.07128	21
22	.52189	15.93692	.06275	.42196	14.45112	.06920	22
23	.50669	16.44361	.06081	.40573	14.85684	.06731	23
24	.49193	16.93554	.05905	.39012	15.24696	.06559	24
25	.47761	17.41315	.05743	.37512	15.62208	.06401	25
26	.46369	17.87684	.05594	.36069	15.98277	.06257	26
27	.45019	18.32703	.05456	.34682	16.32959	.06124	27
28	.43708	18.76411	.05329	.33348	16.66306	.06001	28
29	.42435	19.18845	.05211	.32065	16.98371	.05888	29
30	.41199	19.60044	.05102	.30832	17.29203	.05783	30
31	.39999	20.00043	.05000	.29646	17.58849	.05686	31
32	.38834	20.38877	.04905	.28506	17.87355	.05595	32
33	.37703	20.76579	.04816	.27409	18.14765	.05510	33
34	.36604	21.13184	.04732	.26355	18.41120	.05431	34
35	.35538	21.48722	.04654	.25342	18.66461	.05358	35
36	.34503	21.83225	.04580	.24367	18.90828	.05289	36
37	.33498	22.16724	.04511	.23430	19.14258	.05224	37
38	.32523	22.49246	.04446	.22529	19.36786	.05163	38
39	.31575	22.80822	.04384	.21662	19.58448	.05106	39
40	.30656	23.11477	.04326	.20829	19.79277	.05052	40
41	.29763	23.41240	.04271	.20028	19.99305	.05002	41
42	.28896	23.70136	.04219	.19257	20.18563	.04954	42
43	.28054	23.98190	.04170	.18517	20.37079	.04909	43
44	.27237	24.25427	.04123	.17805	20.54884	.04866	44
45	.26444	24.51871	.04079	.17120	20.72004	.04826	45
46	.25674	24.77545	.04036	.16461	20.88465	.04788	46
47	.24926	25.02471	.03996	.15828	21.04294	.04752	47
48	.24200	25.26671	.03958	.15219	21.19513	.04718	48
49	.23495	25.50166	.03921	.14634	21.34147	.04686	49
50	.22811	25.72976	.03887	.14071	21.48218	.04655	50

ANNUAL COMPOUND INTEREST AND ANNUITY TABLES

		4½%				5%		
Period	PW 1	PW 1/P	PR	PW 1	PW 1/P	PR	Period
1	.95694	.95694	1.04500	.95238	.95238	1.05000	1
2	.91573	1.87267	.53400	.90703	1.85941	.53780	2
3	.87630	2.74896	.36377	.86384	2.72325	.36721	3
4	.83856	3.58753	.27874	.82270	3.54595	.28201	4
5	.80245	4.38998	.22779	.78353	4.32948	.23097	5
6	.76790	5.15787	.19388	.74622	5.07569	.19702	6
7	.73483	5.89270	.16970	.71068	5.78637	.17282	7
8	.70319	6.59589	.15161	.67684	6.46321	.15472	8
9	.67290	7.26879	.13757	.64461	7.10782	.14069	9
10	.64393	7.91272	.12638	.61391	7.72173	.12950	10
11	.61620	8.52892	.11725	.58468	8.30641	.12039	11
12	.58966	9.11858	.10967	.55684	8.86325	.11283	12
13	.56427	9.68285	.10328	.53032	9.39357	.10646	13
14	.53997	10.22283	.09782	.50507	9.89864	.10102	14
15	.51672	10.73955	.09311	.48102	10.37966	.09634	15
16	.49447	11.23402	.08902	.45811	10.83777	.09227	16
17	.47318	11.70719	.08542	.43630	11.27407	.08870	17
18	.45280	12.15999	.08224	.41552	11.68959	.08555	18
19	.43330	12.59329	.07941	.39573	12.08532	.08275	19
20	.41464	13.00794	.07688	.37689	12.46221	.08024	20
21	.39679	13.40472	.07460	.35894	12.82115	.07800	21
22	.37970	13.78442	.07255	.34185	13.16300	.07597	22
23	.36335	14.14777	.07068	.32557	13.48857	.07414	23
24	.34770	14.49548	.06899	.31007	13.79864	.07247	24
25	.33273	14.82821	.06744	.29530	14.09394	.07095	25
26	.31840	15.14661	.06602	.28124	14.37519	.06956	26
27	.30469	15.45130	.06472	.26785	14.64303	.06829	27
28	.29157	15.74287	.06352	.25509	14.89813	.06712	28
29	.27902	16.02189	.06241	.24295	15.14107	.06605	29
30	.26700	16.28889	.06139	.23138	15.37245	.06505	30
31	.25550	16.54439	.06044	.22036	15.59281	.06413	31
32	.24450	16.78889	.05956	.20987	15.80268	.06328	32
33	.23397	17.02286	.05874	.19987	16.00255	.06249	33
34	.22390	17.24676	.05798	.19035	16.19290	.06176	34
35	.21425	17.46101	.05727	.18129	16.37419	.06107	35
36	.20503	17.66604	.05661	.17266	16.54685	.06043	36
37	.19620	17.86224	.05598	.16444	16.71129	.05984	37
38	.18775	18.04999	.05540	.15661	16.86789	.05928	38
39	.17967	18.22966	.05486	.14915	17.01704	.05876	39
40	.17193	18.40158	.05434	.14205	17.15909	.05828	40
41	.16453	18.56611	.05386	.13528	17.29437	.05782	41
42	.15744	18.72355	.05341	.12884	17.42321	.05739	42
43	.15066	18.87421	.05298	.12270	17.54591	.05699	43
44	.14417	19.01838	.05258	.11686	17.66277	.05662	44
45	.13796	19.15635	.05220	.11130	17.77407	.05626	45
46	.13202	19.28837	.05184	.10600	17.88007	.05593	46
47	.12634	19.41471	.05151	.10095	17.98102	.05561	47
48	.12090	19.53561	.05119	.09614	18.07716	.05532	48
49	.11569	19.65130	.05089	.09156	18.16872	.05504	49
50	.11071	19.76201	.05060	.08720	18.25593	.05478	50

ANNUAL COMPOUND INTEREST AND ANNUITY TABLES

	5½%				6%		
Period	PW 1	PW 1/P	PR	PW 1	PW 1/P	PR	Period
1	.94787	.94787	1.05500	.94340	.94340	1.06000	1
2	.89845	1.84632	.54162	.89000	1.83339	.54544	2
3	.85161	2.69793	.37065	.83962	2.67301	.37411	3
4	.80722	3.50515	.28529	.79209	3.46511	.28859	4
5	.76513	4.27028	.23418	.74726	4.21236	.23740	5
6	.72525	4.99553	.20018	.70496	4.91732	.20336	6
7	.68744	5.68297	.17596	.66506	5.58238	.17914	7
8	.65160	6.33457	.15786	.62741	6.20979	.16104	8
9	.61763	6.95220	.14384	.59190	6.80169	.14702	9
10	.58543	7.53763	.13267	.55839	7.36009	.13587	10
11	.55491	8.09254	.12357	.52679	7.88687	.12679	11
12	.52598	8.61852	.11603	.49697	8.38384	.11928	12
13	.49856	9.11708	.10968	.46884	8.85268	.11296	13
14	.47257	9.58965	.10428	.44230	9.29498	.10758	14
15	.44793	10.03758	.09963	.41727	9.71225	.10296	15
16	.42458	10.46216	.09558	.39365	10.10590	.09895	16
17	.40245	10.86461	.09204	.37136	10.47726	.09544	17
18	.38147	11.24607	.08892	.35034	10.82760	.09236	18
19	.36158	11.60765	.08615	.33051	11.15812	.08962	19
20	.34273	11.95038	.08368	.31180	11.46992	.08718	20
21	.32486	12.27524	.08146	.29416	11.76408	.08500	21
22	.30793	12.58317	.07947	.27751	12.04158	.08305	22
23	.29187	12.87504	.07767	.26180	12.30338	.08128	23
24	.27666	13.15170	.07604	.24698	12.55036	.07968	24
25	.26223	13.41393	.07455	.23300	12.78336	.07823	25
26	.24856	13.66250	.07319	.21981	13.00317	.07690	26
27	.23560	13.89810	.07195	.20737	13.21053	.07570	27
28	.22332	14.12142	.07081	.19563	13.40616	.07459	28
29	.21168	14.33310	.06977	.18456	13.59072	.07358	29
30	.20064	14.53375	.06881	.17411	13.76483	.07265	30
31	.19018	14.72393	.06792	.16425	13.92909	.07179	31
32	.18027	14.90420	.06710	.15496	14.08404	.07100	32
33	.17087	15.07507	.06633	.14619	14.23023	.07027	33
34	.16196	15.23703	.06563	.13791	14.36814	.06960	34
35	.15352	15.39055	.06497	.13011	14.49825	.06897	35
36	.14552	15.53607	.06437	.12274	14.62099	.06839	36
37	.13793	15.67400	.06380	.11579	14.73678	.06786	37
38	.13074	15.80474	.06327	.10924	14.84602	.06736	38
39	.12392	15.92866	.06278	.10306	14.94907	.06689	39
40	.11746	16.04612	.06232	.09722	15.04630	.06646	40
41	.11134	16.15746	.06189	.09172	15.13802	.06606	41
42	.10554	16.26300	.06149	.08653	15.22454	.06568	42
43	.10003	16.36303	.06111	.08163	15.30617	.06533	43
44	.09482	16.45785	.06076	.07701	15.38318	.06501	44
45	.08988	16.54773	.06043	.07265	15.45583	.06470	45
46	.08519	16.63292	.06012	.06854	15.52437	.06441	46
47	.08075	16.71366	.05983	.06466	15.58903	.06415	47
48	.07654	16.79020	.05956	.06100	15.65003	.06390	48
49	.07255	16.86275	.05930	.05755	15.70757	.06366	49
50	.06877	16.93152	.05906	.05429	15.76186	.06344	50

ANNUAL COMPOUND INTEREST AND ANNUITY TABLES

6½%   7%

Period	PW 1	PW 1/P	PR	PW 1	PW 1/P	PR	Period
1	.93897	.93897	1.06500	.93458	.93458	1.07000	1
2	.88166	1.82063	.54926	.87344	1.80802	.55309	2
3	.82785	2.64848	.37758	.81630	2.62432	.38105	3
4	.77732	3.42580	.29190	.76290	3.38721	.29523	4
5	.72988	4.15568	.24063	.71299	4.10020	.24389	5
6	.68533	4.84101	.20657	.66634	4.76654	.20980	6
7	.64351	5.48452	.18233	.62275	5.38929	.18555	7
8	.60423	6.08875	.16424	.58201	5.97130	.16747	8
9	.56735	6.65610	.15024	.54393	6.51523	.15349	9
10	.53273	7.18883	.13910	.50835	7.02358	.14238	10
11	.50021	7.68904	.13006	.47509	7.49867	.13336	11
12	.46968	8.15873	.12257	.44401	7.94269	.12590	12
13	.44102	8.59974	.11628	.41496	8.35765	.11965	13
14	.41410	9.01384	.11094	.38782	8.74547	.11434	14
15	.38883	9.40267	.10635	.36245	9.10791	.10979	15
16	.36510	9.76776	.10238	.33873	9.44665	.10586	16
17	.34281	10.11058	.09891	.31657	9.76322	.10243	17
18	.32189	10.43247	.09585	.29586	10.05909	.09941	18
19	.30224	10.73471	.09316	.27651	10.33560	.09675	19
20	.28380	11.01851	.09076	.25842	10.59401	.09439	20
21	.26648	11.28498	.08861	.24151	10.83553	.09229	21
22	.25021	11.53520	.08669	.22571	11.06124	.09041	22
23	.23494	11.77014	.08496	.21095	11.27219	.08871	23
24	.22060	11.99074	.08340	.19715	11.46933	.08719	24
25	.20714	12.19788	.08198	.18425	11.65358	.08581	25
26	.19450	12.39237	.08069	.17220	11.82578	.08456	26
27	.18263	12.57500	.07952	.16093	11.98671	.08343	27
28	.17148	12.74648	.07845	.15040	12.13711	.08239	28
29	.16101	12.90749	.07747	.14056	12.27767	.08145	29
30	.15119	13.05868	.07658	.13137	12.40904	.08059	30
31	.14196	13.20063	.07575	.12277	12.53181	.07980	31
32	.13329	13.33393	.07500	.11474	12.64656	.07907	32
33	.12516	13.45909	.07430	.10723	12.75379	.07841	33
34	.11752	13.57661	.07366	.10022	12.85401	.07780	34
35	.11035	13.68696	.07306	.09366	12.94767	.07723	35
36	.10361	13.79057	.07251	.08754	13.03521	.07672	36
37	.09729	13.88786	.07201	.08181	13.11702	.07624	37
38	.09135	13.97921	.07153	.07646	13.19347	.07580	38
39	.08578	14.06499	.07110	.07146	13.26493	.07539	39
40	.08054	14.14553	.07069	.06678	13.33171	.07501	40
41	.07563	14.22115	.07032	.06241	13.39412	.07466	41
42	.07101	14.29216	.06997	.05833	13.45245	.07434	42
43	.06668	14.35884	.06964	.05451	13.50696	.07404	43
44	.06261	14.42144	.06934	.05095	13.55791	.07376	44
45	.05879	14.48023	.06906	.04761	13.60552	.07350	45
46	.05520	14.53543	.06880	.04450	13.65002	.07326	46
47	.05183	14.58725	.06855	.04159	13.69161	.07304	47
48	.04867	14.63592	.06833	.03887	13.73047	.07283	48
49	.04570	14.68161	.06811	.03632	13.76680	.07264	49
50	.04291	14.72452	.06791	.03395	13.80075	.07246	50

ANNUAL COMPOUND INTEREST AND ANNUITY TABLES

	7½%				8%		
Period	PW 1	PW 1/P	PR	PW 1	PW 1/P	PR	Period
1	.93023	.93023	1.07500	.92593	.92593	1.08000	1
2	.86533	1.79557	.55693	.85734	1.78326	.56077	2
3	.80496	2.60053	.38454	.79383	2.57710	.38803	3
4	.74880	3.34933	.29857	.73503	3.31213	.30192	4
5	.69656	4.04588	.24716	.68058	3.99271	.25046	5
6	.64796	4.69385	.21304	.63017	4.62288	.21632	6
7	.60275	5.29660	.18880	.58349	5.20637	.19207	7
8	.56070	5.85730	.17073	.54027	5.74664	.17401	8
9	.52158	6.37889	.15677	.50025	6.24689	.16008	9
10	.48519	6.86408	.14569	.46319	6.71008	.14903	10
11	.45134	7.31542	.13670	.42888	7.13896	.14008	11
12	.41985	7.73528	.12928	.39711	7.53608	.13270	12
13	.39056	8.12584	.12306	.36770	7.90378	.12652	13
14	.36331	8.48915	.11780	.34046	8.24424	.12130	14
15	.33797	8.82712	.11329	.31524	8.55948	.11683	15
16	.31439	9.14151	.10939	.29189	8.85137	.11298	16
17	.29245	9.43396	.10600	.27027	9.12164	.10963	17
18	.27205	9.70601	.10303	.25025	9.37189	.10670	18
19	.25307	9.95908	.10041	.23171	9.60360	.10413	19
20	.23541	10.19449	.09809	.21455	9.81815	.10185	20
21	.21899	10.41348	.09603	.19866	10.01680	.09983	21
22	.20371	10.61719	.09419	.18394	10.20074	.09803	22
23	.18950	10.80669	.09254	.17032	10.37106	.09642	23
24	.17628	10.98297	.09105	.15770	10.52876	.09498	24
25	.16398	11.14695	.08971	.14602	10.67478	.09368	25
26	.15254	11.29948	.08850	.13520	10.80998	.09251	26
27	.14190	11.44138	.08740	.12519	10.93516	.09145	27
28	.13200	11.57338	.08641	.11591	11.05108	.09049	28
29	.12279	11.69617	.08550	.10733	11.15841	.08962	29
30	.11422	11.81039	.08467	.09938	11.25778	.08883	30
31	.10625	11.91664	.08392	.09202	11.34980	.08811	31
32	.09884	12.01548	.08323	.08520	11.43500	.08745	32
33	.09194	12.10742	.08259	.07889	11.51389	.08685	33
34	.08553	12.19295	.08201	.07305	11.58693	.08630	34
35	.07956	12.27251	.08148	.06763	11.65457	.08580	35
36	.07401	12.34652	.08099	.06262	11.71719	.08534	36
37	.06885	12.41537	.08055	.05799	11.77518	.08492	37
38	.06404	12.47941	.08013	.05369	11.82887	.08454	38
39	.05958	12.53899	.07975	.04971	11.87858	.08419	39
40	.05542	12.59441	.07940	.04603	11.92461	.08386	40
41	.05155	12.64596	.07908	.04262	11.96723	.08356	41
42	.04796	12.69392	.07878	.03946	12.00670	.08329	42
43	.04461	12.73853	.07850	.03654	12.04324	.08303	43
44	.04150	12.78003	.07825	.03383	12.07707	.08280	44
45	.03860	12.81863	.07801	.03133	12.10840	.08259	45
46	.03591	12.85454	.07779	.02901	12.13741	.08239	46
47	.03340	12.88794	.07759	.02686	12.16427	.08221	47
48	.03107	12.91902	.07741	.02487	12.18914	.08204	48
49	.02891	12.94792	.07723	.02303	12.21216	.08189	49
50	.02689	12.97481	.07707	.02132	12.23348	.08174	50

ANNUAL COMPOUND INTEREST AND ANNUITY TABLES

8½%   9%

Period	PW 1	PW 1/P	PR	PW 1	PW 1/P	PR	Period
1	.92166	.92166	1.08500	.91743	.91743	1.09000	1
2	.84946	1.77111	.56462	.84168	1.75911	.56847	2
3	.78291	2.55402	.39154	.77218	2.53129	.39505	3
4	.72157	3.27560	.30529	.70843	3.23972	.30867	4
5	.66505	3.94064	.25377	.64993	3.88965	.25709	5
6	.61295	4.55359	.21961	.59627	4.48592	.22292	6
7	.56493	5.11851	.19537	.54703	5.03295	.19869	7
8	.52067	5.63918	.17733	.50187	5.53482	.18067	8
9	.47988	6.11906	.16342	.46043	5.99525	.16680	9
10	.44229	6.56135	.15241	.42241	6.41766	.15582	10
11	.40764	6.96898	.14349	.38753	6.80519	.14695	11
12	.37570	7.34469	.13615	.35553	7.16073	.13965	12
13	.34627	7.69095	.13002	.32618	7.48690	.13357	13
14	.31914	8.01010	.12484	.29925	7.78615	.12843	14
15	.29414	8.30424	.12042	.27454	8.06069	.12406	15
16	.27110	8.57533	.11661	.25187	8.31256	.12030	16
17	.24986	8.82519	.11331	.23107	8.54363	.11705	17
18	.23028	9.05548	.11043	.21199	8.75563	.11421	18
19	.21224	9.26772	.10790	.19449	8.95011	.11173	19
20	.19562	9.46334	.10567	.17843	9.12855	.10955	20
21	.18029	9.64363	.10370	.16370	9.29224	.10762	21
22	.16617	9.80980	.10194	.15018	9.44243	.10590	22
23	.15315	9.96295	.10037	.13778	9.58021	.10438	23
24	.14115	10.10410	.09897	.12640	9.70661	.10302	24
25	.13009	10.23419	.09771	.11597	9.82258	.10181	25
26	.11990	10.35409	.09658	.10639	9.92897	.10072	26
27	.11051	10.46460	.09556	.09761	10.02658	.09973	27
28	.10185	10.56645	.09464	.08955	10.11613	.09885	28
29	.09387	10.66033	.09381	.08215	10.19828	.09806	29
30	.08652	10.74684	.09305	.07537	10.27365	.09734	30
31	.07974	10.82658	.09237	.06915	10.34280	.09669	31
32	.07349	10.90008	.09174	.06344	10.40624	.09610	32
33	.06774	10.96781	.09118	.05820	10.46444	.09556	33
34	.06243	11.03024	.09066	.05339	10.51784	.09508	34
35	.05754	11.08778	.09019	.04899	10.56682	.09464	35
36	.05303	11.14081	.08976	.04494	10.61176	.09424	36
37	.04888	11.18969	.08937	.04123	10.65299	.09387	37
38	.04505	11.23474	.08901	.03783	10.69082	.09354	38
39	.04152	11.27625	.08868	.03470	10.72552	.09324	39
40	.03827	11.31452	.08838	.03184	10.75736	.09296	40
41	.03527	11.34979	.08811	.02921	10.78657	.09271	41
42	.03251	11.38229	.08786	.02680	10.81337	.09248	42
43	.02996	11.41225	.08763	.02458	10.83795	.09227	43
44	.02761	11.43986	.08741	.02255	10.86051	.09208	44
45	.02545	11.46531	.08722	.02069	10.88120	.09190	45
46	.02345	11.48877	.08704	.01898	10.90018	.09174	46
47	.02162	11.51038	.08688	.01742	10.91760	.09160	47
48	.01992	11.53031	.08673	.01598	10.93358	.09146	48
49	.01836	11.54867	.08659	.01466	10.94823	.09134	49
50	.01692	11.56560	.08646	.01345	10.96168	.09123	50

ANNUAL COMPOUND INTEREST AND ANNUITY TABLES

10% 11%

Period	PW 1	PW 1/P	PR	PW 1	PW 1/P	PR	Period
1	.90909	.90909	1.10000	.90090	.90090	1.11000	1
2	.82645	1.73554	.57619	.81162	1.71252	.58393	2
3	.75131	2.48685	.40211	.73119	2.44371	.40921	3
4	.68301	3.16987	.31547	.65873	3.10245	.32233	4
5	.62092	3.79079	.26380	.59345	3.69590	.27057	5
6	.56447	4.35526	.22961	.53464	4.23054	.23638	6
7	.51316	4.86842	.20541	.48166	4.71220	.21222	7
8	.46651	5.33493	.18744	.43393	5.14612	.19432	8
9	.42410	5.75902	.17364	.39092	5.53705	.18060	9
10	.38554	6.14457	.16275	.35218	5.88923	.16980	10
11	.35049	6.49506	.15396	.31728	6.20652	.16112	11
12	.31863	6.81369	.14676	.28584	6.49236	.15403	12
13	.28966	7.10336	.14078	.25751	6.74987	.14815	13
14	.26333	7.36669	.13575	.23199	6.98187	.14323	14
15	.23939	7.60608	.13147	.20900	7.19087	.13907	15
16	.21763	7.82371	.12782	.18829	7.37916	.13552	16
17	.19784	8.02155	.12466	.16963	7.54879	.13247	17
18	.17986	8.20141	.12193	.15282	7.70162	.12984	18
19	.16351	8.36492	.11955	.13768	7.83929	.12756	19
20	.14864	8.51356	.11746	.12403	7.96333	.12558	20
21	.13513	8.64869	.11562	.11174	8.07507	.12384	21
22	.12285	8.77154	.11401	.10067	8.17574	.12231	22
23	.11168	8.88322	.11257	.09069	8.26643	.12097	23
24	.10153	8.98474	.11130	.08170	8.34814	.11979	24
25	.09230	9.07704	.11017	.07361	8.42174	.11874	25
26	.08391	9.16095	.10916	.06631	8.48806	.11781	26
27	.07628	9.23722	.10826	.05974	8.54780	.11699	27
28	.06934	9.30657	.10745	.05382	8.60162	.11626	28
29	.06304	9.36961	.10673	.04849	8.65011	.11561	29
30	.05731	9.42691	.10608	.04368	8.69379	.11502	30
31	.05210	9.47901	.10550	.03935	8.73315	.11451	31
32	.04736	9.52638	.10497	.03545	8.76860	.11404	32
33	.04306	9.56943	.10450	.03194	8.80054	.11363	33
34	.03914	9.60857	.10407	.02878	8.82932	.11326	34
35	.03558	9.64416	.10369	.02592	8.85524	.11293	35
36	.03235	9.67651	.10334	.02335	8.87859	.11263	36
37	.02941	9.70592	.10303	.02104	8.89963	.11236	37
38	.02673	9.73265	.10275	.01896	8.91859	.11213	38
39	.02430	9.75696	.10249	.01708	8.93567	.11191	39
40	.02210	9.77905	.10226	.01538	8.95105	.11172	40
41	.02009	9.79914	.10205	.01386	8.96491	.11155	41
42	.01826	9.81740	.10186	.01249	8.97740	.11139	42
43	.01660	9.83400	.10169	.01125	8.98865	.11125	43
44	.01509	9.84909	.10153	.01013	8.99878	.11113	44
45	.01372	9.86281	.10139	.00913	9.00791	.11101	45
46	.01247	9.87528	.10126	.00823	9.01614	.11091	46
47	.01134	9.88662	.10115	.00741	9.02355	.11082	47
48	.01031	9.89693	.10104	.00668	9.03022	.11074	48
49	.00937	9.90630	.10095	.00601	9.03624	.11067	49
50	.00852	9.91481	.10086	.00542	9.04165	.11060	50

ANNUAL COMPOUND INTEREST AND ANNUITY TABLES

		12%				13%		
Period	PW 1	PW 1/P	PR		PW 1	PW 1/P	PR	Period
1	.89286	.89286	1.12000		.88496	.88496	1.13000	1
2	.79719	1.69005	.59170		.78315	1.66810	.59948	2
3	.71178	2.40183	.41635		.69305	2.36115	.42352	3
4	.63552	3.03735	.32923		.61332	2.97447	.33619	4
5	.56743	3.60478	.27741		.54276	3.51723	.28431	5
6	.50663	4.11141	.24323		.48032	3.99755	.25015	6
7	.45235	4.56376	.21912		.42506	4.42261	.22611	7
8	.40388	4.96764	.20130		.37616	4.79877	.20839	8
9	.36061	5.32825	.18768		.33288	5.13166	.19487	9
10	.32197	5.65022	.17698		.29459	5.42624	.18429	10
11	.28748	5.93770	.16842		.26070	5.68694	.17584	11
12	.25668	6.19437	.16144		.23071	5.91765	.16899	12
13	.22917	6.42355	.15568		.20416	6.12181	.16335	13
14	.20462	6.62817	.15087		.18068	6.30249	.15867	14
15	.18270	6.81086	.14682		.15989	6.46238	.15474	15
16	.16312	6.97399	.14339		.14150	6.60388	.15143	16
17	.14564	7.11963	.14046		.12522	6.72909	.14861	17
18	.13004	7.24967	.13794		.11081	6.83991	.14620	18
19	.11611	7.36578	.13576		.09806	6.93797	.14413	19
20	.10367	7.46944	.13388		.08678	7.02475	.14235	20
21	.09256	7.56200	.13224		.07680	7.10155	.14081	21
22	.08264	7.64465	.13081		.06796	7.16951	.13948	22
23	.07379	7.71843	.12956		.06014	7.22966	.13832	23
24	.06588	7.78432	.12846		.05323	7.28288	.13731	24
25	.05882	7.84314	.12750		.04710	7.32998	.13643	25
26	.05252	7.89566	.12665		.04168	7.37167	.13565	26
27	.04689	7.94255	.12590		.03689	7.40856	.13498	27
28	.04187	7.98442	.12524		.03264	7.44120	.13439	28
29	.03738	8.02181	.12466		.02889	7.47009	.13387	29
30	.03338	8.05518	.12414		.02557	7.49565	.13341	30
31	.02980	8.08499	.12369		.02262	7.51828	.13301	31
32	.02661	8.11159	.12328		.02002	7.53830	.13266	32
33	.02376	8.13535	.12292		.01772	7.55602	.13234	33
34	.02121	8.15656	.12260		.01568	7.57170	.13207	34
35	.01894	8.17550	.12232		.01388	7.58557	.13183	35
36	.01691	8.19241	.12206		.01228	7.59785	.13162	36
37	.01510	8.20751	.12184		.01087	7.60872	.13143	37
38	.01348	8.22099	.12164		.00962	7.61833	.13126	38
39	.01204	8.23303	.12146		.00851	7.62684	.13112	39
40	.01075	8.24378	.12130		.00753	7.63438	.13099	40
41	.00960	8.25337	.12116		.00666	7.64104	.13087	41
42	.00857	8.26194	.12104		.00590	7.64694	.13077	42
43	.00765	8.26959	.12092		.00522	7.65216	.13068	43
44	.00683	8.27642	.12083		.00462	7.65678	.13060	44
45	.00610	8.28252	.12074		.00409	7.66086	.13053	45
46	.00544	8.28796	.12066		.00362	7.66448	.13047	46
47	.00486	8.29282	.12059		.00320	7.66768	.13042	47
48	.00434	8.29716	.12052		.00283	7.67052	.13037	48
49	.00388	8.30104	.12047		.00251	7.67302	.13033	49
50	.00346	8.30450	.12042		.00222	7.67524	.13029	50

ANNUAL COMPOUND INTEREST AND ANNUITY TABLES

		14%				15%		
Period	PW 1	PW 1/P	PR	PW 1	PW 1/P	PR	Period
---	---	---	---	---	---	---	---
1	.87719	.87719	1.14000	.86957	.86957	1.15000	1
2	.76947	1.64666	.60729	.75614	1.62571	.61512	2
3	.67497	2.32163	.43073	.65752	2.28323	.43798	3
4	.59208	2.91371	.34320	.57175	2.85498	.35027	4
5	.51937	3.43308	.29128	.49718	3.35216	.29832	5
6	.45559	3.88867	.25716	.43233	3.78448	.26424	6
7	.39964	4.28830	.23319	.37594	4.16042	.24036	7
8	.35056	4.63886	.21557	.32690	4.48732	.22285	8
9	.30751	4.94637	.20217	.28426	4.77158	.20957	9
10	.26974	5.21612	.19171	.24718	5.01877	.19925	10
11	.23662	5.45273	.18339	.21494	5.23371	.19107	11
12	.20756	5.66029	.17667	.18691	5.42062	.18448	12
13	.18207	5.84236	.17116	.16253	5.58315	.17911	13
14	.15971	6.00207	.16661	.14133	5.72448	.17469	14
15	.14010	6.14217	.16281	.12289	5.84737	.17102	15
16	.12289	6.26506	.15962	.10686	5.95423	.16795	16
17	.10780	6.37286	.15692	.09293	6.04716	.16537	17
18	.09456	6.46742	.15462	.08081	6.12797	.16319	18
19	.08295	6.55037	.15266	.07027	6.19823	.16134	19
20	.07276	6.62313	.15099	.06110	6.25933	.15976	20
21	.06383	6.68696	.14954	.05313	6.31246	.15842	21
22	.05599	6.74294	.14830	.04620	6.35866	.15727	22
23	.04911	6.79206	.14723	.04017	6.39884	.15628	23
24	.04308	6.83514	.14630	.03493	6.43377	.15543	24
25	.03779	6.87293	.14550	.03038	6.46415	.15470	25
26	.03315	6.90608	.14480	.02642	6.49056	.15407	26
27	.02908	6.93515	.14419	.02297	6.51353	.15353	27
28	.02551	6.96066	.14366	.01997	6.53351	.15306	28
29	.02237	6.98304	.14320	.01737	6.55088	.15265	29
30	.01963	7.00266	.14280	.01510	6.56598	.15230	30
31	.01722	7.01988	.14245	.01313	6.57911	.15200	31
32	.01510	7.03498	.14215	.01142	6.59053	.15173	32
33	.01325	7.04823	.14188	.00993	6.60046	.15150	33
34	.01162	7.05985	.14165	.00864	6.60910	.15131	34
35	.01019	7.07005	.14144	.00751	6.61661	.15113	35
36	.00894	7.07899	.14126	.00653	6.62314	.15099	36
37	.00784	7.08683	.14111	.00568	6.62881	.15086	37
38	.00688	7.09371	.14097	.00494	6.63375	.15074	38
39	.00604	7.09975	.14085	.00429	6.63805	.15065	39
40	.00529	7.10504	.14075	.00373	6.64178	.15056	40
41	.00464	7.10969	.14065	.00325	6.64502	.15049	41
42	.00407	7.11376	.14057	.00282	6.64785	.15042	42
43	.00357	7.11733	.14050	.00245	6.65030	.15037	43
44	.00313	7.12047	.14044	.00213	6.65244	.15032	44
45	.00275	7.12322	.14039	.00186	6.65429	.15028	45
46	.00241	7.12563	.14034	.00161	6.65591	.15024	46
47	.00212	7.12774	.14030	.00140	6.65731	.15021	47
48	.00186	7.12960	.14026	.00122	6.65853	.15018	48
49	.00163	7.13123	.14023	.00106	6.65959	.15016	49
50	.00143	7.13266	.14020	.00092	6.66051	.15014	50

ANNUAL COMPOUND INTEREST AND ANNUITY TABLES

	16%			18%			
Period	PW 1	PW 1/P	PR	PW 1	PW 1/P	PR	Period
1	.86207	.86207	1.16000	.84746	.84746	1.18000	1
2	.74316	1.60523	.62296	.71818	1.56564	.63872	2
3	.64066	2.24589	.44526	.60863	2.17427	.45992	3
4	.55229	2.79818	.35738	.51579	2.69006	.37174	4
5	.47611	3.27429	.30541	.43711	3.12717	.31978	5
6	.41044	3.68474	.27139	.37043	3.49760	.28591	6
7	.35383	4.03857	.24761	.31393	3.81153	.26236	7
8	.30503	4.34359	.23022	.26604	4.07757	.24524	8
9	.26295	4.60654	.21708	.22546	4.30302	.23239	9
10	.22668	4.83323	.20690	.19106	4.49409	.22251	10
11	.19542	5.02864	.19886	.16192	4.65601	.21478	11
12	.16846	5.19711	.19242	.13722	4.79322	.20863	12
13	.14523	5.34233	.18718	.11629	4.90951	.20369	13
14	.12520	5.46753	.18290	.09855	5.00806	.19968	14
15	.10793	5.57546	.17936	.08352	5.09158	.19640	15
16	.09304	5.66850	.17641	.07078	5.16235	.19371	16
17	.08021	5.74870	.17395	.05998	5.22233	.19149	17
18	.06914	5.81785	.17189	.05083	5.27316	.18964	18
19	.05961	5.87746	.17014	.04308	5.31624	.18810	19
20	.05139	5.92884	.16867	.03651	5.35275	.18682	20
21	.04430	5.97314	.16742	.03094	5.38368	.18575	21
22	.03819	6.01133	.16635	.02622	5.40990	.18485	22
23	.03292	6.04425	.16545	.02222	5.43212	.18409	23
24	.02838	6.07263	.16467	.01883	5.45095	.18345	24
25	.02447	6.09709	.16401	.01596	5.46691	.18292	25
26	.02109	6.11818	.16345	.01352	5.48043	.18247	26
27	.01818	6.13636	.16296	.01146	5.49189	.18209	27
28	.01567	6.15204	.16255	.00971	5.50160	.18177	28
29	.01351	6.16555	.16219	.00823	5.50983	.18149	29
30	.01165	6.17720	.16189	.00697	5.51681	.18126	30
31	.01004	6.18724	.16162	.00591	5.52272	.18107	31
32	.00866	6.19590	.16140	.00501	5.52773	.18091	32
33	.00746	6.20336	.16120	.00425	5.53197	.18077	33
34	.00643	6.20979	.16104	.00360	5.53557	.18065	34
35	.00555	6.21534	.16089	.00305	5.53862	.18055	35
36	.00478	6.22012	.16077	.00258	5.54120	.18047	36
37	.00412	6.22424	.16066	.00219	5.54339	.18039	37
38	.00355	6.22779	.16057	.00186	5.54525	.18033	38
39	.00306	6.23086	.16049	.00157	5.54682	.18028	39
40	.00264	6.23350	.16042	.00133	5.54815	.18024	40
41	.00228	6.23577	.16037	.00113	5.54928	.18020	41
42	.00196	6.23774	.16032	.00096	5.55024	.18017	42
43	.00169	6.23943	.16027	.00081	5.55105	.18015	43
44	.00146	6.24089	.16023	.00069	5.55174	.18012	44
45	.00126	6.24214	.16020	.00058	5.55232	.18010	45
46	.00108	6.24323	.16017	.00049	5.55281	.18009	46
47	.00093	6.24416	.16015	.00042	5.55323	.18008	47
48	.00081	6.24497	.16013	.00035	5.55359	.18006	48
49	.00069	6.24566	.16011	.00030	5.55389	.18005	49
50	.00060	6.24626	.16010	.00025	5.55414	.18005	50

ANNUAL COMPOUND INTEREST AND ANNUITY TABLES

	20%				25%			
Period	PW 1	PW 1/P	PR	PW 1	PW 1/P	PR	Period
1	.83333	.83333	1.20000	.80000	.80000	1.25000	1
2	.69444	1.52778	.65455	.64000	1.44000	.69444	2
3	.57870	2.10648	.47473	.51200	1.95200	.51230	3
4	.48225	2.58873	.38629	.40960	2.36160	.42344	4
5	.40188	2.99061	.33438	.32768	2.68928	.37185	5
6	.33490	3.32551	.30071	.26214	2.95142	.33882	6
7	.27908	3.60459	.27742	.20972	3.16114	.31634	7
8	.23257	3.83716	.26061	.16777	3.32891	.30040	8
9	.19381	4.03097	.24808	.13422	3.46313	.28876	9
10	.16151	4.19247	.23852	.10737	3.57050	.28007	10
11	.13459	4.32706	.23110	.08590	3.65640	.27349	11
12	.11216	4.43922	.22526	.06872	3.72512	.26845	12
13	.09346	4.53268	.22062	.05498	3.78010	.26454	13
14	.07789	4.61057	.21689	.04398	3.82408	.26150	14
15	.06491	4.67547	.21388	.03518	3.85926	.25912	15
16	.05409	4.72956	.21144	.02815	3.88741	.25724	16
17	.04507	4.77463	.20944	.02252	3.90993	.25576	17
18	.03756	4.81219	.20781	.01801	3.92794	.25459	18
19	.03130	4.84350	.20646	.01441	3.94235	.25366	19
20	.02608	4.86958	.20536	.01153	3.95388	.25292	20
21	.02174	4.89132	.20444	.00922	3.96311	.25233	21
22	.01811	4.90943	.20369	.00738	3.97049	.25186	22
23	.01509	4.92453	.20307	.00590	3.97639	.25148	23
24	.01258	4.93710	.20255	.00472	3.98111	.25119	24
25	.01048	4.94759	.20212	.00378	3.98489	.25095	25
26	.00874	4.95632	.20176	.00302	3.98791	.25076	26
27	.00728	4.96360	.20147	.00242	3.99033	.25061	27
28	.00607	4.96967	.20122	.00193	3.99226	.25048	28
29	.00506	4.97472	.20102	.00155	3.99381	.25039	29
30	.00421	4.97894	.20085	.00124	3.99505	.25031	30
31	.00351	4.98245	.20070	.00099	3.99604	.25025	31
32	.00293	4.98537	.20059	.00079	3.99683	.25020	32
33	.00244	4.98781	.20049	.00063	3.99746	.25016	33
34	.00203	4.98984	.20041	.00051	3.99797	.25013	34
35	.00169	4.99154	.20034	.00041	3.99838	.25010	35
36	.00141	4.99295	.20028	.00032	3.99870	.25008	36
37	.00118	4.99412	.20024	.00026	3.99896	.25006	37
38	.00098	4.99510	.20020	.00021	3.99917	.25005	38
39	.00082	4.99592	.20016	.00017	3.99934	.25004	39
40	.00068	4.99660	.20014	.00013	3.99947	.25003	40
41	.00057	4.99717	.20011	.00011	3.99957	.250027	41
42	.00047	4.99764	.20009	.00009	3.99966	.250021	42
43	.00039	4.99803	.20008	.00007	3.99973	.250017	43
44	.00033	4.99836	.20007	.00005	3.99978	.250014	44
45	.00027	4.99863	.20006	.00004	3.99983	.250011	45
46	.00023	4.99886	.20005	.000035	3.99986	.250009	46
47	.00019	4.99905	.20004	.000028	3.99989	.250007	47
48	.00016	4.99921	.20003	.000022	3.99991	.250006	48
49	.00013	4.99934	.20003	.000018	3.99993	.250005	49
50	.00011	4.99945	.20002	.000014	3.99994	.250004	50

OAR TABLES

Precomputed OVER-ALL RATES
To Implement the "Instant"
Mortgage-Equity Technique[1]

Variable factors "built into" the OAR's:

Equity Yield Rates: 10%, 12%, 14%, 15%, 16%, 20%

Holding Period: 5, 10, and 15 years

Loan Ratios: 60%, 70%, 75%, 80%, 90%

Interest Rates: 6%, 7%, 8%, 9%, 10%, 12%

Loan Amortization Terms: 15, 20, 25, 30 years

Appreciation or Depreciation: +40%, +20%, 0%, −20%

(Computations are based on monthly loan payments. Annual amortization schedules would call for slightly but not significantly higher over-all rates. In the precomputed rates, rounded to five decimal places, the final digit has been rounded upward.)

---

[1] NOTE: Tables containing nearly 150,000 precomputed over-all rates, covering a more extensive range of variables, appear in "The Instant Mortgage-Equity Techniques," by Irvin E. Johnson (D.C. Heath and Company, Lexington, Massachusetts, 1972).

OVER-ALL RATES

10% EQUITY YIELD
5 Year Holding Period
60% Loan Ratio

Term In Yrs.	Appr. or Dep.	Interest Rate					
		6%	7%	8%	9%	10%	12%
15	+40%	.01167	.01700	.02243	.02792	.03350	.04483
	+20%	.04443	.04976	.05518	.06068	.06626	.07759
	0%	.07719	.08252	.08794	.09344	.09902	.11035
	−20%	.10994	.11528	.12070	.12620	.13177	.14311
20	+40%	.01123	.01680	.02245	.02817	.03395	.04565
	+20%	.04399	.04956	.05521	.06093	.06671	.07841
	0%	.07675	.08232	.08797	.09369	.09947	.11117
	−20%	.10951	.11508	.12073	.12645	.13222	.14393
25	+40%	.01098	.01669	.02246	.02830	.03418	.04605
	+20%	.04374	.04945	.05522	.06106	.06694	.07881
	0%	.07650	.08221	.08798	.09382	.09970	.11157
	−20%	.10926	.11497	.12074	.12658	.13246	.14433
30	+40%	.01083	.01662	.02247	.02837	.03430	.04625
	+20%	.04359	.04938	.05523	.06113	.06706	.07901
	0%	.07635	.08214	.08799	.09389	.09982	.11177
	−20%	.10911	.11490	.12075	.12665	.13258	.14453

10% EQUITY YIELD
5 Year Holding Period
70% Loan Ratio

Term In Yrs.	Appr. or Dep.	Interest Rate					
		6%	7%	8%	9%	10%	12%
15	+40%	.00786	.01409	.02042	.02683	.03333	.04656
	+20%	.04062	.04685	.05317	.05959	.06609	.07932
	0%	.07338	.07961	.08593	.09235	.09885	.11208
	−20%	.10614	.11237	.11869	.12511	.13161	.14484
20	+40%	.00735	.01385	.02044	.02712	.03386	.04751
	+20%	.04011	.04661	.05320	.05987	.06662	.08027
	0%	.07287	.07937	.08596	.09263	.09937	.11303
	−20%	.10563	.11213	.11872	.12539	.13213	.14579
25	+40%	.00706	.01372	.02046	.02727	.03413	.04797
	+20%	.03982	.04648	.05322	.06002	.06689	.08073
	0%	.07258	.07924	.08598	.09278	.09964	.11349
	−20%	.10534	.11200	.11874	.12554	.13240	.14625
30	+40%	.00688	.01364	.02047	.02735	.03427	.04821
	+20%	.03964	.04640	.05323	.06011	.06703	.08097
	0%	.07240	.07916	.08599	.09287	.09979	.11373
	−20%	.10516	.11192	.11875	.12563	.13255	.14649

OVER-ALL RATES

10% EQUITY YIELD
5 Year Holding Period
75% Loan Ratio

Term In Yrs.	Appr. or Dep.	Interest Rate					
		6%	7%	8%	9%	10%	12%
15	+40%	.00596	.01263	.01941	.02628	.03325	.04742
	+20%	.03872	.04539	.05217	.05904	.06601	.08018
	0%	.07148	.07815	.08493	.09180	.09877	.11294
	−20%	.10424	.11091	.11769	.12456	.13153	.14570
20	+40%	.00541	.01238	.01944	.02659	.03381	.04844
	+20%	.03817	.04514	.05220	.05935	.06657	.08120
	0%	.07093	.07790	.08496	.09211	.09933	.11396
	−20%	.10369	.11066	.11772	.12487	.13209	.14672
25	+40%	.00511	.01224	.01946	.02675	.03410	.04894
	+20%	.03786	.04500	.05222	.05951	.06686	.08170
	0%	.07062	.07776	.08498	.09227	.09962	.11446
	−20%	.10338	.11052	.11774	.12503	.13238	.14722
30	+40%	.00491	.01215	.01947	.02684	.03426	.04919
	+20%	.03767	.04491	.05223	.05960	.06702	.08195
	0%	.07043	.07767	.08499	.09236	.09978	.11471
	−20%	.10319	.11043	.11775	.12512	.13254	.14747

10% EQUITY YIELD
5 Year Holding Period
80% Loan Ratio

Term In Yrs.	Appr. or Dep.	Interest Rate					
		6%	7%	8%	9%	10%	12%
15	+40%	.00406	.01118	.01840	.02574	.03317	.04828
	+20%	.03682	.04394	.05116	.05850	.06593	.08104
	0%	.06958	.07670	.08392	.09126	.09869	.11380
	−20%	.10234	.10945	.11668	.12402	.13144	.14656
20	+40%	.00348	.01091	.01844	.02606	.03377	.04937
	+20%	.03624	.04367	.05120	.05882	.06653	.08213
	0%	.06900	.07643	.08396	.09158	.09928	.11489
	−20%	.10176	.10918	.11672	.12434	.13204	.14765
25	+40%	.00315	.01076	.01846	.02623	.03407	.04990
	+20%	.03591	.04352	.05122	.05899	.06683	.08266
	0%	.06867	.07628	.08398	.09175	.09959	.11542
	−20%	.10143	.10903	.11674	.12451	.13235	.14818
30	+40%	.00294	.01067	.01847	.02633	.03424	.05017
	+20%	.03570	.04343	.05123	.05909	.06700	.08293
	0%	.06846	.07618	.08399	.09185	.09976	.11569
	−20%	.10122	.10894	.11675	.12461	.13252	.14845

OVER-ALL RATES

10% EQUITY YIELD
5 Year Holding Period
90% Loan Ratio

Term In Yrs.	Appr. or Dep.	Interest Rate					
		6%	7%	8%	9%	10%	12%
15	+40%	.00026	.00826	.01639	.02464	.03300	.05001
	+20%	.03302	.04102	.04915	.05740	.06576	.08276
	0%	.06578	.07378	.08191	.09016	.09852	.11552
	−20%	.09853	.10654	.11467	.12292	.13128	.14828
20	+40%	− .00041	.00796	.01643	.02501	.03368	.05123
	+20%	.03236	.04072	.04919	.05777	.06644	.08399
	0%	.06512	.07348	.08195	.09053	.09919	.11675
	−20%	.09788	.10624	.11471	.12329	.13195	.14951
25	+40%	− .00078	.00779	.01645	.02520	.03402	.05183
	+20%	.03199	.04055	.04921	.05796	.06678	.08459
	0%	.06475	.07331	.08197	.09072	.09954	.11735
	−20%	.09751	.10607	.11473	.12348	.13230	.15011
30	+40%	− .00101	.00769	.01647	.02531	.03421	.05213
	+20%	.03176	.04045	.04922	.05807	.06697	.08489
	0%	.06452	.07321	.08198	.09083	.09973	.11765
	−20%	.09728	.10597	.11474	.12359	.13249	.15041

OVER-ALL RATES

12% EQUITY YIELD
5 Year Holding Period
60% Loan Ratio

Term In Yrs.	Appr. or Dep.	Interest Rate					
		6%	7%	8%	9%	10%	12%
15	+40%	.02314	.02842	.03379	.03924	.04477	.05601
	+20%	.05462	.05991	.06528	.07073	.07625	.08750
	0%	.08610	.09139	.09676	.10221	.10773	.11898
	−20%	.11759	.12287	.12824	.13369	.13921	.15046
20	+40%	.02236	.02788	.03348	.03916	.04489	.05652
	+20%	.05384	.05937	.06497	.07064	.07637	.08800
	0%	.08533	.09085	.09645	.10212	.10786	.11949
	−20%	.11681	.12233	.12793	.13360	.13934	.15097
25	+40%	.02192	.02758	.03332	.03911	.04496	.05677
	+20%	.05340	.05906	.06480	.07059	.07644	.08825
	0%	.08489	.09055	.09628	.10207	.10792	.11973
	−20%	.11637	.12203	.12776	.13356	.13940	.15121
30	+40%	.02165	.02740	.03322	.03908	.04499	.05689
	+20%	.05313	.05888	.06470	.07057	.07647	.08838
	0%	.08461	.09036	.09618	.10205	.10796	.11986
	−20%	.11610	.12185	.12766	.13353	.13944	.15134

12% EQUITY YIELD
5 Year Holding Period
70% Loan Ratio

Term In Yrs.	Appr. or Dep.	Interest Rate					
		6%	7%	8%	9%	10%	12%
15	+40%	.01749	.02366	.02992	.03628	.04272	.05584
	+20%	.04897	.05514	.06140	.06776	.07420	.08732
	0%	.08045	.08662	.09288	.09924	.10569	.11881
	−20%	.11194	.11810	.12437	.13072	.13717	.15029
20	+40%	.01658	.02302	.02956	.03618	.04287	.05644
	+20%	.04807	.05451	.06104	.06766	.07435	.08792
	0%	.07955	.08599	.09252	.09914	.10583	.11940
	−20%	.11103	.11747	.12400	.13062	.13731	.15088
25	+40%	.01607	.02267	.02936	.03612	.04294	.05672
	+20%	.04755	.05415	.06084	.06760	.07442	.08820
	0%	.07903	.08564	.09232	.09909	.10591	.11969
	−20%	.11052	.11712	.12381	.13057	.13739	.15117
30	+40%	.01575	.02246	.02925	.03609	.04298	.05687
	+20%	.04723	.05394	.06073	.06757	.07446	.08835
	0%	.07871	.08542	.09221	.09905	.10595	.11983
	−20%	.11020	.11691	.12369	.13054	.13743	.15132

OVER-ALL RATES

12% EQUITY YIELD
5 Year Holding Period
75% Loan Ratio

Term In Yrs.	Appr. or Dep.	Interest Rate					
		6%	7%	8%	9%	10%	12%
15	+40%	.01467	.02127	.02798	.03479	.04170	.05576
	+20%	.04615	.05275	.05946	.06628	.07318	.08724
	0%	.07763	.08423	.09095	.09776	.10466	.11872
	−20%	.10911	.11572	.12243	.12924	.13614	.15020
20	+40%	.01369	.02059	.02759	.03468	.04185	.05639
	+20%	.04518	.05208	.05908	.06617	.07334	.08787
	0%	.07666	.08356	.09056	.09765	.10482	.11936
	−20%	.10814	.11504	.12204	.12913	.13630	.15084
25	+40%	.01314	.02022	.02738	.03463	.04193	.05670
	+20%	.04462	.05170	.05887	.06611	.07342	.08818
	0%	.07611	.08318	.09035	.09759	.10490	.11966
	−20%	.10759	.11466	.12183	.12907	.13638	.15115
30	+40%	.01280	.01999	.02726	.03459	.04198	.05686
	+20%	.04428	.05147	.05874	.06608	.07346	.08834
	0%	.07577	.08295	.09022	.09756	.10494	.11982
	−20%	.10725	.11444	.12171	.12904	.13642	.15130

12% EQUITY YIELD
5 Year Holding Period
80% Loan Ratio

Term In Yrs.	Appr. or Dep.	Interest Rate					
		6%	7%	8%	9%	10%	12%
15	+40%	.01184	.01889	.02605	.03331	.04068	.05567
	+20%	.04332	.05037	.05753	.06479	.07216	.08715
	0%	.07480	.08185	.08901	.09628	.10364	.11864
	−20%	.10629	.11333	.12049	.12776	.13512	.15012
20	+40%	.01080	.01816	.02563	.03319	.04084	.05635
	+20%	.04229	.04965	.05711	.06468	.07232	.08783
	0%	.07377	.08113	.08859	.09616	.10381	.11931
	−20%	.10525	.11261	.12008	.12764	.13529	.15080
25	+40%	.01022	.01776	.02541	.03313	.04093	.05668
	+20%	.04170	.04925	.05689	.06461	.07241	.08816
	0%	.07318	.08073	.08837	.09610	.10389	.11964
	−20%	.10466	.11221	.11985	.12758	.13537	.15112
30	+40%	.00985	.01752	.02527	.03310	.04097	.05685
	+20%	.04133	.04900	.05676	.06458	.07246	.08833
	0%	.07282	.08048	.08824	.09606	.10394	.11981
	−20%	.10430	.11197	.11972	.12754	.13542	.15129

OVER-ALL RATES

12% EQUITY YIELD
5 Year Holding Period
90% Loan Ratio

Term In Yrs.	Appr. or Dep.	Interest Rate					
		6%	7%	8%	9%	10%	12%
15	+40%	..00619	.01412	.02217	.03034	.03863	.05550
	+20%	.03767	.04560	.05365	.06183	.07011	.08698
	0%	.06915	.07708	.08513	.09331	.10159	.11846
	−20%	.10064	.10856	.11662	.12479	.13308	.14995
20	+40%	.00502	.01330	.02170	.03021	.03882	.05626
	+20%	.03651	.04479	.05319	.06170	.07030	.08775
	0%	.06799	.07627	.08467	.09318	.10178	.11923
	−20%	.09947	.10775	.11615	.12466	.13326	.15071
25	+40%	.00436	.01285	.02145	..03014	.03891	.05663
	+20%	.03585	.04434	.05293	.06163	.07040	.08811
	0%	.06733	.07582	.08442	.09311	.10188	.11960
	−20%	.09881	.10730	.11590	.12459	.13336	.15108
30	+40%	.00395	.01258	.02130	.03010	.03897	.05682
	+20%	.03544	.04406	.05279	.06159	.07045	.08830
	0%	.06692	.07554	.08427	.09307	.10193	.11979
	−20%	.09840	.10703	.11575	.12455	.13341	.15127

OVER-ALL RATES

14% EQUITY YIELD
5 Year Holding Period
60% Loan Ratio

Term In Yrs.	Appr. or Dep.	Interest Rate					
		6%	7%	8%	9%	10%	12%
15	+40%	.03447	.03971	.04503	.05043	.05590	.06707
	+20%	.06473	.06996	.07528	.08068	.08616	.09732
	0%	.09499	.10022	.10554	.11094	.11642	.12758
	−20%	.12524	.13048	.13580	.14120	.14667	.15784
20	+40%	.03337	.03884	.04439	.05002	.05572	.06728
	+20%	.06363	.06910	.07465	.08028	.08597	.09753
	0%	.09388	.09935	.10491	.11054	.11623	.12779
	−20%	.12414	.12961	.13516	.14079	.14649	.15805
25	+40%	.03274	.03836	.04405	.04981	.05562	.06738
	+20%	.06300	.06861	.07431	.08006	.08588	.09764
	0%	.09326	.09887	.10456	.11032	.11613	.12789
	−20%	.12351	.12913	.13482	.14058	.14639	.15815
30	+40%	.03236	.03807	.04385	.04969	.05557	.06743
	+20%	.06261	.06832	.07410	.07994	.08582	.09769
	0%	.09287	.09858	.10436	.11020	.11608	.12794
	−20%	.12313	.12884	.13462	.14046	.14634	.15820

14% EQUITY YIELD
5 Year Holding Period
70% Loan Ratio

Term In Yrs.	Appr. or Dep.	Interest Rate					
		6%	7%	8%	9%	10%	12%
15	+40%	.02697	.03307	.03928	.04558	.05197	.06499
	+20%	.05723	.06333	.06954	.07584	.08223	.09525
	0%	.08748	.09359	.09979	.10610	.11249	.12551
	−20%	.11774	.12384	.13005	.13635	.14274	.15576
20	+40%	.02568	.03206	.03854	.04511	.05175	.06524
	+20%	.05594	.06232	.06880	.07537	.08201	.09550
	0%	.08619	.09258	.09906	.10562	.11227	.12575
	−20%	.11645	.12283	.12931	.13588	.14252	.15601
25	+40%	.02495	.03150	.03814	.04486	.05164	.06536
	+20%	.05521	.06176	.06840	.07512	.08190	.09562
	0%	.08547	.09202	.09866	.10537	.11216	.12587
	−20%	.11572	.12227	.12891	.13563	.14241	.15613
30	+40%	.02450	.03116	.03791	.04472	.05158	.06542
	+20%	.05476	.06142	.06816	.07497	.08184	.09568
	0%	.08501	.09168	.09842	.10523	.11209	.12593
	−20%	.11527	.12193	.12868	.13549	.14235	.15619

OVER-ALL RATES

14% EQUITY YIELD
5 Year Holding Period
75% Loan Ratio

Term In Yrs.	Appr. or Dep.	Interest Rate					
		6%	7%	8%	9%	10%	12%
15	+40%	.02322	.02976	.03641	.04316	.05001	.06396
	+20%	.05348	.06002	.06667	.07342	.08026	.09422
	0%	.08373	.09027	.09692	.10367	.11052	.12447
	−20%	.11399	.12053	.12718	.13393	.14078	.15473
20	+40%	.02184	.02868	.03562	.04265	.04977	.06422
	+20%	.05209	.05893	.06587	.07291	.08003	.09448
	0%	.08235	.08919	.09613	.10317	.11029	.12474
	−20%	.11261	.11945	.12639	.13342	.14054	.15499
25	+40%	.02106	.02807	.03519	.04239	.04965	.06435
	+20%	.05131	.05833	.06545	.07264	.07991	.09461
	0%	.08157	.08859	.09570	.10290	.11017	.12486
	−20%	.11183	.11884	.12596	.13316	.14042	.15512
30	+40%	.02057	.02771	.03494	.04223	.04959	.06442
	+20%	.05083	.05797	.06519	.07249	.07984	.09467
	0%	.08108	.08822	.09545	.10275	.11010	.12493
	−20%	.11134	.11848	.12571	.13300	.14036	.15519

14% EQUITY YIELD
5 Year Holding Period
80% Loan Ratio

Term In Yrs.	Appr. or Dep.	Interest Rate					
		6%	7%	8%	9%	10%	12%
15	+40%	.01947	.02644	.03354	.04074	.04804	.06292
	+20%	.04972	.05670	.06379	.07100	.07830	.09318
	0%	.07998	.08696	.09405	.10125	.10856	.12344
	−20%	.11024	.11721	.12431	.13151	.13881	.15369
20	+40%	.01799	.02529	.03269	.04020	.04779	.06320
	+20%	.04825	.05554	.06295	.07045	.07805	.09346
	0%	.07851	.08580	.09321	.11071	.10831	.12372
	−20%	.10876	.11606	.12346	.13097	.13856	.15397
25	+40%	.01716	.02465	.03224	.03991	.04766	.06334
	+20%	.04742	.05490	.06249	.07017	.07792	.09360
	0%	.07767	.08516	.09275	.10043	.10818	.12385
	−20%	.10793	.11542	.12301	.13068	.13843	.15411
30	+40%	.01664	.02426	.03197	.03975	.04759	.06341
	+20%	.04690	.05452	.06222	.07001	.07785	.09367
	0%	.07716	.08477	.09248	.10026	.10811	.12392
	−20%	.10741	.11503	.12274	.13052	.13836	.15418

OVER-ALL RATES

14% EQUITY YIELD
5 Year Holding Period
90% Loan Ratio

Term In Yrs.	Appr. or Dep.	Interest Rate					
		6%	7%	8%	9%	10%	12%
15	+40%	.01196	.01981	.02779	.03589	.04411	.06085
	+20%	.04222	.05007	.05805	.06615	.07437	.09111
	0%	.07248	.08033	.08831	.09641	.10462	.12137
	−20%	.10273	.11058	.11856	.12666	.13488	.15162
20	+40%	.01031	.01851	.02684	.03529	.04383	.06117
	+20%	.04056	.04877	.05710	.06554	.07409	.09143
	0%	.07082	.07903	.08736	.09580	.10434	.12168
	−20%	.10108	.10928	.11761	.12606	.13460	.15194
25	+40%	.00937	.01779	.02633	.03497	.04369	.06132
	+20%	.03963	.04805	.05659	.06552	.07394	.09158
	0%	.06988	.07830	.08684	.09548	.10420	.12184
	−20%	.10014	.10856	.11710	.12574	.13446	.15209
30	+40%	.00879	.01735	.02603	.03478	.04360	.06140
	+20%	.03904	.04761	.05628	.06504	.07386	.09166
	0%	.06930	.07787	.08654	.09530	.10412	.12191
	−20%	.09956	.10812	.11680	.12555	.13438	.15217

OVER-ALL RATES

15% EQUITY YIELD
5 Year Holding Period
60% Loan Ratio

Term In Yrs.	Appr. or Dep.	Interest Rate					
		6%	7%	8%	9%	10%	12%
15	+40%	.04009	.04529	.05059	.05597	.06142	.07254
	+20%	.06975	.07496	.08025	.08563	.09109	.10221
	0%	.09941	.10462	.10992	.11530	.12075	.13187
	−20%	.12908	.13428	.13958	.14496	.15041	.16153
20	+40%	.03882	.04427	.04980	.05541	.06109	.07261
	+20%	.06849	.07393	.07947	.08507	.09075	.10227
	0%	.09815	.10360	.10913	.11474	.12041	.13194
	−20%	.12781	.13326	.13879	.14440	.15008	.16160
25	+40%	.03811	.04370	.04937	.05511	.06091	.07264
	+20%	.06777	.07337	.07904	.08478	.09058	.10231
	0%	.09744	.10303	.10870	.11444	.12024	.13197
	−20%	.12710	.13269	.13836	.14410	.14990	.16163
30	+40%	.03767	.04336	.04912	.05495	.06082	.07266
	+20%	.06733	.07302	.07879	.08461	.09048	.10232
	0%	.09699	.10269	.10845	.11427	.12014	.13199
	−20%	.12666	.13235	.13811	.14394	.14981	.16165

15% EQUITY YIELD
5 Year Holding Period
70% Loan Ratio

Term In Yrs.	Appr. or Dep.	Interest Rate					
		6%	7%	8%	9%	10%	12%
15	+40%	.03166	.03773	.04391	.05018	.05655	.06952
	+20%	.06132	.06739	.07357	.07985	.08621	.09918
	0%	.09098	.09706	.10324	.10951	.11588	.12885
	−20%	.12065	.12672	.13290	.13917	.14554	.15851
20	+40%	.03018	.03654	.04299	.04953	.05615	.06960
	+20%	.05985	.06620	.07265	.07919	.08582	.09926
	0%	.08951	.09586	.10232	.10886	.11548	.12893
	−20%	.11917	.12553	.13198	.13852	.14514	.15859
25	+40%	.02935	.03587	.04249	.04919	.05595	.06964
	+20%	.05901	.06554	.07215	.07885	.08561	.09930
	0%	.08867	.09520	.10182	.10851	.11528	.12896
	−20%	.11834	.12486	.13148	.13818	.14494	.15863
30	+40%	.02883	.03547	.04220	.04899	.05584	.06966
	+20%	.05849	.06514	.07186	.07865	.08550	.09932
	0%	.08816	.09480	.10152	.10832	.11516	.12898
	−20%	.11782	.12446	.13119	.13798	.14483	.15865

OVER-ALL RATES

15% EQUITY YIELD
5 Year Holding Period
75% Loan Ratio

Term In Yrs.	Appr. or Dep.	Interest Rate					
		6%	7%	8%	9%	10%	12%
15	+40%	.02744	.03395	.04057	.04729	.05411	.06801
	+20%	.05710	.06361	.07023	.07695	.08377	.09767
	0%	.08677	.09327	.09989	.10662	.11344	.12734
	−20%	.11643	.12294	.12956	.13628	.14310	.15700
20	+40%	.02586	.03267	.03958	.04659	.05369	.06809
	+20%	.05552	.06233	.06925	.07626	.08335	.09776
	0%	.08519	.09199	.09891	.10592	.11301	.12742
	−20%	.11485	.12166	.12857	.13558	.14268	.15708
25	+40%	.02497	.03196	.03905	.04622	.05347	.06813
	+20%	.05463	.06162	.06871	.07589	.08313	.09780
	0%	.08429	.09128	.09837	.10555	.11280	.12746
	−20%	.11396	.12095	.12804	.13521	.14246	.15712
30	+40%	.02441	.03153	.03873	.04601	.05335	.06816
	+20%	.05408	.06119	.06840	.07568	.08301	.09782
	0%	.08374	.09085	.09806	.10534	.11268	.12748
	−20%	.11340	.12052	.12772	.13500	.14234	.15714

15% EQUITY YIELD
5 Year Holding Period
80% Loan Ratio

Term In Yrs.	Appr. or Dep.	Interest Rate					
		6%	7%	8%	9%	10%	12%
15	+40%	.02322	.03017	.03723	.04440	.05167	.06650
	+20%	.05289	.05983	.06689	.07406	.08134	.09616
	0%	.08255	.08949	.09655	.10373	.11100	.12582
	−20%	.11221	.11916	.12622	.13339	.14066	.15549
20	+40%	.02154	.02880	.03618	.04365	.05122	.06659
	+20%	.05120	.05846	.06584	.07332	.08088	.09625
	0%	.08087	.08813	.09550	.10298	.11055	.12591
	−20%	.11053	.11779	.12517	.13264	.14021	.15558
25	+40%	.02059	.02804	.03561	.04326	.05099	.06663
	+20%	.05025	.05771	.06527	.07292	.08065	.09629
	0%	.07991	.08737	.09493	.10259	.11032	.12596
	−20%	.10958	.11703	.12460	.13225	.13998	.15562
30	+40%	.01999	.02759	.03527	.04303	.05086	.06665
	+20%	.04966	.05725	.06493	.07270	.08052	.09632
	0%	.07932	.08691	.09460	.10236	.11019	.12598
	−20%	.10898	.11657	.12426	.13202	.13985	.15564

OVER-ALL RATES

15% EQUITY YIELD
5 Year Holding Period
90% Loan Ratio

Term In Yrs.	Appr. or Dep.	Interest Rate					
		6%	7%	8%	9%	10%	12%
15	+40%	.01479	.02260	.03055	.03861	.04680	.06348
	+20%	.04445	.05227	.06021	.06828	.07646	.09314
	0%	.07412	.08193	.08987	.09794	.10612	.12280
	−20%	.10378	.11159	.11954	.12760	.13579	.15247
20	+40%	.01290	.02107	.02936	.03778	.04629	.06358
	+20%	.04256	.05073	.05903	.06744	.07595	.09324
	0%	.07222	.08039	.08869	.09710	.10562	.12290
	−20%	.10189	.11006	.11835	.12676	.13528	.15257
25	+40%	.01182	.02021	.02872	.03733	.04603	.06363
	+20%	.04149	.04988	.05839	.06700	.07569	.09329
	0%	.07115	.07954	.08805	.09666	.10535	.12295
	−20%	.10081	.10920	.11771	.12632	.13502	.15261
30	+40%	.01116	.01970	.02834	.03708	.04588	.06365
	+20%	.04082	.04936	.05801	.06674	.07555	.09331
	0%	.07049	.07902	.08767	.09641	.10521	.12298
	−20%	.10015	.10869	.11733	.12607	.13487	.15264

OVER-ALL RATES

16% EQUITY YIELD
5 Year Holding Period
60% Loan Ratio

Term In Yrs.	Appr. or Dep.	Interest Rate					
		6%	7%	8%	9%	10%	12%
15	+40%	.04567	.05085	.05612	.06148	.06691	.07799
	+20%	.07475	.07993	.08521	.09056	.09599	.10707
	0%	.10383	.10901	.11429	.11964	.12508	.13615
	−20%	.13291	.13810	.14337	.14872	.15416	.16524
20	+40%	.04425	.04967	.05518	.06077	.06643	.07792
	+20%	.07333	.07875	.08426	.08985	.09551	.10700
	0%	.10241	.10784	.11335	.11893	.12459	.13608
	−20%	.13150	.13692	.14243	.14802	.15367	.16516
25	+40%	.04345	.04902	.05467	.06039	.06618	.07788
	+20%	.07253	.07810	.08375	.08948	.09526	.10696
	0%	.10161	.10718	.11284	.11856	.12434	.13605
	−20%	.13069	.13626	.14192	.14764	.15342	.16513
30	+40%	.04295	.04862	.05437	.06018	.06604	.07786
	+20%	.07203	.07771	.08345	.08926	.09512	.10694
	0%	.10111	.10679	.11254	.11834	.12420	.13603
	−20%	.13020	.13587	.14162	.14743	.15328	.16511

16% EQUITY YIELD
5 Year Holding Period
70% Loan Ratio

Term In Years	Appr. or Dep.	Interest Rate					
		6%	7%	8%	9%	10%	12%
15	+40%	.03631	.04235	.04850	.05475	.06109	.07402
	+20%	.06539	.07143	.07759	.08383	.09017	.10310
	0%	.09447	.10052	.10667	.11292	.11926	.13218
	−20%	.12355	.12960	.13575	.14200	.14834	.16126
20	+40%	.03465	.04098	.04741	.05392	.06052	.07393
	+20%	.06373	.07006	.07649	.08301	.08961	.10301
	0%	.09282	.09914	.10557	.11209	.11869	.13209
	−20%	.12190	.12822	.13465	.14117	.14777	.16118
25	+40%	.03372	.04022	.04681	.05349	.06023	.07389
	+20%	.06280	.06930	.07589	.08257	.08931	.10297
	0%	.09188	.09838	.10497	.11165	.11840	.13205
	−20%	.12096	.12746	.13406	.14073	.14748	.16113
30	+40%	.03313	.03975	.04646	.05324	.06007	.07387
	+20%	.06222	.06884	.07554	.08232	.08915	.10295
	0%	.09130	.09792	.10462	.11140	.11823	.13203
	−20%	.12038	.12700	.13371	.14048	.14732	.16111

OVER-ALL RATES

16% EQUITY YIELD
5 Year Holding Period
75% Loan Ratio

Term In Yrs.	Appr. or Dep.	Interest Rate					
		6%	7%	8%	9%	10%	12%
15	+40%	.03163	.03810	.04469	.05139	.05818	.07203
	+20%	.06071	.06719	.07378	.08047	.08726	.10111
	0%	.08979	.09627	.10286	.10955	.11634	.13019
	−20%	.11887	.12535	.13194	.13863	.14543	.15927
20	+40%	.02985	.03663	.04352	.05050	.05757	.07194
	+20%	.05893	.06571	.07260	.07958	.08665	.10102
	0%	.08802	.09479	.10168	.10867	.11574	.13010
	−20%	.11710	.12388	.13076	.13775	.14482	.15918
25	+40%	.02885	.03581	.04288	.05003	.05726	.07189
	+20%	.05793	.06490	.07196	.07911	.08634	.10097
	0%	.08701	.09398	.10104	.10820	.11542	.13006
	−20%	.11609	.12306	.13013	.13728	.14451	.15914
30	+40%	.02823	.03532	.04250	.04976	.05709	.07187
	+20%	.05731	.06440	.07159	.07885	.08617	.10095
	0%	.08639	.09348	.10067	.10793	.11525	.13003
	−20%	.11547	.12256	.12975	.13701	.14433	.15911

16% EQUITY YIELD
5 Year Holding Period
80% Loan Ratio

Terms In Yrs.	Appr. or Dep.	Interest Rate					
		6%	7%	8%	9%	10%	12%
15	+40%	.02694	.03385	.04088	.04802	.05527	.07004
	+20%	.05603	.06294	.06997	.07711	.08435	.09912
	0%	.08511	.09202	.09905	.10619	.11343	.12820
	−20%	.11419	.12110	.12813	.13527	.14252	.15729
20	+40%	.02505	.03228	.03963	.04708	.05462	.06994
	+20%	.05414	.06136	.06871	.07616	.08370	.09902
	0%	.08322	.09045	.09779	.10524	.11279	.12811
	−20%	.11230	.11953	.12687	.13432	.14187	.15719
25	+40%	.02398	.03141	.03895	.04658	.05429	.06989
	+20%	.05306	.06049	.06803	.07566	.08337	.09898
	0%	.08215	.08958	.09711	.10474	.11245	.12806
	−20%	.11123	.11866	.12619	.13382	.14153	.15714
30	+40%	.02332	.03088	.03855	.04629	.05410	.06987
	+20%	.05240	.05997	.06763	.07537	.08319	.09895
	0%	.08148	.08905	.09671	.10446	.11227	.12803
	−20%	.11056	.11813	.12579	.13354	.14135	.15712

OVER-ALL RATES

16% EQUITY YIELD
5 Year Holding Period
90% Loan Ratio

Term In Yrs.	Appr. or Dep.	Interest Rate					
		6%	7%	8%	9%	10%	12%
15	+40%	.01758	.02536	.03326	.04130	.04945	.06607
	+20%	.04666	.05444	.06235	.07038	.07853	.09515
	0%	.07575	.08352	.09143	.09946	.10761	.12423
	−20%	.10483	.11260	.12051	.12854	.13669	.15331
20	+40%	.01545	.02359	.03185	.04023	.04872	.06595
	+20%	.04454	.05267	.06093	.06932	.07780	.09504
	0%	.07362	.08175	.09002	.09840	.10688	.12412
	−20%	.10270	.11083	.11910	.12748	.13596	.15320
25	+40%	.01425	.02261	.03109	.03967	.04834	.06590
	+20%	.04333	.05169	.06017	.06875	.07743	.09498
	0%	.07241	.08077	.08925	.09783	.10651	.12407
	−20%	.10150	.10985	.11833	.12692	.13559	.15315
30	+40%	.01350	.02201	.03064	.03935	.04814	.06587
	+20%	.04259	.05110	.05972	.06843	.07722	.09496
	0%	.07167	.08018	.08880	.09751	.10630	.12404
	−20%	.10075	.10926	.11788	.12660	.13538	.15312

OVER-ALL RATES

20% EQUITY YIELD
5 Year Holding Period
60% Loan Ratio

Term In Yrs.	Appr. or Dep.	Interest Rate					
		6%	7%	8%	9%	10%	12%
15	+40%	.06767	.07276	.07794	.08321	.08856	.09948
	+20%	.09454	.09963	.10482	.11009	.11544	.12636
	0%	.12142	.12651	.13169	.13696	.14231	.15324
	−20%	.14830	.15339	.15857	.16384	.16919	.18011
20	+40%	.06566	.07099	.07642	.08193	.08751	.09888
	+20%	.09254	.09787	.10330	.10880	.11439	.12575
	0%	.11941	.12475	.13017	.13568	.14126	.15263
	−20%	.14629	.15162	.15705	.16256	.16814	.17950
25	+40%	.06453	.07002	.07560	.08125	.08697	.09858
	+20%	.09140	.09689	.10247	.10813	.11385	.12546
	0%	.11828	.12377	.12935	.13500	.14073	.15233
	−20%	.14515	.15064	.15622	.16188	.16760	.17921
30	+40%	.06382	.06942	.07511	.08086	.08668	.09843
	+20%	.09070	.09630	.10199	.10774	.11355	.12531
	0%	.11757	.12318	.12886	.13462	.14043	.15218
	−20%	.14445	.15005	.15574	.16149	.16730	.17906

20% EQUITY YIELD
5 Year Holding Period
70% Loan Ratio

Term In Yrs.	Appr. or Dep.	Interest Rate					
		6%	7%	8%	9%	10%	12%
15	+40%	.05457	.06051	.06655	.07270	.07895	.09169
	+20%	.08145	.08738	.09343	.09958	.10582	.11857
	0%	.10832	.11426	.12031	.12645	.13270	.14544
	−20%	.13520	.14114	.14718	.15333	.15957	.17232
20	+40%	.05223	.05845	.06478	.07121	.07772	.09098
	+20%	.07911	.08533	.09166	.09808	.10460	.11786
	0%	.10598	.11220	.11853	.12496	.13147	.14473
	−20%	.13286	.13908	.14541	.15184	.15835	.17161
25	+40%	.05090	.05731	.06382	.07042	.07709	.09064
	+20%	.07778	.08419	.09069	.09729	.10397	.11751
	0%	.10466	.11106	.11757	.12417	.13085	.14439
	−20%	.13153	.13794	.14445	.15105	.15772	.17126
30	+40%	.05008	.05662	.06325	.06997	.07675	.09046
	+20%	.07696	.08349	.09013	.09684	.10362	.11733
	0%	.10383	.11037	.11700	.12372	.13050	.14421
	−20%	.13071	.13725	.14388	.15059	.15738	.17109

OVER-ALL RATES

20% EQUITY YIELD
5 Year Holding Period
75% Loan Ratio

Term In Yrs.	Appr. or Dep.	Interest Rate					
		6%	7%	8%	9%	10%	12%
15	+40%	.04802	.05438	.06086	.06745	.07414	.08779
	+20%	.07490	.08126	.08774	.09433	.10101	.11467
	0%	.10177	.10814	.11461	.12120	.12789	.14154
	−20%	.12865	.13501	.14149	.14808	.15477	.16842
20	+40%	.04551	.05218	.05896	.06585	.07283	.08703
	+20%	.07239	.07906	.08584	.09272	.09970	.11391
	0%	.09927	.10593	.11271	.11960	.12658	.14078
	−20%	.12614	.13281	.13959	.14648	.15346	.16766
25	+40%	.04409	.05096	.05793	.06500	.07215	.08666
	+20%	.07097	.07783	.08481	.09188	.09903	.11354
	0%	.09785	.10471	.11168	.11875	.12591	.14041
	−20%	.12472	.13158	.13856	.14563	.15278	.16729
30	+40%	.04321	.05022	.05732	.06452	.07178	.08647
	+20%	.07009	.07009	.08420	.09139	.09866	.11335
	0%	.09696	.10397	.11108	.11827	.12553	.14023
	−20%	.12384	.13084	.13795	.14515	.15241	.16710

20% EQUITY YIELD
5 Year Holding Period
80% Loan Ratio

Term In Yrs.	Appr. or Dep.	Interest Rate					
		6%	7%	8%	9%	10%	12%
15	+40%	.04147	.04826	.05517	.06220	.06933	.08390
	+20%	.06835	.07513	.08205	.08907	.09621	.11077
	0%	.09522	.10201	.10892	.11595	.12308	.13765
	−20%	.12210	.12889	.13580	.14282	.14996	.16452
20	+40%	.03880	.04591	.05314	.06049	.06793	.08308
	+20%	.06567	.07278	.08002	.08736	.09481	.10996
	0%	.09255	.09966	.10689	.11424	.12168	.13683
	−20%	.11943	.12654	.13377	.14111	.14856	.16371
25	+40%	.03728	.04460	.05204	.05958	.06721	.08269
	+20%	.06416	.07148	.07892	.08646	.09409	.10957
	0%	.09104	.09836	.10579	.11334	.12097	.13644
	−20%	.11791	.12523	.13267	.14021	.14784	.16332
30	+40%	.03634	.04381	.05139	.05907	.06682	.08249
	+20%	.06322	.07069	.07827	.08594	.09369	.10936
	0%	.09010	.09757	.10515	.11282	.12057	.13624
	−20%	.11697	.12444	.13202	.13970	.14745	.16312

OVER-ALL RATES

20% EQUITY YIELD
5 Year Holding Period
90% Loan Ratio

Term In Yrs.	Appr. or Dep.	Interest Rate					
		6%	7%	8%	9%	10%	12%
15	+40%	.02838	.03601	.04378	.05169	.05971	.07610
	+20%	.05525	.06289	.07066	.07856	.08659	.10298
	0%	.08213	.08976	.09754	.10544	.11347	.12985
	−20%	.10900	.11664	.12441	.13232	.14034	.15673
20	+40%	.02537	.03336	.04150	.04977	.05814	.07519
	+20%	.05224	.06024	.06838	.07664	.08502	.10206
	0%	.07912	.08712	.09525	.10352	.11189	.12894
	−20%	.10599	.11399	.12213	.13039	.13877	.15581
25	+40%	.02366	.03190	.04027	.04875	.05733	.07474
	+20%	.05054	.05877	.06714	.07563	.08421	.10162
	0%	.07741	.08565	.09402	.10250	.11109	.12850
	−20%	.10429	.11252	.12089	.12938	.13796	.15537
30	+40%	.02260	.03101	.03954	.04817	.05689	.07452
	+20%	.04948	.05788	.06641	.07505	.08376	.10139
	0%	.07636	.08476	.09329	.10192	.11064	.12827
	−20%	.10323	.11164	.12017	.12880	.13752	.15515

OVER-ALL RATES

10% EQUITY YIELD
10 Year Holding Period
60% Loan Ratio

Term In Yrs.	Appr. or Dep.	Interest Rate					
		6%	7%	8%	9%	10%	12%
15	+40%	.05445	.05906	.06381	.06868	.07367	.08398
	+20%	.06700	.07161	.07636	.08123	.08622	.09653
	0%	.07955	.08416	.08891	.09378	.09877	.10908
	−20%	.09210	.09671	.10146	.10633	.11132	.12163
20	+40%	.05314	.05822	.06344	.06878	.07423	.08543
	+20%	.06569	.07077	.07599	.08133	.08678	.09798
	0%	.07824	.08332	.08854	.09388	.09933	.11053
	−20%	.09078	.09587	.10109	.10643	.11188	.12308
25	+40%	.05239	.05775	.06324	.06883	.07452	.08613
	+20%	.06494	.07030	.07579	.08138	.08707	.09868
	0%	.07749	.08285	.08833	.09393	.09962	.11123
	−20%	.09004	.09540	.10088	.10648	.11217	.12378
30	+40%	.05193	.05747	.06312	.06886	.07468	.08649
	+20%	.06448	.07002	.07567	.08141	.08723	.09904
	0%	.07703	.08257	.08822	.09396	.09978	.11159
	−20%	.08958	.09512	.10076	.10651	.11233	.12414

10% EQUITY YIELD
10 Year Holding Period
70% Loan Ratio

Term In Yrs.	Appr. or Dep.	Interest Rate					
		6%	7%	8%	9%	10%	12%
15	+40%	.05104	.05642	.06196	.06764	.07347	.08550
	+20%	.06359	.06897	.07451	.08019	.08602	.09805
	0%	.07614	.08152	.08706	.09274	.09856	.11060
	−20%	.08869	.09407	.09961	.10529	.11111	.12314
20	+40%	.04951	.05544	.06153	.06776	.07412	.08719
	+20%	.06206	.06799	.07408	.08031	.08667	.09973
	0%	.07461	.08054	.08662	.09286	.09922	.11228
	−20%	.08716	.09309	.09917	.10541	.11177	.12483
25	+40%	.04864	.05489	.06129	.06782	.07446	.08800
	+20%	.06119	.06744	.07384	.08037	.08701	.10055
	0%	.07374	.07999	.08639	.09292	.09956	.11310
	−20%	.08629	.09254	.09894	.10547	.11210	.12565
30	+40%	.04810	.05456	.06115	.06785	.07464	.08842
	+20%	.06065	.06711	.07370	.08040	.08719	.10097
	0%	.07320	.07966	.08625	.09295	.09974	.11352
	−20%	.08575	.09221	.09880	.10550	.11229	.12607

OVER-ALL RATES

10% EQUITY YIELD
10 Year Holding Period
75% Loan Ratio

Term In Yrs.	Appr. or Dep.	Interest Rate					
		6%	7%	8%	9%	10%	12%
15	+40%	.04934	.05510	.06104	.06713	.07336	.08625
	+20%	.06189	.06765	.07359	.07967	.08591	.09880
	0%	.07443	.08020	.08613	.09222	.09846	.11135
	−20%	.08698	.09275	.09868	.10477	.11101	.12390
20	+40%	.04769	.05405	.06057	.06725	.07406	.08806
	+20%	.06024	.06660	.07312	.07980	.08661	.10061
	0%	.07279	.07915	.08567	.09235	.09916	.11316
	−20%	.08534	.09170	.09822	.10489	.11171	.12571
25	+40%	.04677	.05346	.06032	.06731	.07443	.08894
	+20%	.05932	.06601	.07287	.07986	.08697	.10148
	0%	.07186	.07856	.08542	.09241	.09952	.11403
	−20%	.08441	.09111	.09797	.10496	.11207	.12658
30	+40%	.04619	.05311	.06017	.06735	.07462	.08939
	+20%	.05874	.06566	.07272	.07990	.08717	.10193
	0%	.07129	.07821	.08527	.09245	.09972	.11448
	−20%	.08384	.09076	.09782	.10500	.11227	.12703

10% EQUITY YIELD
10 Year Holding Period
80% Loan Ratio

Term In Yrs.	Appr. or Dep.	Interest Rate					
		6%	7%	8%	9%	10%	12%
15	+40%	.04763	.05378	.06011	.06661	.07326	.08701
	+20%	.06018	.06633	.07266	.07916	.08581	.09956
	0%	.07273	.07888	.08521	.09171	.09836	.11211
	−20%	.08528	.09143	.09776	.10425	.11091	.12466
20	+40%	.04588	.05266	.05961	.06674	.07401	.08894
	+20%	.05843	.06521	.07216	.07929	.08656	.10149
	0%	.07098	.07776	.08471	.09184	.09911	.11404
	−20%	.08353	.09030	.09726	.10438	.11166	.12659
25	+40%	.04489	.05203	.05935	.06681	.07439	.08987
	+20%	.05744	.06458	.07189	.07936	.08694	.10242
	0%	.06999	.07713	.08444	.09190	.09949	.11497
	−20%	.08254	.08968	.09699	.10445	.11204	.12752
30	+40%	.04428	.05165	.05919	.06685	.07461	.09035
	+20%	.05682	.06420	.07174	.07939	.08715	.10290
	0%	.06937	.07675	.08429	.09194	.09970	.11545
	−20%	.08192	.08930	.09683	.10449	.11225	.12800

OVER-ALL RATES

10% EQUITY YIELD
10 Year Holding Period
90% Loan Ratio

Term In Yrs.	Appr. or Dep.	Interest Rate					
		6%	7%	8%	9%	10%	12%
15	+40%	.04422	.05114	.05826	.06557	.07305	.08852
	+20%	.05677	.06369	.07081	.07812	.08560	.10107
	0%	.06932	.07624	.08336	.09067	.09815	.11362
	−20%	.08187	.08879	.09591	.10322	.11070	.12617
20	+40%	.04225	.04988	.05770	.06572	.07390	.09069
	+20%	.05480	.06243	.07025	.07826	.08645	.10324
	0%	.06735	.07497	.08280	.09081	.09899	.11579
	−20%	.07990	.08752	.09535	.10336	.11154	.12834
25	+40%	.04114	.04917	.05740	.06579	.07433	.09174
	+20%	.05369	.06172	.06995	.07834	.08688	.10429
	0%	.06624	.07427	.08250	.09089	.09943	.11684
	−20%	.07878	.08682	.09505	.10344	.11198	.12939
30	+40%	.04045	.04875	.05722	.06584	.07457	.09228
	+20%	.05300	.06130	.06977	.07839	.08712	.10483
	0%	.06554	.07385	.08232	.09094	.09967	.11738
	−20%	.07809	.08640	.09487	.10348	.11221	.12993

OVER-ALL RATES

12% EQUITY YIELD
10 Year Holding Period
60% Loan Ratio

Term In Yrs.	Appr. or Dep.	Interest Rate					
		6%	7%	8%	9%	10%	12%
15	+40%	.06670	.07126	.07594	.08075	.08569	.09588
	+20%	.07810	.08265	.08734	.09215	.09708	.10728
	0%	.08950	.09405	.09874	.10355	.10848	.11867
	−20%	.10089	.10545	.11013	.11494	.11988	.13007
20	+40%	.06467	.06967	.07482	.08009	.08547	.09654
	+20%	.07606	.08107	.08621	.09148	.09687	.10794
	0%	.08746	.09247	.09761	.10288	.10826	.11933
	−20%	.09886	.10386	.10901	.11428	.11966	.13073
25	+40%	.06352	.06879	.07421	.07973	.08536	.09686
	+20%	.07491	.08019	.08560	.09113	.09676	.10825
	0%	.08631	.09159	.09700	.10253	.10815	.11965
	−20%	.09771	.10299	.10840	.11392	.11955	.13105
30	+40%	.06280	.06826	.07385	.07953	.08530	.09702
	+20%	.07420	.07966	.08524	.09093	.09670	.10842
	0%	.08560	.09106	.09664	.10232	.10809	.11982
	−20%	.09699	.10245	.10804	.11372	.11949	.13121

12% EQUITY YIELD
10 Year Holding Period
70% Loan Ratio

Term In Yrs.	Appr. or Dep.	Interest Rate					
		6%	7%	8%	9%	10%	12%
15	+40%	.06162	.06693	.07240	.07801	.08376	.09566
	+20%	.07301	.07833	.08379	.08941	.09516	.10706
	0%	.08441	.08972	.09519	.10080	.10656	.11845
	−20%	.09581	.10112	.10659	.11220	.11795	.12985
20	+40%	.05924	.06508	.07108	.07723	.08351	.09643
	+20%	.07064	.07648	.08248	.08863	.09491	.10782
	0%	.08204	.08788	.09388	.10003	.10631	.11922
	−20%	.09343	.09927	.10527	.11142	.11770	.13062
25	+40%	.05790	.06406	.07037	.07682	.08338	.09680
	+20%	.06930	.07546	.08177	.08822	.09478	.10820
	0%	.08069	.08685	.09316	.09961	.10618	.11959
	−20%	.09209	.09825	.10456	.11101	.11757	.13099
30	+40%	.05707	.06344	.06995	.07658	.08331	.09699
	+20%	.06846	.07483	.08135	.08798	.09471	.10839
	0%	.07986	.08623	.09275	.09938	.10611	.11978
	−20%	.09126	.09763	.10414	.11077	.11750	.13118

OVER-ALL RATES

12% EQUITY YIELD
10 Year Holding Period
75% Loan Ratio

Term In Yrs.	Appr. or Dep.	Interest Rate					
		6%	7%	8%	9%	10%	12%
15	+40%	.05908	.06477	.07063	.07664	.08280	.09555
	+20%	.07047	.07617	.08202	.08804	.09420	.10694
	0%	.08187	.08756	.09342	.09943	.10560	.11834
	−20%	.09327	.09896	.10482	.11083	.11699	.12974
20	+40%	.05653	.06279	.06922	.07580	.08253	.09637
	+20%	.06793	.07419	.08061	.08720	.09393	.10777
	0%	.07933	.08558	.09201	.09860	.10533	.11917
	−20%	.09072	.09698	.10341	.10999	.11673	.13056
25	+40%	.05509	.06169	.06845	.07536	.08240	.09677
	+20%	.06649	.07309	.07985	.08676	.09379	.10817
	0%	.07789	.08448	.09125	.09816	.10519	.11956
	−20%	.08928	.09588	.10264	.10955	.11659	.13096
30	+40%	.05420	.06103	.06800	.07511	.08232	.09697
	+20%	.06560	.07242	.07940	.08651	.09372	.10837
	0%	.07699	.08382	.09080	.09790	.10511	.11977
	−20%	.08839	.09522	.10219	.10930	.11651	.13116

12% EQUITY YIELD
10 Year Holding Period
80% Loan Ratio

Term In Yrs.	Appr. or Dep.	Interest Rate					
		6%	7%	8%	9%	10%	12%
15	+40%	.05653	.06261	.06885	.07527	.08184	.09544
	+20%	.06793	.07400	.08025	.08667	.09324	.10683
	0%	.07933	.08540	.09165	.09806	.10464	.11823
	−20%	.09072	.09680	.10304	.10946	.11603	.12963
20	+40%	.05382	.06049	.06735	.07438	.08156	.09632
	+20%	.06522	.07189	.07875	.08577	.09295	.10771
	0%	.07661	.08329	.09014	.09717	.10435	.11911
	−20%	.08801	.09468	.10154	.10857	.11575	.13051
25	+40%	.05228	.05932	.06654	.07391	.08141	.09674
	+20%	.06368	.07072	.07793	.08530	.09281	.10814
	0%	.07508	.08212	.08933	.09670	.10420	.11953
	−20%	.08647	.09351	.10073	.10810	.11560	.13093
30	+40%	.05133	.05861	.06606	.07364	.08133	.09696
	+20%	.06273	.07001	.07745	.08503	.09272	.10835
	0%	.07413	.08141	.08885	.09643	.10412	.11975
	−20%	.08552	.09280	.10025	.10783	.11552	.13115

OVER-ALL RATES

12% EQUITY YIELD
10 Year Holding Period
90% Loan Ratio

Term In Yrs.	Appr. or Dep.	Interest Rate					
		6%	7%	8%	9%	10%	12%
15	+40%	.05145	.05828	.06531	.07253	.07992	.09521
	+20%	.06285	.06968	.07670	.08392	.09132	.10661
	0%	.07424	.08107	.08810	.09532	.10272	.11801
	−20%	.08564	.09247	.09950	.10672	.11411	.12941
20	+40%	.04840	.05590	.06362	.07152	.07960	.09620
	+20%	.05979	.06730	.07502	.08292	.09100	.10760
	0%	.07119	.07870	.08641	.09432	.10239	.11900
	−20%	.08259	.09009	.09781	.10571	.11379	.13039
25	+40%	.04667	.05459	.06270	.07099	.07943	.09668
	+20%	.05807	.06598	.07410	.08239	.09083	.10808
	0%	.06946	.07738	.08550	.09379	.10223	.11947
	−20%	.08086	.08878	.09689	.10518	.11362	.13087
30	+40%	.04560	.05379	.06216	.07069	.07934	.09693
	+20%	.05699	.06519	.07356	.08209	.09074	.10832
	0%	.06839	.07658	.08496	.09348	.10214	.11972
	−20%	.07979	.08798	.09635	.10488	.11353	.13112

OVER-ALL RATES

14% EQUITY YIELD
10 Year Holding Period
60% Loan Ratio

Term In Yrs.	Appr. or Dep.	Interest Rate					
		6%	7%	8%	9%	10%	12%
15	+40%	.07859	.08309	.08772	.09248	.09736	.10744
	+20%	.08894	.09343	.09807	.10282	.10770	.11779
	0%	.09928	.10378	.10841	.11317	.11804	.12813
	−20%	.10962	.11412	.11875	.12351	.12838	.13847
20	+40%	.07590	.08083	.08591	.09111	.09643	.10738
	+20%	.08624	.09117	.09625	.10145	.10677	.11773
	0%	.09658	.10152	.10659	.11180	.11712	.12807
	−20%	.10693	.11186	.11693	.12214	.12746	.13841
25	+40%	.07437	.07958	.08492	.09039	.09596	.10735
	+20%	.08471	.08992	.09526	.10073	.10630	.11770
	0%	.09506	.10026	.10561	.11107	.11664	.12804
	−20%	.10540	.11061	.11595	.12141	.12698	.13838
30	+40%	.07343	.07882	.08434	.08997	.09569	.10734
	+20%	.08377	.08916	.09469	.10032	.10604	.11768
	0%	.09411	.09951	.10503	.11066	.11638	.12802
	−20%	.10445	.10985	.11537	.12100	.12672	.13837

14% EQUITY YIELD
10 Year Holding Period
70% Loan Ratio

Term In Yrs.	Appr. or Dep.	Interest Rate					
		6%	7%	8%	9%	10%	12%
15	+40%	.07181	.07705	.08246	.08801	.09370	.10547
	+20%	.08215	.08740	.09280	.09835	.10404	.11581
	0%	.09249	.09774	.10314	.10869	.11438	.12615
	−20%	.10283	.10808	.11348	.11903	.12472	.13649
20	+40%	.06866	.07442	.08034	.08641	.09262	.10539
	+20%	.07900	.08476	.09068	.09675	.10296	.11574
	0%	.08935	.09510	.10102	.10709	.11330	.12608
	−20%	.09969	.10545	.11137	.11744	.12364	.13642
25	+40%	.06688	.07295	.07919	.08556	.09206	.10536
	+20%	.07722	.08330	.08953	.09591	.10240	.11570
	0%	.08757	.09364	.09987	.10625	.11275	.12604
	−20%	.09791	.10398	.11022	.11659	.12309	.13639
30	+40%	.06578	.07207	.07851	.08508	.09176	.10534
	+20%	.07612	.08241	.08886	.09542	.10210	.11568
	0%	.08646	.09276	.09920	.10577	.11244	.12603
	−20%	.09680	.10310	.10954	.11611	.12278	.13637

OVER-ALL RATES

14% EQUITY YIELD
10 Year Holding Period
75% Loan Ratio

Term In Yrs.	Appr. or Dep.	Interest Rate					
		6%	7%	8%	9%	10%	12%
15	+40%	.06841	.07404	.07982	.08577	.09187	.10448
	+20%	.07875	.08438	.09017	.09611	.10221	.11482
	0%	.08910	.09472	.10051	.10646	.11255	.12516
	−20%	.09944	.10506	.11085	.11680	.12289	.13550
20	+40%	.06504	.07121	.07755	.08406	.09071	.10440
	+20%	.07539	.08155	.08790	.09440	.10105	.11474
	0%	.08573	.09190	.09824	.10474	.11139	.12508
	−20%	.09607	.10224	.10858	.11509	.12174	.13543
25	+40%	.06314	.06964	.07632	.08315	.09012	.10436
	+20%	.07348	.07999	.08667	.09350	.10046	.11470
	0%	.08382	.09033	.09701	.10384	.11080	.12505
	−20%	.09416	.10067	.10735	.11418	.12114	.13539
30	+40%	.06195	.06869	.07560	.08264	.08979	.10434
	+20%	.07229	.07904	.08594	.09298	.10013	.11469
	0%	.08264	.08938	.09628	.10332	.11047	.12503
	−20%	.09298	.09972	.10663	.11366	.12081	.13537

14% EQUITY YIELD
10 Year Holding Period
80% Loan Ratio

Term In Yrs.	Appr. or Dep.	Interest Rate					
		6%	7%	8%	9%	10%	12%
15	+40%	.06502	.07102	.07719	.08353	.09004	.10349
	+20%	.07536	.08136	.08753	.09388	.10038	.11383
	0%	.08570	.09170	.09788	.10422	.11072	.12417
	−20%	.09605	.10204	.10822	.11456	.12106	.13451
20	+40%	.06142	.06800	.07477	.08171	.08880	.10340
	+20%	.07177	.07835	.08511	.09205	.09914	.11375
	0%	.08211	.08869	.09545	.10239	.10949	.12409
	−20%	.09245	.09903	.10580	.11274	.11983	.13443
25	+40%	.05939	.06633	.07346	.08074	.08817	.10336
	+20%	.06973	.07667	.08380	.09108	.09851	.11371
	0%	.08008	.08702	.09414	.10143	.10885	.12405
	−20%	.09042	.09736	.10448	.11177	.11920	.13439
30	+40%	.05813	.06532	.07268	.08019	.08782	.10334
	+20%	.06847	.07566	.08303	.09053	.09816	.11369
	0%	.07881	.08601	.09337	.10088	.10850	.12403
	−20%	.08916	.09635	.10371	.11122	.11885	.13437

OVER-ALL RATES

14% EQUITY YIELD
10 Year Holding Period
90% Loan Ratio

Term In Yrs.	Appr. or Dep.	Interest Rate					
		6%	7%	8%	9%	10%	12%
15	+40%	.05823	.06498	.07192	.07906	.08637	.10151
	+20%	.06857	.07532	.08227	.08940	.09672	.11185
	0%	.07892	.08566	.09261	.09974	.10706	.12219
	−20%	.08926	.09601	.10295	.11009	.11740	.13254
20	+40%	.05419	.06159	.06920	.07701	.08499	.10141
	+20%	.06453	.07193	.07954	.08735	.09533	.11176
	0%	.07487	.08227	.08989	.09769	.10567	.12210
	−20%	.08521	.09262	.10023	.10803	.11602	.13244
25	+40%	.05190	.05971	.06772	.07592	.08427	.10137
	+20%	.06224	.07005	.07807	.08626	.09462	.11171
	0%	.07258	.08039	.08841	.09661	.10496	.12206
	−20%	.08293	.09074	.09875	.10695	.11530	.13240
30	+40%	.05048	.05857	.06685	.07530	.08388	.10135
	+20%	.06082	.06891	.07720	.08564	.09422	.11169
	0%	.07116	.07925	.08754	.09599	.10457	.12203
	−20%	.08151	.08960	.09788	.10633	.11491	.13237

OVER-ALL RATES

15% EQUITY YIELD
10 Year Holding Period
60% Loan Ratio

Term In Yrs.	Appr. or Dep.	Interest Rate					
		6%	7%	8%	9%	10%	12%
15	+40%	.08441	.08888	.09349	.09822	.10307	.11311
	+20%	.09426	.09873	.10334	.10807	.11292	.12296
	0%	.10411	.10858	.11319	.11792	.12277	.13281
	−20%	.11396	.11843	.12304	.12777	.13262	.14266
20	+40%	.08141	.08631	.09135	.09652	.10181	.11271
	+20%	.09126	.09616	.10120	.10637	.11166	.12256
	0%	.10111	.10601	.11105	.11622	.12152	.13241
	−20%	.11096	.11586	.12090	.12607	.13137	.14226
25	+40%	.07971	.08488	.09019	.09563	.10117	.11252
	+20%	.08956	.09473	.10004	.10548	.11102	.12237
	0%	.09941	.10458	.10989	.11533	.12087	.13222
	−20%	.10926	.11443	.11974	.12518	.13072	.14207
30	+40%	.07865	.08401	.08951	.09511	.10081	.11242
	+20%	.08850	.09386	.09936	.10496	.11066	.12227
	0%	.09835	.10371	.10921	.11481	.12051	.13212
	−20%	.10820	.11357	.11906	.12467	.13036	.14197

15% EQUITY YIELD
10 Year Holding Period
70% Loan Ratio

Term In Yrs.	Appr. or Dep.	Interest Rate					
		6%	7%	8%	9%	10%	12%
15	+40%	.07676	.08198	.08735	.09287	.09853	.11024
	+20%	.08661	.09183	.09720	.10272	.10838	.12009
	0%	.09646	.10168	.10705	.11257	.11823	.12994
	−20%	.10631	.11153	.11690	.12242	.12808	.13979
20	+40%	.07326	.07897	.08486	.09089	.09707	.10978
	+20%	.08311	.08882	.09471	.10074	.10692	.11963
	0%	.09296	.09868	.10456	.11059	.11677	.12948
	−20%	.10281	.10853	.11441	.12044	.12662	.13933
25	+40%	.07127	.07731	.08351	.08985	.09631	.10955
	+20%	.08112	.08716	.09336	.09970	.10616	.11940
	0%	.09097	.09701	.10321	.10955	.11601	.12926
	−20%	.10082	.10686	.11306	.11940	.12586	.13911
30	+40%	.07004	.07630	.08271	.08925	.09590	.10944
	+20%	.07989	.08615	.09256	.09910	.10575	.11929
	0%	.08974	.09600	.10241	.10895	.11560	.12914
	−20%	.09959	.10585	.11226	.11880	.12545	.13899

OVER-ALL RATES

15% EQUITY YIELD
10 Year Holding Period
75% Loan Ratio

Term In Yrs.	Appr. or Dep.	Interest Rate					
		6%	7%	8%	9%	10%	12%
15	+40%	.07294	.07853	.08428	.09020	.09626	.10881
	+20%	.08279	.08838	.09413	.10005	.10611	.11866
	0%	.09264	.09823	.10398	.10990	.11596	.12851
	−20%	.10249	.10808	.11384	.11975	.12581	.13836
20	+40%	.06918	.07531	.08161	.08808	.09469	.10831
	+20%	.07903	.08516	.09146	.09793	.10454	.11816
	0%	.08888	.09501	.10131	.10778	.11439	.12801
	−20%	.09873	.10486	.11116	.11763	.12424	.13786
25	+40%	.06706	.07352	.08016	.08696	.09388	.10807
	+20%	.07691	.08337	.09001	.09681	.10374	.11792
	0%	.08676	.09322	.09986	.10666	.11359	.12777
	−20%	.09661	.10307	.10971	.11651	.12344	.13762
30	+40%	.06574	.07244	.07931	.08632	.09344	.10795
	+20%	.07559	.08229	.08916	.09617	.10329	.11780
	0%	.08544	.09214	.09901	.10602	.11314	.12765
	−20%	.09529	.10199	.10886	.11587	.12299	.13750

15% EQUITY YIELD
10 Year Holding Period
80% Loan Ratio

Term In Yrs.	Appr. or Dep.	Interest Rate					
		6%	7%	8%	9%	10%	12%
15	+40%	.06911	.07508	.08122	.08752	.09399	.10738
	+20%	.07896	.08493	.09107	.09737	.10384	.11723
	0%	.08881	.09478	.10092	.10723	.11369	.12708
	−20%	.09866	.10463	.11077	.11708	.12354	.13693
20	+40%	.06511	.07164	.07837	.08526	.09232	.10685
	+20%	.07496	.08149	.08822	.09511	.10217	.11670
	0%	.08481	.09134	.09807	.10496	.11202	.12655
	−20%	.09466	.10119	.10792	.11481	.12187	.13640
25	+40%	.06284	.06974	.07682	.08407	.09146	.10659
	+20%	.07269	.07959	.08667	.09392	.10131	.11644
	0%	.08254	.08944	.09652	.10377	.11116	.12629
	−20%	.09239	.09929	.10637	.11362	.12101	.13614
30	+40%	.06143	.06858	.07591	.08338	.09098	.10646
	+20%	.07128	.07843	.08576	.09323	.10083	.11631
	0%	.08113	.08828	.09561	.10308	.11068	.12616
	−20%	.09098	.09813	.10546	.11293	.12053	.13601

OVER-ALL RATES

15% EQUITY YIELD
10 Year Holding Period
90% Loan Ratio

Term In Yrs.	Appr. or Dep.	Interest Rate					
		6%	7%	8%	9%	10%	12%
15	+40%	.06146	.06817	.07508	.08218	.08945	.10451
	+20%	.07131	.07802	.08493	.09203	.09930	.11436
	0%	.08116	.08787	.09478	.10188	.10916	.12421
	−20%	.09101	.09772	.10463	.11173	.11901	.13406
20	+40%	.05696	.06431	.07187	.07963	.08757	.10391
	+20%	.06681	.07416	.08172	.08948	.09742	.11376
	0%	.07666	.08401	.09157	.09933	.10727	.12362
	−20%	.08651	.09386	.10142	.10918	.11712	.13347
25	+40%	.05441	.06217	.07013	.07829	.08660	.10363
	+20%	.06426	.07202	.07998	.08814	.09645	.11348
	0%	.07411	.08187	.08983	.09799	.10630	.12333
	−20%	.08396	.09172	.09969	.10784	.11615	.13318
30	+40%	.05282	.06087	.06911	.07752	.08607	.10348
	+20%	.06267	.07072	.07896	.08737	.09592	.11333
	0%	.07253	.08057	.08881	.09722	.10577	.12318
	−20%	.08238	.09042	.09866	.10707	.11562	.13303

OVER-ALL RATES

16% EQUITY YIELD
10 Year Holding Period
60% Loan Ratio

Term In Yrs.	Appr. or Dep.	Interest Rate					
		6%	7%	8%	9%	10%	12%
15	+40%	.09015	.09459	.09917	.10388	.10871	.11870
	+20%	.09953	.10397	.10855	.11326	.11809	.12808
	0%	.10891	.11335	.11793	.12264	.12747	.13746
	−20%	.11829	.12273	.12732	.13202	.13685	.14684
20	+40%	.08685	.09172	.09673	.10187	.10714	.11798
	+20%	.09623	.10110	.10611	.11125	.11652	.12736
	0%	.10561	.11048	.11549	.12063	.12590	.13674
	−20%	.11499	.11986	.12487	.13001	.13528	.14612
25	+40%	.08498	.09012	.09540	.10081	.10633	.11763
	+20%	.09436	.09950	.10478	.11019	.11571	.12701
	0%	.10374	.10888	.11416	.11957	.12509	.13639
	−20%	.11312	.11826	.12354	.12895	.13447	.14577
30	+40%	.08382	.08915	.09462	.10020	.10588	.11745
	+20%	.09320	.09853	.10400	.10958	.11526	.12683
	0%	.10258	.10791	.11338	.11896	.12464	.13621
	−20%	.11196	.11730	.12276	.12834	.13402	.14559

16% EQUITY YIELD
10 Year Holding Period
70% Loan Ratio

Term In Yrs.	Appr. or Dep.	Interest Rate					
		6%	7%	8%	9%	10%	12%
15	+40%	.08163	.08682	.09216	.09765	.10329	.11494
	+20%	.09101	.09620	.10154	.10703	.11267	.12432
	0%	.10039	.10558	.11092	.11641	.12205	.13370
	−20%	.10977	.11496	.12030	.12579	.13143	.14308
20	+40%	.07778	.08346	.08931	.09531	.10145	.11410
	+20%	.08716	.09284	.09869	.10469	.11083	.12348
	0%	.09654	.10222	.10807	.11407	.12021	.13286
	−20%	.10592	.11160	.11745	.12345	.12959	.14224
25	+40%	.07560	.08160	.08776	.09407	.10051	.11370
	+20%	.08498	.09098	.09714	.10345	.10989	.12308
	0%	.09436	.10036	.10652	.11283	.11927	.13246
	−20%	.10374	.10974	.11590	.12221	.12865	.14184
30	+40%	.07425	.08047	.08685	.09336	.09999	.11349
	+20%	.08363	.08985	.09623	.10274	.10937	.12287
	0%	.09301	.09923	.10561	.11212	.11875	.13225
	−20%	.10239	.10861	.11499	.12150	.12813	.14163

OVER-ALL RATES

16% EQUITY YIELD
10 Year Holding Period
75% Loan Ratio

Term In Yrs.	Appr. or Dep.	Interest Rate					
		6%	7%	8%	9%	10%	12%
15	+40%	.07737	.08293	.08866	.09454	.10057	.11306
	+20%	.08675	.09231	.09804	.10392	.10995	.12244
	0%	.09613	.10169	.10742	.11330	.11933	.13182
	−20%	.10551	.11107	.11680	.12268	.12872	.14120
20	+40%	.07325	.07933	.08560	.09203	.09861	.11216
	+20%	.08263	.08871	.09498	.10141	.10799	.12154
	0%	.09201	.09809	.10436	.11079	.11737	.13092
	−20%	.10139	.10747	.11374	.12017	.12675	.14030
25	+40%	.07091	.07734	.08394	.09070	.09760	.11173
	+20%	.08029	.08672	.09332	.10008	.10698	.12111
	0%	.08967	.09610	.10270	.10946	.11636	.13049
	−20%	.09905	.10548	.11208	.11884	.12574	.13987
30	+40%	.06947	.07613	.08297	.08994	.09704	.11150
	+20%	.07885	.08551	.09235	.09932	.10642	.12089
	0%	.08823	.09489	.10173	.10870	.11580	.13027
	−20%	.09761	.10427	.11111	.11808	.12518	.13965

16% EQUITY YIELD
10 Year Holding Period
80% Loan Ratio

Term In Yrs.	Appr. or Dep.	Interest Rate					
		6%	7%	8%	9%	10%	12%
15	+40%	.07311	.07904	.08515	.09143	.09786	.11118
	+20%	.08249	.08842	.09453	.10081	.10724	.12056
	0%	.09187	.09780	.10391	.11019	.11662	.12994
	−20%	.10125	.10718	.11329	.11957	.12600	.13932
20	+40%	.06871	.07521	.08189	.08875	.09577	.11022
	+20%	.07809	.08459	.09127	.09813	.10515	.11960
	0%	.08747	.09397	.10065	.10751	.11453	.12898
	−20%	.09685	.10335	.11003	.11689	.12391	.13836
25	+40%	.06623	.07308	.08012	.08733	.09469	.10976
	+20%	.07561	.08246	.08950	.09671	.10407	.11914
	0%	.08499	.09184	.09888	.10609	.11345	.12852
	−20%	.09437	.10122	.10826	.11547	.12283	.13790
30	+40%	.06468	.07179	.07908	.08652	.09409	.10952
	+20%	.07406	.08117	.08846	.09590	.10347	.11890
	0%	.08344	.09055	.09784	.10528	.11285	.12828
	−20%	.09282	.09993	.10722	.11466	.12223	.13766

OVER-ALL RATES

16% EQUITY YIELD
10 Year Holding Period
90% Loan Ratio

Terms In Yrs.	Appr. or Dep.	Interest Rate					
		6%	7%	8%	9%	10%	12%
15	+40%	.06460	.07127	.07814	.08520	.09244	.10743
	+20%	.07398	.08065	.08752	.09458	.10182	.11681
	0%	.08336	.09003	.09690	.10396	.11120	.12619
	−20%	.09274	.09941	.10628	.11334	.12058	.13557
20	+40%	.05965	.06695	.07447	.08219	.09008	.10635
	+20%	.06903	.07633	.08385	.09157	.09946	.11573
	0%	.07841	.08571	.09323	.10095	.10884	.12511
	−20%	.08779	.09509	.10261	.11033	.11822	.13449
25	+40%	.05685	.06456	.07248	.08059	.08887	.10583
	+20%	.06623	.07394	.08186	.08997	.09825	.11521
	0%	.07561	.08332	.09124	.09935	.10763	.12459
	−20%	.08499	.09270	.10062	.10873	.11701	.13397
30	+40%	.05511	.06311	.07131	.07968	.08820	.10556
	+20%	.06449	.07249	.08069	.08906	.09758	.11494
	0%	.07387	.08187	.09007	.09844	.10696	.12432
	−20%	.08325	.09125	.09945	.10782	.11634	.13370

OVER-ALL RATES

20% EQUITY YIELD
10 Year Holding Period
60% Loan Ratio

Term In Yrs.	Appr. or Dep.	Interest Rate					
		6%	7%	8%	9%	10%	12%
15	+40%	.11233	.11669	.12118	.12580	.13054	.14037
	+20%	.12003	.12439	.12889	.13351	.13825	.14807
	0%	.12774	.13210	.13659	.14121	.14595	.15577
	−20%	.13544	.13980	.14430	.14892	.15366	.16348
20	+40%	.10798	.11274	.11764	.12268	.12784	.13850
	+20%	.11569	.12044	.12535	.13038	.13555	.14620
	0%	.12339	.12815	.13305	.13809	.14325	.15391
	−20%	.13110	.13585	.14075	.14579	.15096	.16161
25	+40%	.10552	.11055	.11572	.12103	.12645	.13760
	+20%	.11322	.11825	.12343	.12873	.13416	.14530
	0%	.12093	.12595	.13113	.13644	.14186	.15301
	−20%	.12863	.13366	.13883	.14414	.14957	.16071
30	+40%	.10399	.10922	.11459	.12009	.12569	.13714
	+20%	.11170	.11692	.12229	.12779	.13339	.14484
	0%	.11940	.12463	.13000	.13550	.14110	.15254
	−20%	.12711	.13233	.13770	.14320	.14880	.16025

20% EQUITY YIELD
10 Year Holding Period
70% Loan Ratio

Term In Yrs.	Appr. or Dep.	Interest Rate					
		6%	7%	8%	9%	10%	12%
15	+40%	.10028	.10537	.11061	.11600	.12154	.13299
	+20%	.10799	.11308	.11832	.12371	.12924	.14070
	0%	.11569	.12078	.12602	.13141	.13694	.14840
	−20%	.12340	.12849	.13373	.13912	.14465	.15611
20	+40%	.09521	.10076	.10648	.11236	.11838	.13082
	+20%	.10292	.10847	.11419	.12006	.12609	.13852
	0%	.11062	.11617	.12189	.12777	.13379	.14623
	−20%	.11833	.12388	.12960	.13547	.14150	.15393
25	+40%	.09234	.09820	.10424	.11043	.11676	.12977
	+20%	.10005	.10591	.11195	.11814	.12447	.13747
	0%	.10775	.11361	.11965	.12584	.13217	.14517
	−20%	.11545	.12132	.12736	.13355	.13988	.15288
30	+40%	.09056	.09666	.10292	.10933	.11587	.12922
	+20%	.09826	.10436	.11063	.11704	.12357	.13693
	0%	.10597	.11207	.11833	.12474	.13128	.14463
	−20%	.11367	.11977	.12604	.13245	.13898	.15234

OVER-ALL RATES

20% EQUITY YIELD
10 Year Holding Period
75% Loan Ratio

Terms In Yrs.	Appr. or Dep.	Interest Rate					
		6%	7%	8%	9%	10%	12%
15	+40%	.09426	.09971	.10533	.11111	.11703	.12931
	+20%	.10197	.10742	.11303	.11881	.12474	.13701
	0%	.10967	.11512	.12074	.12651	.13244	.14472
	−20%	.11738	.12283	.12844	.13422	.14015	.15242
20	+40%	.08883	.09477	.10090	.10720	.11365	.12698
	+20%	.09653	.10248	.10861	.11491	.12136	.13468
	0%	.10424	.11018	.11631	.12261	.12906	.14238
	−20%	.11194	.11789	.12402	.13031	.13677	.15009
25	+40%	.08575	.09203	.09850	.10514	.11192	.12585
	+20%	.09346	.09974	.10621	.11284	.11962	.13355
	0%	.10116	.10744	.11391	.12055	.12733	.14126
	−20%	.10886	.11515	.12162	.12825	.13503	.14896
30	+40%	.08384	.09037	.09709	.10396	.11096	.12527
	+20%	.09155	.09808	.10479	.11166	.11866	.13297
	0%	.09925	.10578	.11250	.11937	.12637	.14068
	−20%	.10696	.11349	.12020	.12707	.13407	.14838

20% EQUITY YIELD
10 Year Holding Period
80% Loan Ratio

Term In Yrs.	Appr. or Dep.	Interest					
		6%	7%	8%	9%	10%	12%
15	+40%	.08824	.09405	.10005	.10621	.11253	.12562
	+20%	.09594	.10176	.10775	.11391	.12023	.13333
	0%	.10365	.10946	.11545	.12161	.12794	.14103
	−20%	.11135	.11717	.12316	.12932	.13564	.14874
20	+40%	.08244	.08879	.09532	.10204	.10893	.12313
	+20%	.09015	.09649	.10303	.10975	.11663	.13084
	0%	.09785	.10419	.11073	.11745	.12433	.13854
	−20%	.10556	.11190	.11844	.12515	.13204	.14625
25	+40%	.07916	.08586	.09276	.09984	.10707	.12193
	+20%	.08687	.09357	.10047	.10754	.11478	.12964
	0%	.09457	.10127	.10817	.11525	.12248	.13734
	−20%	.10228	.10898	.11588	.12295	.13019	.14505
30	+40%	.07713	.08409	.09125	.09858	.10605	.12131
	+20%	.08483	.09180	.09896	.10629	.11376	.12902
	0%	.09253	.09950	.10666	.11399	.12146	.13672
	−20%	.10024	.10721	.11437	.12170	.12916	.14443

OVER-ALL RATES

20% EQUITY YIELD
10 Year Holding Period
90% Loan Ratio

Term In Yrs.	Appr. or Dep.	Interest Rate					
		6%	7%	8%	9%	10%	12%
15	+40%	.07620	.08274	.08948	.09641	.10352	.11825
	+20%	.08390	.09044	.09718	.10411	.11122	.12595
	0%	.09160	.09815	.10489	.11182	.11893	.13366
	−20%	.09931	.10585	.11259	.11952	.12663	.14136
20	+40%	.06967	.07681	.08416	.09172	.09947	.11545
	+20%	.07738	.08451	.09187	.09943	.10717	.12316
	0%	.08508	.09222	.09957	.10713	.11488	.13086
	−20%	.09279	.09992	.10728	.11483	.12258	.13857
25	+40%	.06598	.07352	.08128	.08925	.09738	.11410
	+20%	.07369	.08123	.08899	.09695	.10509	.12180
	0%	.08139	.08893	.09669	.10465	.11279	.12951
	−20%	.08910	.09663	.10440	.11236	.12050	.13721
30	+40%	.06369	.07153	.07959	.08783	.09623	.11340
	+20%	.07140	.07923	.08729	.09554	.10394	.12111
	0%	.07910	.08694	.09500	.10324	.11164	.12881
	−20%	.08681	.09464	.10270	.11094	.11935	.13652

OVER-ALL RATES

10% EQUITY YIELD
15 Year Holding Period
60% Loan Ratio

Term In Yrs.	Appr. or Dep.	Interest Rate					
		6%	7%	8%	9%	10%	12%
15	+40%	.06929	.07325	.07734	.08156	.08590	.09494
	+20%	.07558	.07954	.08363	.08785	.09220	.10124
	0%	.08188	.08584	.08993	.09415	.09849	.10753
	−20%	.08817	.09213	.09622	.10044	.10479	.11383
20	+40%	.06711	.07175	.07655	.08150	.08659	.09716
	+20%	.07341	.07804	.08284	.08779	.09289	.10345
	0%	.07970	.08434	.08914	.09409	.09918	.10975
	−20%	.08600	.09063	.09543	.10038	.10547	.11604
25	+40%	.06588	.07092	.07612	.08146	.08694	.09823
	+20%	.07218	.07721	.08241	.08776	.09324	.10452
	0%	.07847	.08350	.08871	.09405	.09953	.11082
	−20%	.08477	.08980	.09500	.10035	.10583	.11711
30	+40%	.06512	.07041	.07586	.08145	.08714	.09878
	+20%	.07141	.07671	.08216	.08774	.09343	.10507
	0%	.07771	.08300	.08845	.09404	.09973	.11137
	−20%	.08400	.08930	.09475	.10033	.10602	.11766

10% EQUITY YIELD
15 Year Holding Period
70% Loan Ratio

Term In Yrs.	Appr. or Dep.	Interest Rate					
		6%	7%	8%	9%	10%	12%
15	+40%	.06627	.07089	.07566	.08058	.08565	.09620
	+20%	.07256	.07718	.08195	.08688	.09195	.10249
	0%	.07886	.08348	.08825	.09317	.09824	.10879
	−20%	.08515	.08977	.09454	.09947	.10454	.11508
20	+40%	.06373	.06914	.07473	.08051	.08645	.09878
	+20%	.07002	.07543	.08103	.08681	.09275	.10508
	0%	.07632	.08173	.08732	.09310	.09904	.11137
	−20%	.08261	.08802	.09362	.09939	.10534	.11767
25	+40%	.06229	.06816	.07423	.08047	.08686	.10003
	+20%	.06859	.07446	.08053	.08677	.09316	.10632
	0%	.07488	.08075	.08682	.09306	.09945	.11262
	−20%	.08118	.08705	.09312	.09936	.10575	.11891
30	+40%	.06140	.06758	.07394	.08045	.08709	.10067
	+20%	.06769	.07387	.08023	.08675	.09339	.10696
	0%	.07399	.08017	.08653	.09304	.09968	.11326
	−20%	.08028	.08646	.09282	.09933	.10598	.11955

OVER-ALL RATES

10% EQUITY YIELD
15 Year Holding Period
75% Loan Ratio

Term In Yrs.	Appr. or Dep.	Interest Rate					
		6%	7%	8%	9%	10%	12%
15	+40%	.06476	.06971	.07482	.08009	.08553	.09683
	+20%	.07105	.07600	.08111	.08639	.09182	.10312
	0%	.07735	.08229	.08741	.09268	.09811	.10942
	−20%	.08364	.08859	.09370	.09898	.10441	.11571
20	+40%	.06204	.06783	.07383	.08002	.08638	.09959
	+20%	.06833	.07412	.08012	.08631	.09268	.10589
	0%	.07463	.08042	.08642	.09261	.09897	.11218
	−20%	.08092	.08671	.09271	.09890	.10527	.11848
25	+40%	.06050	.06679	.07329	.07998	.08683	.10093
	+20%	.06679	.07308	.07959	.08627	.09312	.10722
	0%	.07309	.07938	.08588	.09257	.09941	.11352
	−20%	.07938	.08567	.09217	.09886	.10571	.11981
30	+40%	.05954	.06616	.07297	.07995	.08707	.10162
	+20%	.06584	.07246	.07927	.08625	.09336	.10791
	0%	.07213	.07875	.08556	.09254	.09966	.11421
	−20%	.07843	.08504	.09186	.09884	.10595	.12050

10% EQUITY YIELD
15 Year Holding Period
80% Loan Ratio

Term In Yrs.	Appr. or Dep.	Interest Rate					
		6%	7%	8%	9%	10%	12%
15	+40%	.06325	.06852	.07398	.07961	.08540	.09745
	+20%	.06954	.07482	.08027	.08590	.09169	.10375
	0%	.07584	.08111	.08657	.09220	.09799	.11004
	−20%	.08213	.08741	.09286	.09849	.10428	.11634
20	+40%	.06035	.06652	.07292	.07952	.08632	.10040
	+20%	.06664	.07282	.07922	.08582	.09261	.10670
	0%	.07293	.07911	.08551	.09211	.09890	.11299
	−20%	.07923	.08541	.09181	.09841	.10520	.11929
25	+40%	.05870	.06541	.07235	.07948	.08679	.10183
	+20%	.06500	.07171	.07864	.08578	.09308	.10813
	0%	.07129	.07800	.08494	.09207	.09938	.11442
	−20%	.07759	.08430	.09123	.09836	.10567	.12071
30	+40%	.05768	.06474	.07201	.07946	.08705	.10256
	+20%	.06398	.07104	.07831	.08575	.09334	.10886
	0%	.07027	.07733	.08460	.09204	.09964	.11515
	−20%	.07657	.08363	.09090	.09834	.10593	.12145

OVER-ALL RATES

10% EQUITY YIELD
15 Year Holding Period
90% Loan Ratio

Term In Yrs.	Appr. or Dep.	Interest Rate					
		6%	7%	8%	9%	10%	12%
15	+40%	.06023	.06616	.07230	.07863	.08515	.09871
	+20%	.06652	.07246	.07859	.08493	.09144	.10500
	0%	.07282	.07875	.08489	.09122	.09774	.11130
	−20%	.07911	.08505	.09118	.09751	.10403	.11759
20	+40%	.05696	.06391	.07111	.07854	.08618	.10203
	+20%	.06326	.07021	.07741	.08483	.09247	.10832
	0%	.06955	.07650	.08370	.09113	.09877	.11462
	−20%	.07585	.08280	.08999	.09742	.10506	.12091
25	+40%	.05511	.06266	.07047	.07849	.08671	.10363
	+20%	.06141	.06896	.07676	.08478	.09300	.10993
	0%	.06770	.07525	.08305	.09108	.09930	.11622
	−20%	.07400	.08155	.08935	.09737	.10559	.12252
30	+40%	.05397	.06191	.07009	.07846	.08700	.10446
	+20%	.06026	.06820	.07638	.08476	.09329	.11075
	0%	.06656	.07450	.08268	.09105	.09959	.11705
	−20%	.07285	.08079	.08897	.09734	.10588	.12334

OVER-ALL RATES

12% EQUITY YIELD
15 Year Holding Period
60% Loan Ratio

Term In Yrs.	Appr. or Dep.	Interest Rate					
		6%	7%	8%	9%	10%	12%
15	+40%	.08194	.08590	.08999	.09421	.09855	.10759
	+20%	.08730	.09126	.09535	.09957	.10392	.11296
	0%	.09267	.09663	.10072	.10494	.10928	.11832
	−20%	.09803	.10199	.10608	.11030	.11465	.12369
20	+40%	.07873	.08330	.08804	.09294	.09797	.10843
	+20%	.08409	.08867	.09341	.09830	.10334	.11379
	0%	.08946	.09403	.09877	.10367	.10870	.11916
	−20%	.09482	.09940	.10414	.10903	.11407	.12452
25	+40%	.07691	.08187	.08699	.09227	.09767	.10883
	+20%	.08228	.08723	.09236	.09763	.10304	.11419
	0%	.08764	.09260	.09772	.10300	.10840	.11956
	−20%	.09301	.09796	.10308	.10836	.11377	.12492
30	+40%	.07578	.08100	.08637	.09188	.09751	.10904
	+20%	.08115	.08636	.09173	.09725	.10287	.11440
	0%	.08651	.09173	.09710	.10261	.10824	.11977
	−20%	.09188	.09709	.10246	.10798	.11360	.12513

12% EQUITY YIELD
15 Year Holding Period
70% Loan Ratio

Term In Yrs.	Appr. or Dep.	Interest Rate					
		6%	7%	8%	9%	10%	12%
15	+40%	.07738	.08200	.08677	.09170	.09677	.10731
	+20%	.08275	.08737	.09214	.09706	.10213	.11268
	0%	.08811	.09273	.09750	.10243	.10750	.11804
	−20%	.09348	.09809	.10287	.10779	.11286	.12341
20	+40%	.07364	.07898	.08451	.09021	.09609	.10828
	+20%	.07900	.08434	.08987	.09558	.10145	.11365
	0%	.08437	.08971	.09524	.10094	.10682	.11901
	−20%	.08973	.09507	.10060	.10631	.11218	.12438
25	+40%	.07152	.07730	.08328	.08943	.09574	.10875
	+20%	.07688	.08266	.08864	.09480	.10111	.11412
	0%	.08225	.08803	.09401	.10016	.10647	.11948
	−20%	.08761	.09339	.09937	.10553	.11184	.12485
30	+40%	.07020	.07628	.08255	.08898	.09555	.10900
	+20%	.07557	.08165	.08792	.09435	.10091	.11436
	0%	.08093	.08701	.09328	.09971	.10628	.11972
	−20%	.08630	.09238	.09865	.10508	.11164	.12509

OVER-ALL RATES

12% EQUITY YIELD
15 Year Holding Period
75% Loan Ratio

Term In Yrs.	Appr. or Dep.	Interest Rate					
		6%	7%	8%	9%	10%	12%
15	+40%	.07510	.08005	.08517	.09044	.09587	.10717
	+20%	.08047	.08542	.09053	.09581	.10124	.11254
	0%	.08583	.09078	.09590	.10117	.10660	.11790
	−20%	.09120	.09615	.10126	.10654	.11197	.12327
20	+40%	.07109	.07681	.08274	.08885	.09515	.10821
	+20%	.07646	.08218	.08810	.09422	.10051	.11358
	0%	.08182	.08754	.09347	.09958	.10588	.11894
	−20%	.08719	.09291	.09883	.10495	.11124	.12431
25	+40%	.06882	.07501	.08142	.08801	.09477	.10872
	+20%	.07419	.08038	.08678	.09338	.10014	.11408
	0%	.07955	.08574	.09215	.09874	.10550	.11945
	−20%	.08491	.09111	.09751	.10411	.11087	.12481
30	+40%	.06741	.07393	.08064	.08753	.09457	.10898
	+20%	.07278	.07929	.08601	.09290	.09993	.11434
	0%	.07814	.08466	.09137	.09826	.10530	.11970
	−20%	.08351	.09002	.09674	.10363	.11066	.12507

12% EQUITY YIELD
15 Year Holding Period
80% Loan Ratio

Term In Yrs.	Appr. or Dep.	Interest Rate					
		6%	7%	8%	9%	10%	12%
15	+40%	.07283	.07810	.08356	.08919	.09498	.10703
	+20%	.07819	.08347	.08892	.09455	.10034	.11240
	0%	.08356	.08883	.09429	.09992	.10571	.11776
	−20%	.08892	.09420	.09965	.10528	.11107	.12313
20	+40%	.06855	.07465	.08097	.08749	.09421	.10814
	+20%	.07391	.08001	.08633	.09286	.09957	.11351
	0%	.07928	.08538	.09170	.09822	.10493	.11887
	−20%	.08464	.09074	.09706	.10359	.11030	.12424
25	+40%	.06612	.07273	.07956	.08660	.09381	.10868
	+20%	.07149	.07809	.08493	.09196	.09917	.11404
	0%	.07685	.08346	.09029	.09733	.10454	.11941
	−20%	.08222	.08882	.09566	.10269	.10990	.12477
30	+40%	.06462	.07157	.07873	.08608	.09359	.10896
	+20%	.06998	.07693	.08410	.09145	.09895	.11432
	0%	.07535	.08230	.08946	.09681	.10432	.11968
	−20%	.08071	.08766	.09483	.10218	.10968	.12505

OVER-ALL RATES

12% EQUITY YIELD
15 Year Holding Period
90% Loan Ratio

Term In Yrs.	Appr. or Dep.	Interest Rate					
		6%	7%	8%	9%	10%	12%
15	+40%	.06827	.07421	.08034	.08667	.09319	.10675
	+20%	.07364	.07957	.08571	.09204	.09856	.11212
	0%	.07900	.08494	.09107	.09740	.10392	.11748
	−20%	.08437	.09030	.09644	.10277	.10929	.12285
20	+40%	.06345	.07032	.07743	.08477	.09232	.10800
	+20%	.06882	.07568	.08279	.09013	.09769	.11337
	0%	.07418	.08105	.08816	.09550	.10305	.11873
	−20%	.07955	.08641	.09352	.10086	.10842	.12410
25	+40%	.06073	.06816	.07585	.08376	.09187	.10860
	+20%	.06609	.07353	.08121	.08913	.09724	.11397
	0%	.07146	.07889	.08658	.09449	.10260	.11933
	−20%	.07682	.08426	.09194	.09986	.10797	.12470
30	+40%	.05904	.06686	.07492	.08319	.09163	.10892
	+20%	.06440	.07222	.08028	.08855	.09699	.11428
	0%	.06977	.07759	.08565	.09391	.10236	.11964
	−20%	.07513	.08295	.09101	.09928	.10772	.12501

OVER-ALL RATES

14% EQUITY YIELD
15 Year Holding Period
60% Loan Ratio

Term In Yrs.	Appr. or Dep.	Interest Rate					
		6%	7%	8%	9%	10%	12%
15	+40%	.09395	.09791	.10200	.10622	.11057	.11961
	+20%	.09852	.10247	.10657	.11079	.11513	.12417
	0%	.10308	.10704	.11113	.11535	.11969	.12873
	−20%	.10764	.11160	.11569	.11991	.12425	.13329
20	+40%	.08985	.09438	.09907	.10391	.10889	.11925
	+20%	.09441	.09894	.10363	.10847	.11346	.12381
	0%	.09897	.10350	.10819	.11303	.11802	.12837
	−20%	.10354	.10806	.11275	.11759	.12258	.13293
25	+40%	.08753	.09242	.09747	.10268	.10803	.11908
	+20%	.09209	.09698	.10203	.10725	.11260	.12364
	0%	.09665	.10154	.10660	.11181	.11716	.12820
	−20%	.10121	.10610	.11116	.11637	.12172	.13276
30	+40%	.08609	.09123	.09654	.10199	.10756	.11899
	+20%	.09065	.09579	.10110	.10655	.11212	.12355
	0%	.09521	.10035	.10566	.11111	.11668	.12811
	−20%	.09977	.10491	.11022	.11567	.12124	.13267

14% EQUITY YIELD
15 Year Holding Period
70% Loan Ratio

Term In Yrs.	Appr. or Dep.	Interest Rate					
		6%	7%	8%	9%	10%	12%
15	+40%	.08780	.09242	.09719	.10211	.10718	.11773
	+20%	.09236	.09698	.10175	.10668	.11174	.12229
	0%	.09692	.10154	.10631	.11124	.11631	.12685
	−20%	.10148	.10610	.11088	.11580	.12087	.13142
20	+40%	.08301	.08829	.09376	.09941	.10523	.11731
	+20%	.08757	.09285	.09832	.10397	.10979	.12187
	0%	.09214	.09742	.10289	.10854	.11435	.12643
	−20%	.09670	.10198	.10745	.11310	.11891	.13100
25	+40%	.08030	.08600	.09191	.09799	.10423	.11711
	+20%	.08486	.09057	.09647	.10255	.10879	.12167
	0%	.08943	.09513	.10103	.10711	.11335	.12623
	−20%	.09399	.09969	.10559	.11167	.11791	.13079
30	+40%	.07862	.08462	.09081	.09717	.10367	.11700
	+20%	.08318	.08918	.09537	.10173	.10823	.12156
	0%	.08775	.09374	.09993	.10629	.11279	.12613
	−20%	.09231	.09830	.10450	.11086	.11736	.13069

OVER-ALL RATES

14% EQUITY YIELD
15 Year Holding Period
75% Loan Ratio

Term In Yrs.	Appr. or Dep.	Interest Rate					
		6%	7%	8%	9%	10%	12%
15	+40%	.08472	.08967	.09478	.10006	.10549	.11679
	+20%	.08928	.09423	.09935	.10462	.11005	.12135
	0%	.09385	.09879	.10391	.10918	.11461	.12591
	−20%	.09841	.10336	.10847	.11374	.11918	.13048
20	+40%	.07959	.08525	.09111	.09717	.10340	.11634
	+20%	.08416	.08981	.09567	.10173	.10796	.12090
	0%	.08872	.09437	.10024	.10629	.11252	.12546
	−20%	.09328	.09894	.10480	.11085	.11708	.13003
25	+40%	.07669	.08280	.08912	.09564	.10232	.11612
	+20%	.08125	.08736	.09368	.10020	.10688	.12069
	0%	.08581	.09192	.09824	.10476	.11144	.12525
	−20%	.09038	.09648	.10281	.10932	.11601	.12981
30	+40%	.07489	.08131	.08795	.09476	.10173	.11601
	+20%	.07945	.08588	.09251	.09932	.10629	.12057
	0%	.08401	.09044	.09707	.10389	.11085	.12514
	−20%	.08857	.09500	.10163	.10845	.11541	.12970

14% EQUITY YIELD
15 Year Holding Period
80% Loan Ratio

Term In Yrs.	Appr. or Dep.	Interest Rate					
		6%	7%	8%	9%	10%	12%
15	+40%	.08164	.08692	.09238	.09800	.10380	.11585
	+20%	.08621	.09148	.09694	.10257	.10836	.12041
	0%	.09077	.09605	.10150	.10713	.11292	.12497
	−20%	.09533	.10061	.10606	.11169	.11748	.12954
20	+40%	.07617	.08221	.08846	.09492	.10156	.11537
	+20%	.08074	.08677	.09302	.09948	.10613	.11993
	0%	.08530	.09133	.09758	.10404	.11069	.12449
	−20%	.08986	.09589	.10215	.10860	.11525	.12906
25	+40%	.07308	.07959	.08634	.09329	.10042	.11514
	+20%	.07764	.08415	.09090	.09785	.10498	.11970
	0%	.08220	.08872	.09546	.10241	.10954	.12426
	−20%	.08676	.09328	.10002	.10697	.11410	.12882
30	+40%	.07116	.07801	.08509	.09235	.09978	.11502
	+20%	.07572	.08257	.08965	.09692	.10434	.11958
	0%	.08028	.08713	.09421	.10148	.10891	.12414
	−20%	.08484	.09170	.09877	.10604	.11347	.12871

OVER-ALL RATES

14% EQUITY YIELD
15 Year Holding Period
90% Loan Ratio

Term In Yrs.	Appr. or Dep.	Interest Rate					
		6%	7%	8%	9%	10%	12%
15	+40%	.07549	.08143	.08756	.09389	.10041	.11397
	+20%	.08005	.08599	.09213	.09846	.10497	.11853
	0%	.08461	.09055	.09669	.10302	.10953	.12310
	−20%	.08918	.09511	.10125	.10758	.11410	.12766
20	+40%	.06934	.07612	.08316	.09042	.09790	.11343
	+20%	.07390	.08069	.08772	.09498	.10246	.11799
	0%	.07846	.08525	.09228	.09955	.10702	.12256
	−20%	.08302	.08981	.09684	.10411	.11159	.12712
25	+40%	.06585	.07318	.08077	.08859	.09661	.11317
	+20%	.07041	.07774	.08533	.09315	.10117	.11773
	0%	.07498	.08231	.08989	.09771	.10573	.12230
	−20%	.07954	.08687	.09445	.10227	.11029	.12686
30	+40%	.06369	.07140	.07936	.08754	.09590	.11304
	+20%	.06825	.07596	.08392	.09210	.10046	.11760
	0%	.07281	.08052	.08849	.09666	.10502	.12216
	−20%	.07738	.08509	.09305	.10122	.10958	.12672

OVER-ALL RATES

15% EQUITY YIELD
15 Year Holding Period
60% Loan Ratio

Term In Yrs.	Appr. or Dep.	Interest Rate					
		6%	7%	8%	9%	10%	12%
15	+40%	.09975	.10370	.10780	.11202	.11636	.12540
	+20%	.10395	.10791	.11200	.11622	.12056	.12960
	0%	.10815	.11211	.11620	.12042	.12477	.13381
	−20%	.11236	.11631	.12041	.12463	.12897	.13801
20	+40%	.09524	.09975	.10441	.10923	.11420	.12451
	+20%	.09945	.10395	.10862	.11344	.11840	.12871
	0%	.10365	.10815	.11282	.11764	.12260	.13292
	−20%	.10785	.11236	.11702	.12184	.12681	.13712
25	+40%	.09270	.09755	.10258	.10776	.11309	.12408
	+20%	.09690	.10176	.10678	.11197	.11729	.12828
	0%	.10110	.10596	.11099	.11617	.12149	.13248
	−20%	.10531	.11016	.11519	.12037	.12570	.13669
30	+40%	.09112	.09622	.10150	.10693	.11247	.12386
	+20%	.09532	.10043	.10571	.11113	.11668	.12806
	0%	.09952	.10463	.10991	.11533	.12088	.13226
	−20%	.10373	.10883	.11411	.11954	.12508	.13647

15% EQUITY YIELD
15 Year Holding Period
70% Loan Ratio

Term In Yrs.	Appr. or Dep.	Interest Rate					
		6%	7%	8%	9%	10%	12%
15	+40%	.09277	.09739	.10216	.10709	.11215	.12270
	+20%	.09697	.10159	.10636	.11129	.11636	.12690
	0%	.10118	.10580	.11057	.11549	.12056	.13111
	−20%	.10538	.11000	.11477	.11970	.12476	.13531
20	+40%	.08752	.09277	.09822	.10384	.10963	.12166
	+20%	.09172	.09698	.10242	.10804	.11383	.12586
	0%	.09593	.10118	.10662	.11225	.11804	.13007
	−20%	.10013	.10538	.11083	.11645	.12224	.13427
25	+40%	.08455	.09021	.09608	.10213	.10833	.12116
	+20%	.08875	.09442	.10028	.10633	.11254	.12536
	0%	.09295	.09862	.10449	.11053	.11674	.12956
	−20%	.09716	.10282	.10869	.11474	.12094	.13377
30	+40%	.08270	.08866	.09482	.10115	.10762	.12090
	+20%	.08691	.09287	.09902	.10535	.11182	.12510
	0%	.09111	.09707	.10323	.10955	.11602	.12931
	−20%	.09531	.10127	.10743	.11376	.12023	.13351

OVER-ALL RATES

15% EQUITY YIELD
15 Year Holding Period
75% Loan Ratio

Term In Yrs.	Appr. or Dep.	Interest Rate					
		6%	7%	8%	9%	10%	12%
15	+40%	.08928	.09423	.09934	.10462	.11005	.12135
	+20%	09349	.09843	.10355	.10882	.11425	.12555
	0%	.09769	.10264	.10775	.11303	.11846	.12976
	−20%	.10189	.10684	.11195	.11723	.12266	.13396
20	+40%	.08366	.08928	.09512	.10114	.10735	.12024
	+20%	.08786	.09349	.09932	.10535	.11155	.12444
	0%	.09206	.09769	.10352	.10955	.11575	.12864
	−20%	.09627	.10189	.10773	.11375	.11996	.13285
25	+40%	.08047	.08654	.09283	.09931	.10596	.11970
	+20%	.08467	.09074	.09703	.10351	.11016	.12390
	0%	.08888	.09495	.10123	.10771	.11436	.12810
	−20%	.09308	.09915	.10544	.11192	.11857	.13231
30	+40%	.07849	.08488	.09148	.09826	.10519	.11942
	+20%	.08270	.08908	.09568	.10246	.10939	.12362
	0%	.08690	.09329	.09988	.10666	.11360	.12783
	−20%	.09110	.09749	.10409	.11087	.11780	.13203

15% EQUITY YIELD
15 Year Holding Period
80% Loan Ratio

Term In Yrs.	Appr. or Dep.	Interest Rate					
		6%	7%	8%	9%	10%	12%
15	+40%	.08580	.09107	.09653	.10215	.10795	.12000
	+20%	.09000	.09528	.10073	.10636	.11215	.12420
	0%	.09420	.09948	.10493	.11056	.11635	.12841
	−20%	.09841	.10368	.10914	.11476	.12056	.13261
20	+40%	.07979	.08580	.09202	.09845	.10506	.11881
	+20%	.08400	.09000	.09622	.10265	.10927	.12302
	0%	.08820	.09420	.10043	.10685	.11347	.12722
	−20%	.09240	.09841	.10463	.11106	.11767	.13142
25	+40%	.07640	.08287	.08958	.09649	.10358	.11824
	+20%	.08060	.08707	.09378	.10069	.10779	.12244
	0%	.08480	.09128	.09798	.10489	.11199	.12664
	−20%	.08901	.09548	.10219	.10910	.11619	.13085
30	+40%	.07429	.08110	.08814	.09537	.10276	.11794
	+20%	.07849	.08530	.09234	.09957	.10697	.12215
	0%	.08269	.08951	.09654	.10377	.11117	.12635
	−20%	.08690	.09371	.10075	.10798	.11537	.13055

OVER-ALL RATES

15% EQUITY YIELD
15 Year Holding Period
90% Loan Ratio

Term In Yrs.	Appr. or Dep.	Interest Rate					
		6%	7%	8%	9%	10%	12%
15	+40%	.07882	.08476	.09089	.09722	.10374	.11730
	+20%	.08302	.08896	.09510	.10143	.10794	.12150
	0%	.08723	.09316	.09930	.10563	.11215	.12571
	−20%	.09143	.09737	.10350	.10983	.11635	.12991
20	+40%	.07207	.07882	.08582	.09305	.10050	.11596
	+20%	.07627	.08303	.09003	.09726	.10470	.12017
	0%	.08047	.08723	.09423	.10146	.10890	.12437
	−20%	.08468	.09143	.09843	.10566	.11311	.12857
25	+40%	.06825	.07553	.08307	.09085	.09883	.11532
	+20%	.07245	.07973	.08728	.09505	.10303	.11952
	0%	.07665	.08394	.09148	.09925	.10724	.12372
	−20%	.08086	.08814	.09568	.10346	.11144	.12793
30	+40%	.06587	.07354	.08145	.08959	.09791	.11499
	+20%	.07008	.07774	.08566	.09379	.10211	.11919
	0%	.07428	.08194	.08986	.09800	.10632	.12339
	−20%	.07848	.08615	.09406	.10220	.11052	.12760

OVER-ALL RATES

16% EQUITY YIELD
15 Year Holding Period
60% Loan Ratio

Term In Yrs.	Appr. or Dep.	Interest Rate					
		6%	7%	8%	9%	10%	12%
15	+40%	.10541	.10936	.11345	.11768	.12202	.13106
	+20%	.10928	.11324	.11733	.12155	.12589	.13493
	0%	.11315	.11711	.12120	.12542	.12976	.13880
	−20%	.11702	.12098	.12507	.12929	.13363	.14267
20	+40%	.10054	.10502	.10966	.11446	.11940	.12968
	+20%	.10441	.10889	.11353	.11833	.12328	.13355
	0%	.10828	.11276	.11741	.12221	.12715	.13742
	−20%	.11215	.11663	.12128	.12608	.13102	.14129
25	+40%	.09778	.10261	.10761	.11276	.11806	.12901
	+20%	.10165	.10648	.11148	.11664	.12193	.13288
	0%	.10552	.11035	.11535	.12051	.12580	.13675
	−20%	.10939	.11422	.11922	.12438	.12968	.14062
30	+40%	.09607	.10115	.10640	.11179	.11732	.12866
	+20%	.09994	.10502	.11027	.11567	.12119	.13253
	0%	.10381	.10889	.11414	.11954	.12506	.13641
	−20%	.10768	.11276	.11801	.12341	.12893	.14028

16% EQUITY YIELD
15 Year Holding Period
70% Loan Ratio

Term In Yrs.	Appr. or Dep.	Interest Rate					
		6%	7%	8%	9%	10%	12%
15	+40%	.09760	.10221	.10699	.11191	.11698	.12753
	+20%	.10147	.10609	.11086	.11578	.12085	.13140
	0%	.10534	.10996	.11473	.11965	.12472	.13527
	−20%	.10921	.11383	.11860	.12353	.12859	.13914
20	+40%	.09191	.09714	.10256	.10816	.11393	.12591
	+20%	.09579	.10101	.10643	.11203	.11780	.12978
	0%	.09966	.10489	.11031	.11591	.12167	.13365
	−20%	.10353	.10876	.11418	.11978	.12554	.13753
25	+40%	.08870	.09433	.10016	.10618	.11236	.12513
	+20%	.09257	.09820	.10404	.11005	.11623	.12900
	0%	.09644	.10207	.10791	.11392	.12010	.13287
	−20%	.10031	.10594	.11178	.11780	.12398	.13674
30	+40%	.08670	.09263	.09875	.10505	.11149	.12473
	+20%	.09057	.09650	.10262	.10892	.11537	.12860
	0%	.09444	.10037	.10650	.11279	.11924	.13247
	−20%	.09832	.10424	.11037	.11666	.12311	.13634

OVER-ALL RATES

16% EQUITY YIELD
15 Year Holding Period
75% Loan Ratio

Term In Yrs.	Appr. or Dep.	Interest Rate					
		6%	7%	8%	9%	10%	12%
15	+40%	.09369	.09864	.10375	.10903	.11446	.12576
	+20%	.09756	.10251	.10762	.11290	.11833	.12963
	0%	.10143	.10638	.11150	.11677	.12220	.13350
	−20%	.10531	.11025	.11537	.12064	.12607	.13737
20	+40%	.08760	.09321	.09901	.10501	.11119	.12403
	+20%	.09147	.09708	.10288	.10888	.11506	.12790
	0%	.09535	.10095	.10676	.11276	.11893	.13177
	−20%	.09922	.10482	.11063	.11663	.12280	.13564
25	+40%	.08416	.09019	.09644	.10289	.10951	.12319
	+20%	.08803	.09406	.10031	.10676	.11338	.12706
	0%	.09190	.09794	.10419	.11063	.11725	.13094
	−20%	.09577	.10181	.10806	.11450	.12112	.13481
30	+40%	.08202	.08837	.09493	.10168	.10858	.12276
	+20%	.08589	.09224	.09880	.10555	.11245	.12663
	0%	.08976	.09611	.10267	.10942	.11632	.13051
	−20%	.09363	.09998	.10654	.11329	.12020	.13438

16% EQUITY YIELD
15 Year Holding Period
80% Loan Ratio

Term In Yrs.	Appr. or Dep.	Interest Rate					
		6%	7%	8%	9%	10%	12%
15	+40%	.08979	.09506	.10052	.10615	.11194	.12399
	+20%	.09366	.09894	.10439	.11002	.11581	.12786
	0%	.09753	.10281	.10826	.11389	.11968	.13174
	−20%	.10140	.10668	.11213	.11776	.12355	.13561
20	+40%	.08329	.08927	.09546	.10186	.10845	.12215
	+20%	.08716	.09314	.09933	.10573	.11232	.12602
	0%	.09104	.09701	.10321	.10961	.11620	.12989
	−20%	.09491	.10088	.10708	.11348	.12007	.13376
25	+40%	.07962	.08605	.09272	.09960	.10666	.12125
	+20%	.08349	.08993	.09659	.10347	.11053	.12513
	0%	.08736	.09380	.10047	.10734	.11440	.12900
	−20%	.09123	.09767	.10434	.11121	.11827	.13287
30	+40%	.07734	.08411	.09111	.09831	.10567	.12080
	+20%	.08121	.08798	.09498	.10218	.10954	.12467
	0%	.08508	.09185	.09885	.10605	.11341	.12854
	−20%	.08895	.09572	.10272	.10992	.11728	.13241

OVER-ALL RATES

16% EQUITY YIELD
15 Year Holding Period
90% Loan Ratio

—Term In Yrs.	Appr. or Dep.	Interest Rate					
		6%	7%	8%	9%	10%	12%
15	+40%	.08198	.08791	.09405	.10038	.10690	.12046
	+20%	.08585	.09179	.09792	.10425	.11077	.12433
	0%	.08972	.09566	.10179	.10812	.11464	.12820
	−20%	.09359	.09953	.10567	.11200	.11851	.13207
20	+40%	.07467	.08139	.08836	.09556	.10298	.11838
	+20%	.07854	.08527	.09223	.09943	.10685	.12225
	0%	.08241	.08914	.09611	.10331	.11072	.12612
	−20%	.08629	.09301	.09998	.10718	.11459	.13000
25	+40%	.07054	.07778	.08528	.09302	.10096	.11738
	+20%	.07441	.08165	.08915	.09689	.10483	.12125
	0%	.07828	.08552	.09302	.10076	.10870	.12512
	−20%	.08215	.08939	.09689	.10463	.11257	.12899
30	+40%	.06797	.07559	.08346	.09156	.09985	.11686
	+20%	.07184	.07946	.08734	.09543	.10372	.12073
	0%	.07571	.08333	.09121	.09930	.10759	.12461
	−20%	.07958	.08720	.09508	.10318	.11146	.12848

OVER-ALL RATES

20% EQUITY YIELD
15 Year Holding Period
60% Loan Ratio

Term In Yrs.	Appr. or Dep.	Interest Rate					
		6%	7%	8%	9%	10%	12%
15	+40%	.12688	.13084	.13493	.13915	.14349	.15254
	+20%	.12966	.13362	.13771	.14193	.14627	.15531
	0%	.13243	.13639	.14048	.14470	.14905	.15809
	−20%	.13521	.13917	.14326	.14748	.15182	.16086
20	+40%	.12079	.12521	.12978	.13451	.13939	.14952
	+20%	.12357	.12798	.13256	.13729	.14216	.15230
	0%	.12635	.13076	.13534	.14007	.14494	.15508
	−20%	.12912	.13354	.13811	.14284	.14772	.15785
25	+40%	.11735	.12208	.12699	.13206	.13728	.14807
	+20%	.12012	.12486	.12977	.13484	.14005	.15085
	0%	.12290	.12763	.13255	.13762	.14283	.15362
	−20%	.12568	.13041	.13532	.14039	.14561	.15640
30	+40%	.11521	.12019	.12535	.13066	.13611	.14732
	+20%	.11799	.12297	.12813	.13344	.13889	.15010
	0%	.12076	.12574	.13090	.13622	.14166	.15287
	−20%	.12354	.12852	.13368	.13899	.14444	.15565

20% EQUITY YIELD
15 Year Holding Period
70% Loan Ratio

Term In Yrs.	Appr. or Dep.	Interest Rate					
		6%	7%	8%	9%	10%	12%
15	+40%	.11562	.12024	.12501	.12993	.13500	.14555
	+20%	.11840	.12301	.12779	.13271	.13778	.14833
	0%	.12117	.12579	.13056	.13549	.14055	.15110
	−20%	.12395	.12857	.13334	.13826	.14333	.15388
20	+40%	.10852	.11367	.11900	.12452	.13021	.14204
	+20%	.11129	.11644	.12178	.12730	.13299	.14481
	0%	.11407	.11922	.12456	.13008	.13576	.14759
	−20%	.11685	.12199	.12733	.13285	.13854	.15037
25	+40%	.10450	.11002	.11575	.12167	.12775	.14034
	+20%	.10727	.11280	.11853	.12444	.13052	.14312
	0%	.11005	.11557	.12130	.12722	.13330	.14589
	−20%	.11283	.11835	.12408	.12999	.13608	.14867
30	+40%	.10200	.10781	.11383	.12003	.12639	.13947
	+20%	.10478	.11059	.11661	.12281	.12916	.14224
	0%	.10755	.11337	.11939	.12559	.13194	.14502
	−20%	.11033	.11614	.12216	.12836	.13472	.14780

OVER-ALL RATES

20% EQUITY YIELD
15 Year Holding Period
75% Loan Ratio

Term In Yrs.	Appr. or Dep.	Interest Rate					
		6%	7%	8%	9%	10%	12%
15	+40%	.10999	.11494	.12005	.12533	.13076	.14206
	+20%	.11276	.11771	.12283	.12810	.13353	.14483
	0%	.11554	.12049	.12560	.13088	.13631	.14761
	−20%	.11832	.12326	.12838	.13365	.13908	.15039
20	+40%	.10238	.10789	.11362	.11953	.12562	.13829
	+20%	.10515	.11067	.11639	.12231	.12840	.14107
	0%	.10793	.11345	.11917	.12508	.13117	.14385
	−20%	.11071	.11622	.12194	.12786	.13395	.14662
25	+40%	.09807	.10399	.11013	.11647	.12298	.13647
	+20%	.10085	.10677	.11290	.11924	.12576	.13925
	0%	.10362	.10954	.11568	.12202	.12854	.14203
	−20%	.10640	.11232	.11846	.12480	.13131	.14480
30	+40%	.09540	.10162	.10807	.11472	.12153	.13554
	+20%	.09817	.10440	.11085	.11749	.12430	.13832
	0%	.10095	.10718	.11363	.12027	.12430	.14109
	−20%	.10373	.10995	.11640	.12305	.12985	.14387

20% EQUITY YIELD
15 Year Holding Period
80% Loan Ratio

Term In Yrs.	Appr. or Dep.	Interest Rate					
		6%	7%	8%	9%	10%	12%
15	+40%	.10436	.10963	.11509	.12072	.12651	.13856
	+20%	.10713	.11241	.11787	.12349	.12929	.14134
	0%	.10991	.11519	.12064	.12627	.13206	.14412
	−20%	.11269	.11796	.12342	.12905	.13484	.14689
20	+40%	.09624	.10212	.10823	.11453	.12103	.13455
	+20%	.09902	.10490	.11100	.11731	.12381	.13732
	0%	.10179	.10768	.11378	.12009	.12659	.14010
	−20%	.10457	.11045	.11656	.12286	.12936	.14288
25	+40%	.09165	.09796	.10451	.11127	.11822	.13261
	+20%	.09442	.10073	.10728	.11404	.12100	.13539
	0%	.09720	.10351	.11006	.11682	.12377	.13816
	−20%	.09997	.10629	.11284	.11960	.12655	.14094
30	+40%	.08879	.09544	.10232	.10940	.11666	.13161
	+20%	.09157	.09821	.10509	.11218	.11944	.13439
	0%	.09435	.10099	.10787	.11495	.12222	.13716
	−20%	.09712	.10377	.11064	.11773	.12499	.13994

OVER-ALL RATES

20% EQUITY YIELD
15 Year Holding Period
90% Loan Ratio

Term In Yrs.	Appr. or Dep.	Interest Rate					
		6%	7%	8%	9%	10%	12%
15	+40%	.09310	.09903	.10517	.11150	.11802	.13158
	+20%	.09587	.10181	.10795	.11428	.12079	.13435
	0%	.09865	.10459	.11072	.11705	.12357	.13713
	−20%	.10142	.10736	.11350	.11983	.12635	.13991
20	+40%	.08396	.09058	.09745	.10454	.11186	.12706
	+20%	.08674	.09336	.10022	.10732	.11463	.12984
	0%	.08952	.09614	.10300	.11010	.11741	.13261
	−20%	.09229	.09891	.10578	.11287	.12018	.13539
25	+40%	.07879	.08590	.09326	.10087	.10869	.12488
	+20%	.08157	.08867	.09604	.10365	.11147	.12766
	0%	.08435	.09145	.09882	.10642	.11424	.13043
	−20%	.08712	.09423	.10159	.10920	.11702	.13321
30	+40%	.07559	.08306	.09080	.09877	.10694	.12376
	+20%	.07836	.08584	.09357	.10155	.10972	.12653
	0%	.08114	.08861	.09635	.10432	.11249	.12931
	−20%	.08392	.09139	.09913	.10710	.11527	.13209

SUPPLEMENTAL TABLES
(Mortgage-Equity Technique)

The following tables of *Loan Balances* and *Loan Constants* will serve two purposes: a quick computation of:
- Loan balance at the end of 5, 10, and 15 year holding periods.
- Annual loan payments so that a determination can be made of "cash flow" (positive or negative) after debt service but before income tax.

LOAN BALANCE OWING AT END OF 5 YEARS
(As a Percent of Original Principal)

Loan Term and Payment Frequency	Interest Rate					
	6%	7%	8%	9%	10%	12%
15 Years						
Monthly	.76022	.77413	.78766	.80068	.81317	.83652
Annual	.75782	.77120	.78394	.79617	.80785	.82959
20 Years						
Monthly	.84900	.86257	.87526	.88707	.89802	.91744
Annual	.84676	.85972	.87180	.88302	.89341	.91183
25 Years						
Monthly	.89932	.91162	.92274	.93273	.94164	.95651
Annual	.89726	.90908	.91975	.92934	.93792	.95235
30 Years						
Monthly	.93054	.94132	.95070	.95880	.96574	.97662
Annual	.92871	.93912	.94821	.95610	.96290	.97368

LOAN BALANCE OWING AT END OF 10 YEARS
(As a Percent of Original Principal)

Loan Term and Payment Frequency	Interest Rate					
	6%	7%	8%	9%	10%	12%
15 Years						
Monthly	.43649	.45393	.47131	.48861	.50577	.53954
Annual	.43372	.45018	.46647	.48255	.49839	.52927
20 Years						
Monthly	.64531	.66774	.68941	.71026	.73024	.76747
Annual	.64169	.66298	.68344	.70303	.72174	.75645
25 Years						
Monthly	76352	.78634	.80763	.82740	.84561	.87754
Annual	.75976	.78155	.80184	.82063	.83795	.86839
30 Years						
Monthly	.83686	.85813	.87725	.89430	.90938	.93417
Annual	.83328	.85373	.87212	.88854	.90312	.92729

LOAN BALANCE OWING AT END OF 15 YEARS
(As a Percent of Original Principal)

Loan Term and Payment Frequency	Interest Rate					
	6%	7%	8%	9%	10%	12%
20 Years						
Monthly	.37058	.39154	.41252	.43343	.45419	.49500
Annual	.36725	.38703	.40667	.42610	.44527	.48261
25 Years						
Monthly	.58034	.60872	.63614	.66248	.68762	.73409
Annual	.57576	.60270	.62859	.65336	.67694	.72040
30 Years						
Monthly	.71049	.74019	.76782	.79331	.81665	.85705
Annual	.70560	.73397	.76032	.78460	.80685	.84553

LOAN CONSTANT
(As an Annual Percent of Original Principal)

Loan Term and Payment Frequency	Interest Rate					
	6%	7%	8%	9%	10%	12%
15 Years						
Monthly	.10127	.10786	.11468	.12171	.12895	.14402
Annual	.10296	.10980	.11683	.12406	.13148	.14683
20 Years						
Monthly	.08597	.09304	.10037	.10800	.11580	.13213
Annual	.08719	.09439	.10185	.10955	.11746	.13388
25 Years						
Monthly	.07732	.08482	.09262	.10071	.10905	.12639
Annual	.07823	.08581	.09368	.10181	.11017	.12750
30 Years						
Monthly	.07195	.07984	.08805	.09656	.10531	.12343
Annual	.07265	.08059	.08883	.09734	.10608	.12415

PRODUCTION NOTES

This book was printed by Interstate Printers and Publishers, Inc., Danville, Illinois. The text is set in Century, and the section and chapter headings in Century Schoolbook. Cover design is by Alvin Parsons, Chicago.

Editing and production is by the Publications Department of the International Association of Assessing Officers. Editor, Carol Thompson, Assistant Editor, Mavis Takeuchi.